HEAVEN AND HELL

Books by Albertus Pretorius:

WHO, WHERE, AND WHAT IS GOD?
JESUS OF NAZARETH: A DELUDED MESSIAH
THE END OF CHRISTIANITY
THE GOSPELS EXPLAINED
TO HELL WITH THE DEVIL

Albrecht Dürer: The Angels Receiving a Soul into Heaven

ALBERTUS PRETORIUS

HEAVEN AND HELL

LIFE AFTER DEATH AS VIEWED FROM SCRIPTURE AND NEUROPSYCHOLOGY

WIPF & STOCK · Eugene, Oregon

Heaven and Hell
Life After Death as Viewed from Scripture and Neuropsychology

Copyright © 2024 Albert Pretorius. All rights reserved. Except for brief quotations in critical publications or reviews, no part of this book may be reproduced in any manner without prior written permission from the publisher. Write: Permissions, Wipf and Stock Publishers, 199 W. 8th Ave., Suite 3, Eugene, OR 97401.

Wipf & Stock
An Imprint of Wipf and Stock Publishers
199 W. 8th Ave., Suite 3
Eugene, OR 97401
www.wipfandstock.com

PAPERBACK ISBN: 979-8-3852-3427-1
HARDCOVER ISBN: 979-8-3852-3428-8
EBOOK ISBN: 979-8-3852-3429-5

Picture on outside cover: Martyred Saints in Heaven with Crowns as Victors. Ravenna: Basilica, Saint Apollinare Nuovo
https://commons.wikimedia.org/wiki/File:Ravenna,_sant%27apollinare_nuovo,_int.,_santi_martiri_offerenti,_epoca_del_vescovo_agnello_07.JPG

CONTENTS

CHAPTER	PAGE
FOREWORD	xi
1. INTRODUCTION: WHO WANTS TO LIVE FOREVER?	1
2. ANIMISM AND THE ORIGINS OF RELIGION	9
3. ANCIENT CIVILIZATIONS	38
4. PRE-EXILIC HEBREW SCRIPTURES	56
5. POST-EXILIC HEBREW SCRIPTURES	73
6. APOCRYPHAL HEBREW SCRIPTURES	86
7. GREEK PHILOSOPHERS	107
8. JESUS OF NAZARETH	121
9. PAUL OF TARSUS	143
10. THE LATER GOSPELS	163
11. JOHN OF PATMOS	174
12. THE QUR'AN	210
13. SCIENTIFIC PERSPECTIVES	215
14. PHILOSOPHICAL PERSPECTIVES	253
BIBLIOGRAPHY	278
LIST OF ILLUSTRATIONS	291

Abbreviations Used:

Enc Brit   Encyclopaedia Brittanica
NW Enc   New World Encyclopedia
WH Enc   World History Encyclopedia

"Hell at last, yawning, received them whole"
(drawing by Gustave Dore)

FOREWORD

While I was serving as a minister of religion in three congregations of the Dutch Reformed Church in South Africa, I often had to deal with death. It was my task to prepare terminally ill members of my congregation for their impending deaths by explaining to them and their families what the Bible teaches us about death and the afterlife. It was my task to conduct funeral services for parishioners who had died and I had to support their loved ones emotionally and spiritually afterwards.

The shadow of death also fell upon me personally. I lost some close family members and I still mourn their absence from my life.

It may be argued that I am well qualified to write a book on the topic of the soul and the afterlife. After my initial training as minister of religion, I kept on studying and I attained two doctorates and other qualifications.

After my retirement from the ministry, I continued with my studies and wrote a number of books. I am interested in various scientific subjects, including the human brain, and I read much about neuropsychology, the discipline dealing with the relationship between human behavior, cognition, and emotions on the one hand and the functioning of the brain and the body on the other hand. This background is invaluable in explaining why people behave the way they do behave and experience the emotions and psychological disorders they do experience.

I am aware of a great number of books written about death and the afterlife. I am, though, confident that I am able to contribute some novel insights and shed some new light on certain mysterious aspects of the human soul, ego, and self-consciousness, that have eluded scientific explanations until now. In the process, I believe that I also provided some original and credible expositions of certain biblical texts.

At this moment, I am past retirement age and during this stage of my life it is inevitable that I often ponder my own approaching end, although I still enjoy life very much by working as a pastoral counselor, writing books, getting exercise, and listening to beautiful music.

Recently, I and my wife attended a music concert to listen to the Requiem of Mozart, performed by a choir, soloists, and an orchestra. A rquiem may be described as a mass for the dead with musical accompaniment. The word *Requiem* is derived from the first words of this mass in Latin: "Requiem aeternum dona eis" (eternal rest be given to them).

This moving musical experience emphasized to us the brevity of human life and the eternal rest afterwards. That inspired and motivated me the next day to start writing this book.

This book is written from the perspective of a retired minister of religion who cannot forget that he spent most of his adult life in the service of the church, but who also wants to knowand understand as much as possible about the world in which we live.

Albertus Pretoriust, South Africa, September 2024

Chapter 1
INTRODUCTION: WHO WANTS TO LIVE FOREVER?

"Who Wants to Live Forever?"

That was the title song of the movie Highlander, sung by the late Freddy Mercury in 1986. It dealt with the story of the fictional warrior Connor MacLeod who was one of a rare class of human beings, the so-called immortals, people who never grew old.

One may truly ask: who wants to live forever? Although man has often hoped to attain immortality, it transpired that nobody lives forever. It is actually a blessing that we all have a limited life span and that death may deal with us at any moment, whether through an accident, illness, or old age. If we had an unlimited amount of time stretching ahead of us, we wouldn't be motivated to achieve anything. There would be no deadlines and we could postpone all our tasks to tomorrow or whenever. Such a life would be very boring and even meaningless. The limited amount of time alotted to each one of us motivates us to make the most of our lives.

It is an inherent quality of all life forms on earth that the ending of life is unavoidable. All living creatures exit and expire and exhale for the last time on some or other occasion.

Human beings, with their inquisitive minds and exploring brains, always wondered what would happen to them after they had died. All cultures through the ages believed that something, the soul, the (self-)consciousness, the mind, the mass of memories, the ego, trhe spirit, and the personality survives and enters an afterlife, somehow or other.

INTRODUCTION

All religions on earth tried to give explanations about what happens when a person dies. Some of them believed that there is a realm of the dead where all the dead souls are gathered and dumped. Others thought that there is a heaven where the souls of the upright and virtuous people enjoy unending bliss and a hell where the souls of godless and evil people arre punished and tortured for all eternity. Still others taught the return of the soul of the decased in another body, while sometimes retaining memories of a previous life.

"Death" by Hendrick Andriessen – Museum of Fine Arts, Ghent

Many cultures had the idea that the spirits of the ancestors were, somehow, still around and that one could communicate with them.

Philosophers through the ages pondered the nature of the soul before and after death and tried to explain where mortal man fits into the bigger picture of the cosmos as a whole.

This book will explain what the religions of the ancient world in Mesopotamia, Egypt, Persia, Greece, and India made of the soul and the afterlife. The views of some Greek philosophers will also be explained. Special focus will be directed at the thoughts in the holy scriptures of Judaism, Christianity, and Islam and it will be explained how these scriptures were influenced and shaped by the religious and intellectual scene of the ancient world in which they originated.

INTRODUCTION

Many practitioners of the disciplines of medicine and psychology have endevored to study death, the soul, and the afterlife scientifically and those insights must also be presented here.

In the end, an effort will be made to provide a rational explanation why scientists were unable to pinpoint the seat of the (self-)consciousness, the soul, the ego, or mind of a person, anywhere in the brain or the body.

It is impossible to give an overview of all the points of view expressed through the centuries regarding heaven and hell. Large stacks of books were written on this topic and it is impossible to deal with all of them here. The goal of this book is merely to provide an easily digestible overview on a very important aspect of life, while providing some novel thoughts and insights from the perspectives of a rational philosophy and the science of neuropsychology.

We all know what the words *heaven* and *hell* mean. They are in common usage. The word *heaven* denotes a perfect, superb, and unsurpassable state of happiness, joy, delight, and euphoria. *Hell*, on the other hand, is the ultimate, worst, ugliest, most torturous, and most horrible, harsh, and horrifying state of affairs imaginable. Most sophisticated religious systems contain a belief in an afterlife, either in heaven or in hell. This book will explain how these concepts were developed through the centuries in different cultures and religions and how people of our age may or ought to understand these concepts pertaining to an existence beyond the grave, either in heaven, or in hell.

A warning at this point is warranted: this book is critical of the sacred scriptures of the religions discussed, especially those of the monotheistic religions. This book may contradict the convictions of some believers. In a previous publication I argued at length that the Bible – Old Testament and New Testament – cannot be regarded as divinely inspired due to all their historical errors, inconsistencies, contradictions, nonsensical notions, irrational ideas, impossible explanations, and confusing claims.[1] In my commentary on the four Gospels of the New Testament, I demonstrated that much of the material about the life and teachings of Jesus of Nazareth is credible when viewed and interpreted from the correct perspective, but that many people's recollections about Jesus also became skewed and distorted before they were eventually written down, some decades after his time. It was shown that he was an ordinary mortal human being who managed to surrvive his crucifixion with the help of his friends after he had been condemned to death for declaring himself the king of the Jews. He was a deluded messiah who unsuccessfully and tragically strove to restore the kingdom of his ancestor, King David, which he called the kingdom of God, with the help of a host of angels from heaven, and with him on the throne in Jerusalem.[2] This point of view will be explained in more detail in another chapter.

In another publication, I demonstrated that the scriptural accounts of the devil, Satan, and his helpers, the demons, contain fundamental contradictions and are ultimately based on ancient pagan supersitions.[3]

The present book, therefore, will dissect the scriptural accounts of the afterlife, heaven as the dwelling of God and hell as the prison of Satan, evil spirits, and unrepentant sinners, as well as the immortality of the soul sympathetivcally, but also rationally, and critically.

This methodology is inevitable. Most educated contemporary believers don't accept the primitive world view of the Scriptures anymore. They don't believe that the earth is the center

---

[1] Pretorius, *The End of Christianity.*
[2] Pretorius, *The Gospels Explained.*
[3] Pretorius, *To Hell with the Devil.*

of the universe, that the earth is a flat disk with edges from which people could fall off, that God resides just beyond the stars, and that the souls of deceased people are gathered inside an abyss below the surface of the earth where they are held captive until Judgment Day. They have decided to abandon the mythical elements in these Scriptures. This book will show that many conventional ideas regarding the afterlife cannot hold water and have to be discarded as outdated myths or superstitions, just as the ancient cosmology has been jettisonned and cast aside.

The object of this book is to provide a scientifically and philosophically credible and valid explanation of the subject matter. That means that descriptions of the concepts of *science* and *philosophy* have to be provided.

So, what is *science*? The late eminent South African philosopher, Herman Stoker (1899–1993), explained convincingly, and correctly that scientific knowledge is not simply a description of phenomena. It is systemised knowledge that endeavors to understand, to explain, and to evaluate. It seeks relationships in order to combine knowledge into a system or a finished whole.[4]

Heyns and Jonker, two eminent theologians, agreed: "Science is systemised knowledge and verified knowledge of reality."[5] Maarten Boudry defined science as "encompassing all legitimate domains of inquiry based on reason and evidence."[6]

Scientific knowledge, therefore, is systematic and tested knowledge; knowledge that may be verified (or hasn't been falsified) by other investigators and observers; knowledge that tries to provide a rational or logical explanation for certain phenomena, and that makes certain predictions possible. Scientific knowledge is

---

[4] Stoker, *Beginseks en Metodes in die Wetenskap,* 135–36.
[5] Heyns and Jonker, *Op Weg met die Teologie,* 28 (own translation).
[6] Boudry, "The Sin of Scientism", 6.1.

the exact opposite and negation of superstition, a belief not supported by solid evidence or rational deductions from established facts and accepted theories.

Nobody can deny that science as a whole has been very successful in unravelling of many mysteries regarding the world and that the application of scientific knowledge has changed the world of our time drastically in comparison with previous centuries. The disciplines of medicine, agriculture, engineering, and psychology provided the world with numerous innovations that work very well in practice. Therefore: it will be foolish to discard or neglect or reject scientific insights, just because they clash with some religious beliefs or prejudices.

How must we understand the academic and intellectual discipline known as *philosophy*?

Stace, who wrote a classic book about Greek philosophy, explained that –

> "… philosophy does not deal with this or that particular sphere of being, but with being as such. It seeks to see the universe as a single coordinated system of things. It might be described as the science of things in general. The world in its most universal aspects is its subject. All sciences tend to generalize, to reduce multitudes of particular facts to single general laws. Philosophy carries this process to its highest limit. It generalizes to the utmost. It seeks to view the entire universe in the light of the fewest possible general principles, in the light, if possible, of a single ultimate principle."[7]

The Encyclopaedia Brittanice reminds us that the word *philosophy*

---

[7] Stace, *Greek Philosophy*, 3.

is a Greek word, φιλοσοφία (*philosophia*), meening "the love of wisdom." It may also be defined as "the critical examination of the grounds for fundamental beliefs and an analysis of the basic concepts employed in the expression of such beliefs."[8]

The Department of Philosophy of the Florida State University explains on its website:

> "In a broad sense, philosophy is an activity people undertake when they seek to understand fundamental truths about themselves, the world in which they live, and their relationships to the world and to each other. As an academic discipline philosophy is much the same. Those who study philosophy are perpetually engaged in asking, answering, and arguing for their answers to life's most basic questions."

Strauss calls philosophy "the science of sciences". He adds that philosophy is the science that is directed towards a coherent vision of the totality of the varieties of reality.[9]

From all this, it is clear that philosophers use reasoning, deduction, generalization, and arguing to reach valid, useful, or acceptable conclusions about the world in general. They all strive to construct a rational explanation of all aspects of reality. It, therefore, seems that the principle of rationality is the most fundamental principle in this academic and intellectual discipline – just as in science in general. In other words: all thought systems, whether they are philosophical, mythological, religious, theological, or scientific in nature, ought to be measured, analyzed, and evaluated in the light of the universal principle of rationality. We must constantly ask: do these idea systems comply with and adhere to the rules of logical

---

[8] Enc Brit, "Philosophy".
[9] Strauss, *Inleiding tot die Kosmologie,* 5, 7.

thinking and argumenttation? Are there any proofs and evidence for their assertions and claims?

This methodology will be applied in the last part of this book after descriptions of a range of religious and philosophical systems have been given.

Chapter 2
ANIMISM AND THE ORIGINS OF RELIGION

DESCRIPTION OF ANIMISM

Animism may be regarded as the most primitive and original form of religion known to cultural anthropologists. It can be described as the "belief in innumerable spiritual beings concerned with human affairs and capable of helping or harming human interests. (…) The term animism denotes not a single creed or doctrine but a view of the world consistent with a certain range of religious beliefs and practices, many of which may survive in more-complex and hierarchical religions."[10]

The term *animism* is derived from the Latin word "animus", which means "spirit, mind, courage, or anger".

Animism is generally regarded as a primitive form of religion, in contrast with more sophisticated religions where a hierarchy of deities or a single God was or is worshipped.

The term *animism* is used as an umbrella name for a great variety of primitive and tribal religions, each with its own beliefs and practices. Their belief in the power of spirits, which may inhabit any part or aspect of the world, as well as a belief in an afterworld for the deceased, are common characteristics.[11]

Sir James Frazer, a famed cultural anthropologist, divided human history into three ages: the age of magic, the age of religion, and the age of science. Advanced civilizations on earth have entered the age of science where people of higher intelligence with advanced

---

[10] Enc Brit, "Animism".
[11] Enc Brit, "Animism"

education are seeking rational explanations for all phenomena. This was preceded by the age of religion during which everybody in the civilized world adhered to some or other religion, especially the more sophisticated religions such as Judaism, Christianity, Islam, Buddhism, or Hinduism, but also the paganism of the ancient Babylonians, Egyptians, Greeks, and Romans. The decay of the age of religion in the West can be seen in the tendency that the more intelligent university students do not enter the ministry anymore, but are choosing other professions. The first age, the age of magic, is characterized by polytheism and animism, the explanation of all natural forces as the result of the use of magic by sorcerers, witches, gods, and spirits. This age still lingers on in primitive societies in remote spots on earth, but certain aspects of this age were incorporated into the age of religion. Animism was usually the religious system of pre-scientific and pre-literate societies.[12]

Various (neuro-)psychological and sociological factors may be identified that led to the formation of animistic religions. They are as follows:

PERSONIFICATION

Detection of Patterns and Agents

The most persuasive explanation for the phenomenon of religion, especially animism, is to be found in the fact that the human brain is hard-wired to personify all phenomena encountered in the world. This tendency is coupled to a propensity to detect patterns and to ascribe human volition and motives to non-human phenomena – animals and inanimate objects.

Shermer points out that the human brain is programmed to

---

[12] Frazer, *The Golden Bough*, 932; Jackson, "Man, God and Civilization", 147–49.

detect patterns because the individual's safety may depend upon it. This faculty is so fine-tuned that humans often detect patterns where there are none. We see faces in the clouds, we hear voices when the wind blows, we detect dangers where there are none, and we imagine regularities when there is nothing of the sort.[13]

It was found that when people were given L-Dopa, the medication used for patients with Parkinson's disease and which increases the levels of the neurotransmitter dopamine in the brain, the propensity to detect patterns where none existed, was enhanced. This mechanism is related to the fact that an overproduction of dopamine in the brain due to the use of certain drugs, such as cannabis, may lead to hallucinations – often with a religious content – and even psychosis.[14]

In addition, we have the propensity to regard non-human phenomena as "agents" – entities with a will, intentions, purposes and even a mind. Natural phenomena and processes such as the stars, the ocean, mountains, trees, lakes, lightning, rain, animals, the seasons, *etcetera* are regarded as beings endowed with invisible spirits – just as humans regard themselves as being comprised of body and spirit. The world is, therefore, haunted by surreal spirits, diabolical demons, ghastly ghosts, silent specters, angry angels, and gruesome gods. Our brains are also hard-wired to imagine and detect all sorts of "presences" – ghosts, spirits, angels and other supernatural agents – during abnormal circumstances, such as extreme cold, lack of oxygen, danger, exhaustion or sleep deprivation. This phenomenon occurs especially during a near-death experience (NDE) or an out-of-the-body experience (OBE) when the person suffers from anoxia, the lack of oxygen to the brain.[15] A lter chapter will deal with

---

[13] Shermer, *The Believing Brain,* 50–86.
[14] Shermer, *The Believing Brain,* 120–21.
[15] Shermer, *The Believing Brain,* 87–110.

NDE's and OBE's in more detail.

According to Dawkins, humans tend to assign purpose to inanimate objects. This is how our brains were programmed by evolution. We had to be ready at all times to face predators and other dangers or to flee. There was no time to make sure what the intentions of the predator were and it had to be assumed that it had the purpose of making a meal of us. Immediate action was, therefore, necessary. Likewise, purpose was automatically ascribed to inanimate objects, just to be on the safe side.[16]

A manual of neuropsychology explains that the brains of primates, humans included, contain so-called mirror neurons or brain cells, which enable them to have empathy with others, to mimic the others' behavior and to read and understand their intentions and emotions. This is the underlying neurological structure for personification. "The attribution of intentions to others is so automatic in people that we humans seem compelled to attribute intentions and other psychological motives to nonhumans and even to abstract animations."[17]

This all explains why primitive people experienced natural phenomena as being inhabited by spirits and having the same emotions and motivations as themselves. This explains why pagan religions devised gods for every aspect of the world – the oceans, the sky, the moon, the sun, starry formations, the weather, fertility, *etcetera*.

The human disposition to anthropomorphize animals and inanimate objects is especially visible in children. They are easily entertained by fictional animals in cartoons and stories. Characters such as Donald Duck, Mickey Mouse, Winnie the Pooh and numerous other animals and even animated robots such as R2D2 are

---

[16] Dawkins, *The God Delusion*, 183–84.

[17] Kolb and Whishaw, *Fundamentals*, 582.

part and parcel of contemporary Western culture. Of course, ducks, mice, teddy bears, and robots cannot talk and think as we do, but these human characteristics are attributed to these characters and especially children experience them as credible. The same mechanism was at work when people created spirits and gods inhabiting natural phenomena.

The ultimate act of personification, seeking patterns and looking for agents, occurs when humans ascribe a soul or a spirit to the world as a whole. This is how a single God may have been invented.[18]

Venus of Willendorf: A statuette, presumably of a fertility goddess, of ±22 000 BC found in Lower Austria near the city of Krems. It is carved from an oolitic limestone and tinted with red ochre. It is at the Vienna Natural History Museum, Austria.

Gerald Benedict finds that "fertility goddess cults" are probably "the earliest religions of which we have evidence in the form of artifacts and artwork." He adds that early religions deified "most, if not all aspects of nature." This form of religion is called "animism" since all elements of nature were seen as being animated by spirits.[19]

Grayling writes that there is a certain evolutionary process visible in the development of gods. It started when people saw spirits

---

[18] Shermer, *The Believing Brain*, 165.
[19] Benedict, *The God Debate*, 15, 17–18.

in all natural phenomena. When understanding of natural phenomena grew, these spirits became gods on mountain tops, such as Olympus or Mount Sinai. When people became even more sophisticated, the gods on the mountain tops were relocated to the sky into a hypothetical heaven.[20]

In our time, relics of this tendency are still part of our Western culture. The ancients identified the visible planets with certain deities and we have retained their names in their Latin translations (Mercury, Venus, Mars, Jupiter, and Saturn). The ancients also identified the constellations in the starry sky with mythical figures and we still use their Greek and Latin names (*e.g.,* Andromeda, Perseus, Orion, Hercules, the Twins [Gemini] or Castor and Pollux, Leo, Pegasus, Coma Berenices, and Sagittarius).

Natural-born Dualists
Dawkins reminds us that research has shown that humans, and especially children, are natural or instinctive dualists and teleologists. We experience the "me" inside ourselves as being different from our physical bodies and regard it as something immaterial or spiritual since it cannot be localized precisely. We see ourselves, therefore, as composed of two different elements, body and soul – a duality.[21]

We also tend to assign purpose (Greek: τελος – *telos,* goal, purpose) to everything in the world – hence teleology, the tendency to look for purposes. If we assign a purpose to the universe as a whole, we easily think that it was created for God's pleasure.

Shermer agrees with Dawkins. He quotes statistics to show that a majority of Americans believe in an afterlife, including heaven and hell. He explains that this belief is connected to the fact that human beings are "natural-born dualists". They experience their

---
[20] Grayling, *The God Argument,* 36.
[21] Dawkins, *The God Delusion,* 180–81.

inner core, their "ego", their self-consciousness, as something different from their bodies. They believe, therefore, that they are composed of a body and a soul, that they are a duality. They also find it difficult to imagine a time when this soul or spirit will not be somewhere and, therefore, they are convinced that there must be an afterlife. Humans also possess the faculty of imagination and it is easy to imagine a continued existence after death in a wonderful heaven.[22]

According to Benedict, the fear of death must have been a powerful impulse for the development and staying power of religions, such as animism. People were always aware of the temporary and fragile nature of life and they had various myths regarding an existence beyond the grave.[23] He adds that –

> "… we can reasonably conclude that human beings have always had the need to believe in something other than themselves, but in a way that fosters an understanding of the nature and meaning of life. Until relatively recently, this need to believe and understand has been determined by the struggle to survive physically, and it remains so in the world's poorer countries."[24]

People who have experienced an OBE or a NDE very often experience hallucinations with a religious character and they believe that they have had encounters with God, Jesus, deities, angels, deceased loved ones, and other supernatural beings.[25] The reports of their visions must certainly have fed and enhanced the belief in an afterlife in all civilizations.

This state of affairs must also be the reason why adherents of

---

[22] Shermer, *The Believing Brain*, 143–45.
[23] Benedict, *The God Debate*, 19–21.
[24] Benedict, *The God Debate*, 24–25.
[25] Cunningham, *Decoding the Language of God*, 210.

so many animistic religions revere and interact with their ancestors. They believe that these ancestors, although in their graves, are actually still invisibly present and could exert an influence on events in the world of the living.

The ideas regarding the world of the spirits of the dead differ from community to community, and these mental pictures are usually vague. The San of the Kalahari in Botswana and Namibia, for instance, thought that the realm of the dead must be somewhere in the west where the dying sun sets.[26]

Many animists think that the spirits of not only humans, but also of animals and other beings may survive death or destruction and continue with a shadowy existence.[27]

DREAMS

All people dream several times every night during normal sleep; they just don't always remember their dreams.

In pre-scientific ages, people regarded dreams as the wanderings of their spirits through strange places and experiencing bizarre events. Even being asleep, without dreaming, was often interpreted as a departure of the soul from the body.[28]

These dreams were often seen as prophetic in nature or as predictions of the future. Martin is convinced that dreams played a major role in the origins of religion. People saw their dreams as an indication of a spirit world filled with gods, demons, deceased loved ones, or ancestors. These were, after all, the beings they encountered during their dreams.[29]

---

[26] Anon. "Religion of the San".
[27] Swancutt, "Animism", 6.
[28] NW Enc, "Animism".
[29] Martin, *Counting Sheep,* 188–90.

The dreams of several biblical characters were interpreted as revelations from God. The following examples come to mind:

- Jacob (Gen 28: 10–12);
- Laban (Gen 31: 24);
- Joseph (Gen 37: 5);
- Pharaoh (Gen 41: 1–13);
- Samuel (1 Sam 3);
- King Solomon (1 Kgs 3: 5);
- King Nebuchadnezzar (Dan 2: 1–13);
- Joseph (Matt 1: 19–20 & 2: 13);
- The wise men from the East (Matt 2: 12); and
- Mrs Pontia Pilata (Matt 27: 13, 19).

Scientific investigations since the fifties of the previous century have demystified the phenomenon of dreaming. Dreams were found to be simply products of the brain, occurring in man and higher animals. They happen several times per night during so-called rapid-eye-movement (REM) sleep and they are a mechanism the brain uses to sort through memories, consolidating important recollections, deleting irrelevant memories, processing unpleasant feelings, and dealing with problems.[30]

In other words: there is nothing supernatural about dreams and they are certainly not divine communications or excursions or expeditions of the spirit of the sleeper. They explain, though, why people are "natural-born dualists" and inclined to believe in gods, spirits, and an existence beyond the grave when their wandering "spirits" meet deceased loved ones or other beings during the night.

---

[30] Kolb & Wishaw, *Fundamentals,* 769–70; Martin, *Counting Sheep,* 99–104, 241–54.

ALTERED STATES OF CONSCIOUSNESS

Hallucinations

Hallucinations may be defined as "perceptual experiences that occur in the absence of external sensory input. They can emerge in any of the sensory modalities and arise from a wide range of conditions as well as in different states of normal consciousness."[31] They may be caused by psychotic disorders, such as schizophrenia or bipolar disorder, by hallucinogens (psychedelic drugs), hypnosis, brain injuries, anoxia, epilepsy, malnutrition, and dehydration.

These hallucinations are caused by an overproduction of the neurotransmitters dopamine or serotonin and their effects are often ascribed to the influence of a demon or a spirit. During hallucinations the distinction between reality and fantasy becomes blurred and the person has the belief that he experiences something real, although the visions he sees or the voices he hears are simply the effect of his altered state of consciousness on the brain.[32]

A strong case can be made that certain biblical figures had hallucinatory visions or revelations – including Jesus of Nazareth when he was tempted by Satan in the desert and the apostle Paul.

Jesus and the Biblical Prophets

Jesus spent forty days in the desert without food and drink. This incident has to be explored in more detail.

Jesus departed for the desert after his baptism by John the Baptist and when he saw the heavens opened, while experiencing the presence of the Holy Spirit. During this time, where he tried to make sense of the events surroundding his baptism, he reportedly

---

[31] Hoffman *et al.*, "Transcranial Magnetic Stimulation", 500–01.
[32] Goetz, "Hallucinogens", 503–04; Temes, *Hypnosis*, 35–36, 49–50; Clark et al., *Pharmacology*, 104.

experienced temptations by Satan, but was afterwards cared for by angels (Mark 1: 9–12; Matt 3: 13–4: 11; Luke 3: 21–22; Luke 4: 1–13).

This period of forty days must be greatly exaggerated. Nobody can survive more than ten days without water, especially not in a hot desert environment where Jesus experienced these temptations.[33] The period of forty days is rather a symbolic number, a reminder of the forty years the Israelites purportedly spent in the desert after escaping from slavery in Egypt. It is also a reminder of Moses who reportedly stayed forty days on the mountain without eating and drinking, while receiving God's commandments (Ex 34: 28).

Anyway, if Jesus fasted for an extended period of time and consequently suffered from malnutrition and dehydration, it is very possible and highly probable that he experienced hallucinations of a religious nature, in which he struggled with demonic forces, had encounters with angels, and which he regarded as a confirmation of his calling from God to establish the kingdom of God in Israel – in other words, a theocracy, free from Roman oppression.

The "angels" who cared for him after Satan had left him were quite likely Bedouins who found the disoriented, dehydrated and undernourished Jesus somewhere in the desert and nursed him back to health.

These experiences must have been so real for Jesus that he afterwards told his friends and disciples about it – and the compilers of the Gospels must have collected these stories from people who heard it from Jesus or from his friends or disciples.

We read in the book of Genesis that the patriarch Abram (later called Abraham) held various conversations with God. We must ask:

---

[33] Craighead and Nemeroff, *The Corsini Encyclopedia*, 1587; Swaab, *Wij Zijn ons Brein*, 247; Encyclopaedia Britannica, "Dehydration".

was he hearing voices in his head – just as people with schizophrenia often do? These voices even told him to sacrifice his own son, Isaac – which must be classified as a case of a religious delusion, coupled with serious child abuse (Gen 22).

Moses, the Israelite lawgiver, received a number of revelations from God. The best-known example is his solo meeting with God on Mount Sinai where he received the Ten Commandments – that is, to say, if the receipt of the Ten Commandments happened as reported.

The first six chapters of his book record the prophet Isaiah's early ministry and visions of God, who sat on his throne and was surrounded by seraphim – hybrid human-animal-bird figures – which is typical of people who hallucinate.

Ezekiel, the priest, received the call to become a prophet during a vision "in the thirtieth year, in the fourth month, on the fifth day" — perhaps July 31, 593 BC. He, likewise, had visions of strange beings, which he interpreted as revelations from God.[34]

Graham Hancock quotes Beny Shanon, professor of psychology at the Hebrew University of Jerusalem, who theorized that the prophet Ezekiel had these visions while under the influence of psychoactive substances. Shanon experimented himself with such substances and claims to have had similar experiences.[35]

The prophet Daniel had strange visions or dreams while asleep. In chapter 7 of his book, he describes hideous beasts and a vision of God on his throne. Chapter 8 mentions a ram and a goat fighting, but also a vision of God. Daniel reports that these visions made him sick. According to chapter 10, he fasted for three weeks and then had more visions of God and of the archangel Michael. Other prophets from the Old Testament claimed to have had direct

---

[34] Rylaarsdam, "Biblical Literature".
[35] Hancock, *Supernatural,* 517–19.

contact with God, who ordered them to convey certain messages to the Israelites.

John of Patmos, the prophet who wrote the book of Revelation, probably also experienced altered states of consciousness while having visions. He repeatedly had an experience of being "in the Spirit" (Rev 1: 10; Rev 4: 2; Rev 17: 3; Rev 21: 10). His altered form of consciousness could not have been a trance in which he became unconscious – it may only have been a light form of hypnosis that enabled him to concentrate strongly on his visions.

Something similar seems to have happened with Muhammad, the prophet of Islam. The description of his first revelation or vision on mount Hira on the night of 17 Ramadan AD 610, as given by Karen Armstrong, makes it clear that he saw and heard an angel, that he fell trembling on the ground and that he was overcome by fear for the unknown God, Allah. He later repeatedly had similar visions.

According to Muslims, these were genuine supernatural events, but it might equally well have been a series of trances with hallucinations. After all, Armstrong relates that Muhammad had the habit of praying and meditating on the mountain before his first vision and that he had clear dreams of Allah appearing to him.[36]

Possible Explanations

How are these visions and revelations of the prophets to be explained? Biblical prophets, it seems, had visions and revelations, which "may be induced by a variety of techniques: by meditation, by mystico-magical formulas and gestures..., by music..., by drumming, dancing, or the ingestion of intoxicants or narcotics."[37]

Ahlström writes:

---

[36] Armstrong, *The Battle for God,* 82–89.
[37] Enc Brit, "Prophet".

"The nature of prophecy is twofold: either inspired (by visions or revelatory auditions), or acquired (by learning certain techniques). In many cases both aspects are present. The goal of learning certain prophetic techniques is to reach an ecstatic state in which revelations can be received. That state might be reached through the use of music, dancing, drums, violent bodily movement, and self-laceration. The ecstatic prophet is regarded as being filled with the divine spirit, and in this state the deity speaks through him. Ecstatic oracles, therefore, are generally delivered by the prophet in the first-person singular pronoun and are spoken in a short, rhythmic style."[38]

Religious ecstasy may be described as –

"… the experience of an inner vision of God or of one's relation to or union with the divine. Various methods have been used to achieve ecstasy, which is a primary goal in most forms of religious mysticism. The most typical consists of four stages: (1) purgation (of bodily desire); (2) purification (of the will); (3) illumination (of the mind); and (4) unification (of one's being or will with the divine). Other methods are dancing (as used by the Mawlawīyah, or whirling dervishes, a Muslim Ṣūfī sect); the use of sedatives and stimulants (as utilized in some Hellenistic mystery religions); and the use of certain drugs, such as peyote, mescaline, hashish, LSD, and similar products (in certain Islamic sects and modern experimental religious groups). Most mystics, both in the East and in the West, frown on the

---

[38] Ahlström, "Prophecy".

use of drugs because no permanent change in the personality (in the mystical sense) has been known to occur.

"In certain ancient Israelite prophetic groups, music was used to achieve the ecstatic state, in which the participants, in their accompanying dancing, were believed to have been seized by the hand of Yahweh, the God of Israel, as in the case of Saul, the 11th-century-BC king of Israel."[39]

On account of all these observations it seems likely that NDE's and OBE's may also be responsible for the altered states of consciousness that may have been experienced by biblical figures – as well as adherents of other religions, such as animism. These experiences can be caused by anoxia, the electrical stimulation of the temporal lobes of the brain, and certain drugs, such as LSD and ketamines. During these processes, people very often have religious experiences in which they "see" a bright light, God, Jesus or other deities or spirits, while receiving messages from these beings.[40]

It may even be argued that no genuine religious vision or revelation ever occurred. Those persons who supposedly had contact with a deity or a supernatural being merely experienced hallucinations, delusions, or other altered states of consciousness, such as intoxication by a drug, an OBE or NDE, a trance (hypnosis), a psychosis, dehydration or epilepsy – all the products of chemical and electrical processes in the brain.

In ages gone by, quite a number of people must have recovered from a NDE in which they had experiences or hallucinations, which they then interpreted as being spiritual in nature. Their reports to their friends, family and others must have convinced people of the reality of an afterlif, gods, and spirits.

---

[39] Enc Brit, "Ecstasy".
[40] Cunningham, *Decoding the Language of God*, 210.

William Temple (1881–1944), who was archbishop of Canterbury during the last two years of his life, is reported as declaring:

> "If you talk to God you are praying; if God talks to you, you have schizophrenia."[41]

Thomas Paine was of the opinion that "prophesying is lying professionally", since nobody is able to verify or confirm the revelations or visions of a prophet.[42]

Evidence of Prehistoric Visions and Trances
In his book, Supernatural, Graham Hancock argues that ancient cave paintings in Europe, depicting strange beings, as well as more recent rock paintings of the San in Southern Africa, were all done by shamans after having experienced altered states of consciousness. During these states, they had visions of spiritual beings – which must have formed the basis or origin of various religious ideas and systems. These states or trances could be achieved by the use of psychedelic drugs derived from various plants, as well as chanting, dancing, dehydration, and sleep deprivation.[43]

Hancock argues that the ingestion of psychedelic drugs, which produced these visions with a religious content, must be related to the increased production of the neurotransmitters dopamine and serotonin in the brains of those who experienced these trances. He is, furthermore, convinced that these trances or altered states of consciousness enabled the participants to get access to real or genuine religious experiences and alternative realities, which were not simply hallucinations.[44]

---

[41] Humphreys, *In God we Doubt,* 219.
[42] Paine, *The Age of Reason,* 129.
[43] Hancock, *SupernaturL,* 163–65, 497, 563–64.
[44] Hancock, *Supernatural,* 519, 577.

San Rock Art, Drakensberg, South Africa

The fact that the shamans of various ages experienced very similar visions may be due to the way the human brain is hard-wired, but it is also proof for him that they all had access "to the same otherworlds and spirits" and with "alternative realities."[45]

According to him, there is evidence that the ancient Greek mystery religion, practiced at Eleusis, was based upon the ingestion of a potion containing an ingredient akin to LSD, which induced religious visions in those who participated in its rituals.[46]

Mike Pitts cites research that suggests that people who lived at the time when structures such as Stonehenge in Britain were being built, about 5 000 years ago, knew "altered states of mind", which could have been induced by herbal drugs or other means. Signs of this can be seen in the artistic designs on pottery from that age, which are typical of the patterns seen during trances.[47]

---

[45] Hancock, *Supernatural*, 567, 577.
[46] Hancock, *Supernatural*, 524–25.
[47] Pitts, *Hengeworld*, 235–36.

Graham Phillips has the interesting hypothesis that the "burning bush", which Moses saw and where he encountered God must have been the weed *datura stramonium* – also known as "thorn apples."[48] This does not seem to be too far-fetched. This plant, which originated in India and was used as a medicine for epilepsy and for inducing religious experiences due to its hallucinatory ingredients such as scalopomine, was well-known throughout the ancient world. It grows mostly in dry areas, including the Sinai Peninsula.[49]

The burning bush that Moses encountered while tending the flocks of his father-in-law, is described as follows in Ex 3: 2 –

> "And the angel of the Lord was seen by him in a flame of fire coming out of a thorn-tree: and he saw that the tree was on fire, but it was not burned up."

Phillips speculates that the text of this verse got altered with its transmission and editing through the ages and that the "burning" experienced by Moses must have been due to the fact that the chemicals in the seeds and the leaves of this bush cause the tongue to feel burnt and that a burning sensation is also experienced throughout the body. Moses' encounter with God may, therefore, have simply been the hallucinations he got by chewing the seeds or brewing the leaves.[50]

Experiments with psilocybin, the active ingredient in "magic mushrooms", with terminally ill cancer patients, led to "remarkable" results. A single high dose of this drug caused a long-lasting effect on the state of mind of these patients – as well as in healthy persons. This drug lifted their depression and despair in the face of death and

---

[48] Phillips, *The Moses Legacy,* 276–78.
[49] Seebauer, "Datura stramonium"; Arnett, "Jimson Weed".
[50] Phillips, *The Moses Legacy,* 276–78.

helped them to experience their lives as meaningful. Dr Stephen Ross, director of addiction psychiatry at the NYU Langone Medical Center explained that psilocybin activates a sub-type of serotonin receptor in the brain:

> "Our brains are hard-wired to have these kinds of experiences – these alterations of consciousness. We have endogenous chemicals in our brain. We have a little system that, when you tickle it, it produces these altered states that have been described as spiritual states, mystical states in different religious branches."[51]

Religious experiences may also be caused by electrical stimulation of the brain (such as during a thunder storm) or by a lack of oxygen (such as during an epileptic fit). When certain parts of the brain are surgically removed, these experiences disappear.[52]

Whether these people really did make contact with an alternative or spiritual reality is, of course, another matter. Benedict correctly remarks that arguments for the existence of God relying on religious experiences may be convincing for those who had them, but due to the fact that they are "subjective and incapable of validation", they may not convince skeptics.[53]

SUPERNATURALISM

A Plurality of Supernatural Forces

People in primitive, pre-scientific, and pre-literate societies tried to make sense of the world in which they lived. They had no rational explanations for a range of natural phenomena. They, therefore, saw

---

[51] Carbonaro et al. "Magic Mushrooms".
[52] Stenger, *The New Atheism*, 180.
[53] Benedict, *The God Debate*, 110.

these phenomena as the result of magical or "supernatural" forces – deities, spirits, and demonic forces.

Man in a pre-scientific age had no idea what the nature of natural phenomena and forces were. Nobody had a rational explanation for lightning, rain, the heat of the sun, the phases of the moon, solar and lunar eclipses, the tides of the ocean, how plants could grow from seeds, how new life could be created through the act of copulation, various illnesses, the nature of the stars, *etcetera*. The only explanation for these phenomena could only be that they must have a "supernatural" origin, that gods, spirits, or even demons and magicians were responsible.

The word "supernatural" was placed in quotation marks above on purpose because animists and people in ancient times did not see a discontinuity between nature and anything outside of or above nature. For them, the whole cosmos was one interconnected system.

Deities, spirits, and demons were part and parcel of everyday reality, although they were invisible and ungraspable; they simply belonged to parts of the cosmos over which humans had no control. In those times, people had no idea how natural forces worked or that natural laws operated throughout the universe. For them, the whole cosmos was under the influence of the gods or spirits who could do whatever they liked.

Mithen cites many instances where archaeologists unearthed the remains of people from the Stone Age and investigated the rock art of ancient humans. They concluded that these humans, who lived millennia ago, must have had a belief in magic, spirits, and other supernatural beings, as well as an existence beyond the grave – an elementary form of religion. It seems probable that some individuals must have claimed a special connection with the spirit world and were regarded as shamans or soothsayers. We have no way of knowing exactly what these people believed and thought, but it could have been something similar to contemporary societies of hunter-gatherers.[54]

HUMAN NEEDS SATISFIED

Human beings, like all life forms, have certain needs that have to be satisfied for them to survive. These needs can be divided into physical or biological needs, psychological needs, and spiritual needs. These needs serve as motivators and determinants of human behavior. If a person has some or other need that has to be satisfied, he is moved to do something about the matter.

One reason why religion – including animism – originated and has survived so long is that it managed to satisfy most of these human needs. A short description of these various needs is necessary before it can be explained how religion satisfies these needs.

Physical Needs

Physical or biological needs of humans and animals are obvious: the need for nourishment, water, sleep and rest, oxygen, protection against the elements, warmth and movement or exercise. Nobody can stay alive or healthy if these needs are not satisfied.

Religious communities are usually geared to provide social support for those in need. There are usually mechanisms or institutions for helping the destitute, the poor, the grieving, and the lonely. The human physical and psychological needs are, therefore, taken care of.

Psychological Needs

There is no consensus among psychologists with regards to the nature

---

[54] Mithen, *The Prehistory of the Mind*, 198–202.

of the psychological needs of humans. The categorization that follows, however, seems to be useful. One can deem psychological needs to include the following (in order of importance): the need for identity, the need for stimulation, and the need for security. Many people would like to add the need for love; that may, however, be seen as a combination of all three above-mentioned needs.[55] These needs have to be explained in more detail:

The Need for Identity
The need for identity means that every human being would like to be recognized as an individual, as a unique person with human dignity. He needs to receive recognition for work well done, to be regarded highly and to be respected by others.

Identity is tied to a person's history, his *past*, the road along which he has travelled to reach the present and the factors in his past that made him the person he has become. People retain memories of their achievements, disappointments, trauma, failures, and successes – and these memories of past events shape their present identity, personality, and self-image.

An individual's identity is largely dependent upon the people and groups to which he belongs: his life partner, his family, his friends, his group of colleagues, his church, and his neighborhood. With these people and within these groups he has a certain status and he performs a certain role.

His identity is coupled with his address: the piece of the earth that he calls home. This is where he is king of his castle. People who do not have a property of their own find it difficult to settle down. Who wants to be bound to a rented apartment on the tenth floor?

It is important for every human being to have a positive identity and self-image, to be respected and to have his human digni-

---

[55] Ardrey, *The Territorial Imperative*, 358–70.

ty recognized.

The need for identity is satisfied within a religious community when the individual feels part of a group and experiences himself as a child of God.

Most believers regard their religion as an important aspect of their lives and they feel offended when others make disparaging remarks regarding their convictions. Their religious beliefs define their personal identity to a large extent and, therefore, they will resist any effort to convince them that what they believe could be wrong.

The Need for Stimulation

The need for stimulation is connected to the way the human brain is hard-wired. We all avoid boredom and a lack of stimulation like the plague. This is why life is so difficult for elderly people, invalids, and patients; they have nothing to occupy themselves with.

People will even suppress their need for security in favor of stimulation. That is why so many people exchange a somewhat safe existence in rural areas for the excitement of city lights and squatter camps. People engage in certain relationships – even dangerous ones – on account of the excitement they experience, even though this may endanger their safe relationships.

Love between people of the opposite sexes wanes when excitement and stimulation disappear from the relationship.

The need for stimulation and excitement is concerned with the *present*. People want to make the most of the moment in which they are living, including having religious experiences.

Especially charismatic groups provide in the need for stimulation and excitement with their ecstatic singing, speaking in tongues, dancing, and rituals such as healing or exorcism.

The Need for Security

The human need for security is fairly obvious. It is reassuring to know where you stand with people, especially with a life partner. A person may toil at a tedious job for many years, as it holds the promise of a secure existence. A person's address also gives security; if there is a "place under the sun" he can call his own he more readily feels safe and secure, and he will – if needs be – fight to keep it his own.

This need is focused on the *future*. People dislike unpleasant surprises and they need to know what they can expect from tomorrow and next year.

The need for security often clashes with the need for stimulation. This may be the source of much stress.

The need for security is satisfied when a believer is reassured that he is a child of God, that his eternal fate in heaven is guaranteed, and that he can rely on the support of other members of the group when experiencing distress.

Spiritual Needs

The highest needs of a human being – his spiritual needs – are his needs for meaning in life and for freedom and responsibility.

It can be said that religion generally fulfill the following three functions: it helps the believer –

- To discover meaning in life;
- To live according to moral norms and standards; and
- To receive social support.[56]

Shermer puts it this way:

"Religion is a social institution that evolved to reinforce

---

[56] Louw, *Pastoraat en Ontmoeting*, 66; Meadow and Kahoe, *Psychology of Religion*, 5.

group cohesion and moral behaviour. It is an integral mechanism of human culture to encourage altruism ... and to reveal the level of commitment to cooperate and reciprocate among members of a social community. Believing in God provides an explanation for our universe, our world, and ourselves; it explains where we came from, why we are here, and where we are going. God is also the ultimate enforcer of the rules, the final arbiter of moral dilemmas, and the pinnacle object of commitment."[57]

It is important for every person to experience that life makes sense. Viktor Frankl has demonstrated convincingly that people are prepared to endure extreme difficulties and hardship as long as it makes sense.[58] Rossouw declares that the question regarding the meaning of life is "the most critical question" that anyone can pose. This question deals with "the humanity of man", and when he seeks an answer without success, he "arrives at an existential crisis" (*own translation*).[59]

It cannot be denied that a great deal of the suffering that people have to endure appears to them to be meaningless and irrational. Christians and other believers are convinced that life and everything connected to it only makes sense if they can experience it in relationship with God.

It may be argued that this need for meaning in life flows from the fact that human beings are rational beings – apart from the fact that they are also emotional beings and beings who act upon their urges and instincts. They seek a reason for their suffering and misfortune that makes sense, that is rational or logical.

---

[57] Shermer, *The Believing Brain*, 186.
[58] Frankl, *Man's Search for Meaning*, 6.
[59] Rossouw, *Die Sin van die Lewe*, 6.

Religion usually provides in this need. Van den Heever theorizes that this search for meaning lies at the root of all forms of religion; the initial naive explanations of pre-scientific people needed the presence of gods and spirits as an explanation for natural phenomena, as well as the vicissitudes of life.[60]

Grayling reminds us that most people are too lazy or unable to think for themselves and that they need an institution, such as the tribe, the temple, or the church, to do their thinking for them and to provide them with a ready-made world view to make sense of life and the world. That is one of the reasons why religion has survived[61]

A sane human being is able to make decisions freely. Accordingly, he also has the need to put this freedom into practice. That means that he seeks to have control over his own life. If he gets caught up in circumstances where this control becomes impossible, then the result is frustration and a feeling of powerlessness.

The down-side of human freedom is responsibility. A person must always be able to justify his decisions towards society and himself in the light of his own ethical principles. A normal human being is endowed with a conscience and it is unpleasant to be plagued by a bad conscience. Therefore, people find it best to practice their freedom of choice with responsibility – unless they are pathological liars and cheaters.

Religion also provides norms and standards for good, decent, acceptable, and right behaviour for adherents. In the Bible, one finds, for instance, the Ten Commandments with certain prescriptions for good and moral behaviour. This provides in the need for freedom and responsibility. People are challenged to make certain decisions and they have to respond to the dictates of their consciences.

---

[60] Van den Heever, *Wat Moet ons met ons Kerk Doen?* 1–2.
[61] Grayling, *The God Argument,* 160.

ORACLES

The existence of oracles, prophets, sages, soothsayers, and seers through the ages aided in the continued existence of all types of religion. People were always interested to know what the future would bring and what the advice of the gods, the spirits, or the ancestors in certain circumstances was – and oracles provided in that need.

These oracles purportedly had the power to communicate with the spirits of the dead ancestors, which gave them much power and influende in their societies.[62]

RITUALS AND CEREMONIES

All religions are characterized by rituals and ceremonies. All religions celebrate important events, such as weddings and funerals, with certain routines and stereotyped actions.

These actions, obviously, convey meaning to the participants. They are symbolic acts to commemorate certain historical events or to give expression to their beliefs and hopes. These actions strengthen the feeling of community between the members of a certain tribe or community and affirm that they share the same belief system, ideals, and values.

Although some of these rituals and ceremonies may seem strange and even bizarre to the uninitiated, it is accepted by all that they convey meaning, that the participants are strengthened in their beliefs, and that they are convinced that they are performing actions and movements that are pleasing to the deity or the spirits. The believers even have the conviction that their gods are present at their ceremonies and meetings – albeit in an invisible way.

---

[62] Enc Brit, "Animism:.

ANIMISM AND THE ORIGIN OF RELIGION

Healing dance by a San tribe, Southern Africa

Animists who perform rituals do so in the belief that they are able to influence the gods, natural forces such as the weather, and the behavior of other people with their actions. If they do not achieve the desired result, it must be that they have committed some or other mistake or sin while performing the rituals and that that displeased the gods and spirits. For that reason, it is necessary to perform the necessary actions correctly during a funeral to send the spirit of the deceased off on his dangerous journey to the world of the spirits in the afterlife and to prevent the spirit of the deceased to turn into a ghost who could haunt or harm the living.[63]

Religion in all its permutations, including animism, has managed to survive through the ages, partly due to the fact that believers and adherents participate in established and traditional customs, formalities, and liturgies in a social setting. Without these, religion would have lost much of its appeal.

---

[63] Enc Brit, "Animism"; NW Enc, "Animism".

How did ancient religions develop from animism into more sophisticated forms? The next chapter deals with this question.

Chapter 3
ANCIENT CIVILIZATIONS

MESOPOTAMIA

Successive Civilizations

It is generally acknowledged that the oldest civilization on earth originated in Mesopotamia, the region between the twin rivers, the Tigris and the Euphrates. The name "Mesopotamia" is derived from Greek and means the region "between the rivers". Ancient Mesopotamia, which included several successive civilizations, was located in what is today Iraq and parts of Turkey and Syria.

King Hammurabi (standing) receiving his royal insignia and laws from a god

The Sumerian civilization is the oldest Mesopotamian civilization and it arose more or less during the period of 4 500 – 4 000 BC. This civilization was later absorbed into the successive civilizations of the Akadians, Babylonians, and Assyrians, until the Neo-Babylonian empire was overthrown by the Persians during 539 BC.

Although Mesopotamia was the home of more than one civilization with its own characteristic languages and traditions, there was also some continuity, especially in the fields of religion and culture.

Mesopotamia is known as the brithplace of the first towns and cites that developed systems of government with codified laws.

City life, where people live in close proximity to each another, can easily lead to disorder, chaos, and strife and, therefore, laws had to be passed by the kings to ensure peace and order. To legitimize these laws, they had to be given the status of divine orders.

Innovations

The art of writing was invented by the Sumerians. They were also responsible for developments in the fields of architecture, engineering, metalurgy, agriculture, astronomy, and mathematics. We inherited from them the convention of dividing a minute into sixty seconds, an hour into sixty minutes, and a circle into 360 degrees. The Bablylonians divided the year into twelve parts.[64]

Astrology was an important part of Mesotaminan religious scene. Althouigh the Sumerians and Akadians left some records of their observations of the sky and the stars, it was especially the Babylonians who developed a system to fathom the will and plans of the gods by noting the positions of the twelve starry constellations through which the sun travels in a year's time (called the Zodiac by the Greeks) and the seven observable planets at the moment of the birth of an important person, for whom a horoscope could be drawn up, giving hints of his fate. These planets were the visible moving heavenly bodies, namely the sun, the moon, Mercury, Venus, Mars, Jupiter, and Saturn – to use their Latin and English names, which are translations of the old Babylonian names.

It was thought that the positions of the stars and the planets relative to the horizon provided insights into the objectives and wishes of the gods and made predictions about the future possible – the outcome of battles, the death of a king, *etcetera*.

---

[64] Enc Brit, "Sumer"; Enc Brit, "Mesopotamia"; Kennedy, "6 Early Human Civilizations".

The astronomers or astrologers of those times were also priests since watching the skies and interpreting the messages of the pantheon of gods was seen as primarily a religious activity.[65]

Subterranean Realm of the Dead

The Mesopotamians believed that the souls of the dead were gathered in a realm of the dead, described as a city or a house from which no one could return or escape. This netherworld was thought to be below the surface of the inhabited world and was the opposite of the heavens where most of the gods resided. This netherworld was not seen as heaven or hell since all the dead were destined to go there, irrespective of their lifestyle while still alive. It was, therefore, not a place of punishment or reward for the dead.

It was important to provide a deceased person with a decent burial with appropriate mourning ceremonies to prevent his ghost from haunting his relatives. The soul had to be kept happy in the netherworld by offerings of food and beverages at his grave because the dark and bleak netherworld could not provide in those needs.

The soul or ghost of a dead person continued to exist after death because mankind was thought to have been created from a mixture of clay (of which Msepotamia had abundant supplies) and the blood of a deity. This ellement of divine blood ensured that the soul of the deceased, situated in either his blood or breath, survived death. Somebody was deemed to be dead if he has lost all his blood or stopped breathing.

The spirit of the deceased did not enter the afterlife immedia-

---

[65] Enc Brit, "Astrology"; Thiel, *And then there was Light,* 35, 43–44; Malina, *On the Genre and Message of Revelation,* 2–10; Gauquelin, *Astrology and Science,* 101–03; Peters, *The Harvest of Hellenism,* 437–39; Hengel, *Judentum und Hellenismus,* 432–33; McGregor and Purdy, *Jew and Greek,* 291–92.

tely and had to be guided through seven gates of the city of the netherworld by the appropriate funerary rites. Upon arrival in the afterlife, the deceased's soul was examined by the god of the underworld. The outcome of this examination was partly determined by the quality of the funeral and mourning ceremonies. If these rites were performed adequately, sometimes even taking seven days, the soul of the deceased could regain his previous social status, which he had while still alive. He could then be welcomed by his ancestors in their midst.[66]

The Israelite elite spent a few decades in Bablylonia after Jerusalem was sacked by Nebukanezar's army in 597 BC. It will be pointed out in the next chapters how much influence the Mesopotamian religiouse ideas and astrology had on the post-exilic Hebrew Scriptures and the New Testament.

EGYPT

Influence

The second-oldest civilization of earth, ancient Egypt, also exerted considerable influence upon the Israelites. Of course, the Israelites were also influnced by the Mesopotamian civilizations and they retained the memory of their patriarch, Abraham, who emigrated from Ur, a Sumerian city, to the land of Canaan. The Hebrews were slaves in Egypt for four centuries before they escaped into the desert and eventually settled in Canaan. At that time, Canaan was nominally Egyptian territory, although it was inhabited by non-Egyptians. Canaanite cultures show considerable influence from the strong and ancient Egyptian example.[67]

---

[66] Segal, *Life after Death*, ch 2; Enc Brit, "Mesopotaminan Religion", Choksi, "Ancient Mesopotamian Beliefs".
[67] Segal, *Life after Death*, ch 1.

That Israel was indeed influenced by Egypt is demonstrated by the fact that certain texts in the Hebrew Scriptures were copied from Egyptian documents. For instance, Psalm 104 is clearly an adaptation of the Hymn to the Aten (the sun god, worshipped by Pharaoh Akhenaten). Proverbs 22: 17 – 24: 22 seemingly relies on the wisdom and instructions of Amenemope. Isaiah 19 seems to be dependent upon Egyptian oracles. Other examples can be cited.[68]

The start of the Egyptian civilization in the Nile valley and the Nile Delta can be dated to around 3 100 BC when the country was united under the first Pharaohs. Archaeologists, though, have found primitive Egyptian graves in the desert dating from more or less 5 500 BC. Writing seems to have been inevnted in Egypt shortly before the unification of the country and the art of writing must have aided the administration of the new state.

There were two basic types of writing – hieroglyphs, which were used for monuments and display, and the cursive form known as hieratic, used for less important documents on wood or papyrus. Hieroglyphs consisted of small pictures that represented sylables in the Egyptian language.[69]

Pantheon

The numerous monuments, tombs, inscriptions, and documents that have survived the centuries, as well as archaeological diggings, provide us with a lively picture of Egyptian religious views and the treatment of their dead. The ancient Egyptian civilization showed a remarkable resilience during the three millennia it endured, although there were certain developments as time went on. The Egyptians worshipped a whole pantheon of gods through the centuries, each one concerned with some or other aspect of the world and life.

---

[68] Schipper, "Egyptian Influences".

[69] Bowman, "Egypt, Ancient"; Brunner and Dorman, "Hieroglyphic Writing".

Just as the animists and the Mesopotamians, the Egyptians believed in an afterlife. For them, the realm of the dead was not situated under the hot desert sands surrounding their country, but between the stars in the sky. The soul had to endure various dangers, including demons, on his way to his eternal destination. Tombs and coffins contained copies of the Book of the Dead, a document that instructed the soul of the deceased how to ward off these dangers and which spells could be used to stay safe.

Weighing of the Heart

Anubis weighing the soul of the scribe Ani, from the Egyptian Book of the Dead, *c.* 1275 BC.

The final stage before reaching heavenly bliss, which was deemed to be a perfected copy of Egyptian life, was the weighing of the heart where the god of death, Anubis (pictured with a jackal's head) weighed the heart of the departed. A questionnaire had to be completed to make sure that the newly arrived soul was not guilty of a long range of wrongs, transgressions, and crimes. His heart was then hung in a balance scale against a feather, which symbolized truth, order, and honesty. This ceremony took place in the presence of Ositis, the chief deity. If the test was passed, the soul could pass into the fields of plenty.

If the test was failed, an ugly beast with the head of a crocodile, the body of a lion and the hind quarters of a hippopotamus, devoured that heart. That meant that that particular soul was extinguished, erased, or eradicated, which was a most horrible fate for the Egyptians who wished to experience the pleasures of the afterlife.[70]

Mummification

It was deemed necessary to preserve the corpse of the deceased as carefully as possible to ensure a safe passage of the soul into the hereafter. People who could afford it, mummified the bodies of their dead relatives and buried them in safe tombs to prevent the looting of the treasures buried with the mummy. Many tombs contained dolls or models of servants who supposedly came to life and served their masters and mistresses in the afterlife.[71]

The bodies of deceased kings and their families received special treatment since the Pharaohs were thought to be divine beings, the offspring of Osiris. The kings of the third royal dynasty were buried in imposing pyramids. Later kings were buried in die Valley of the Kings in subterranean tombs of which the tomb of Tutankhamun is the best known since it was discovered in 1927 with all its contents still inside. It was thought that the Pharaoh would join the other gods after his death and, therefore, special care was given to his funeral and mummification.[72]

---

[70] Oakes and Gahlin, *Ancient Egypt,* 394–95; Bowman, "Egypt, Ancient".
[71] Oakes and Gahlin, *Ancient Egypt,* 396–99; Bowman, "Egypt, Ancient".
[72] Oakes and Gahlin, *Ancient Egypt,* 114–15; 424–25; Bowman, "Egypt, Ancient".

PERSIA

Monotheism and Dualism

Judea became a Persian province in 539 BC when king Cyrus of Persia conquored the Neo-Babylonian empire and allowed the Jewish exiles in Babylonia to return home and granted them limited self-rule. This development inevitably influenced the post-exilic Hebrew Scriptures. It is, therefore, necessay to describe the Persian religion with its beliefs about the afterlife.

The classic Persian religion was the brainchild of the religious reformer Zoroaster or Zarathustra (c. 1500–1000 BC) and it is still being practiced in remote parts of Iran and India today. He convinced the people of his vision to worship a single supreme deity, Ahura Mazda, although many of the gods of the previous polytheistic religion were retained as lesser celestial beings – comparable to the angels found in the Bible. They were also regarded as emanations of Ahura Mazda. This supreme God was seen as the source of all blessings, truth, honesty, goodness, and light.

There was, though, also an evil spirit called Ahriman or Angra Mainyu, the enemy of Ahura Mazda and the source of darkness and all that is evil, bad, wrong, and horrible. A constant battle rages between light and darkness, good and evil, although it was expected that light and goodness would eventually prevail.

Human beings were created by Ahura Mazda with free will and they can, therefore, choose to either lead good and virtuous lives, or to follow the seduction of Ahriman.[73]

Although Zoroastrianism worshipped a chief deity and creator of the world, Ahura Mazda, his opponent, Ahriman, almost had the status of an equal deity and, therefore, the Persian religion is often regarded as dualistic and not a true form of monotheism.

---

[73] Duchesne-Guillemin, "Zoroastrianism"; Mark, "Ancient Persian Religion."

The Fravahar (Farohar or Fravashi) symbolizes the "Divinity within Humanity," the essence of God that dwells in every human being and in all of Creation (Persepolis, c. 500 BC)

The Afterlife

According to Zoroastrianism, the immaterial soul of a person had a pre-existence, before being united with a material body at birth. This soul lingered three days in the vicinity of the corpse after the death of that person. Relatives of the deceased had to spend this time in prayer and fasting to ward off evil demons from the Abyss who threaten the soul on its journey to the afterlife, the spiritual realm.

The soul was then led across a narrow bridge to the afterlife where it was judged by Ahura Mazda, who examined the person's consience, and then sent him either to the House of Song, or to the House of Lies. The House of Song, or heaven, had four divisions and the souls of the dead were assigned to a division according to their former lifestyle. Those on the highest level enjoyed the direct presence of Ahura Mazda.

The House of Lies also had four divisions, from bad to worse, where sinners were being punished. There was, in addition, an intermediate place, a sort of Purgatory, where souls were housed that did not fit into one of the two houses.

Since Ahura Mazda has perfect love, also for the evil sinners in the House of Lies, he was expected to provide a savior at the end of days to salvage these unfortunate souls, although Ahriman, the embodiment of evil, would then be totally vanquised and vaporized.

    Mark finds that post-exilic Judaism, Christianity, and Islam were all certainly influenced by Zoroastrianism. The concepts of Judgment Day, a supreme God, Satan as the personification of evil, demons from the Abyss, a perfect heaven, and a horrible hell are all to be found in each one of these reiligons.[74]

GREECE AND THE HELLENISTIC WORLD

Greek Pantheon

The names of the most important ancient Greek gods are well-known. There were, for instance, Zeus, the chief deity and father of the gods, Aphrodite, the godess of love, Ares, the god of war, Athena, the godess of wisdom, Chronos, the god of time, Poseidon, the god of the sea, Apollo, the god of music and the arts, Artemis, the godess of fertility, and so forth. They lived on top of the highest mountain in Greece, Mount Olympus.[75]

The Soul or Spirit

The ancient Greeks used more than one word for the concept of a human soul. The word *psyche* (Greek: ψυχή) was used for the soul or life force of man, but also for his breath. When a person blew out his last breath on his deathbed, it was seen as the soul leaving that body. The will or the life force of a person was signified by the word *thymos* (Greek: θυμος).

    The ghost or phantom of a dead person after his soul had reached the realm of the dead, Hades, was called an

---

[74] Mark, "Death and Afterlife in Ancient Persia".
[75] Pollard, "Greek Mythology".

εἴδωλον (*eidolon*), which may also mean an "image" or "shadow". The word πνεῦμα (*pneuma*) is usually translated with "spirit". Its literal meaning is also "breath" or "wind".

From all this it is clear that the ancient Greeks conceptualized of the soul or spirit in rather concrete ways. The soul or the spirit was not viewed as a totally immaterial entity, but rather as an attribute of the living physical body.[76]

Hades and Tartarus

The earliest Greek literary works thought of the destination of the souls of all deceased as the netherworld, called *Hades* (Greek: Ἅδης). This was also the name of the Greek deity in charge of this netherworld, which was to be found in a deep abyss. During later times, it was thought that evil and wicked people were condemned to *Tartarus* (Greek: Τάρταρος), the deepest pit in Hades where the gods also kept their enemies locked up. Virtuous people's souls were, though, thought to be taken to the fields of *Elysium* (Greek: Ἠλύσιον), also part of the netherworld, where a happy existence awaited them. It was also sometimes regarded as a land at the edge of the world or as a remote island. The happiness in Elysium was also dependent upon the way the living on earth remembered the dead and honored their memory.[77]

To reach Hades, the souls or shaddows of the demised had to be rowed over the Styx, a river filled with dark and poisonous water. The souls were taken by die boat man Charon, who demanded payment from every soul for his services and for that reason a coin was usually placed in the mouth of a corpse before burial.[78]

---

[76] Mackay, "Early Greek Theories".
[77] Mark, "The Afterlife in Ancient Greece".
[78] Enc. Brit, "Charon"; Enc Brit, "Styx".

The Hellenistic World

The young king of Macedonia, Alexander the Great, who was a military genius, conquored the whole of Greece, Palestine, Egypt, and Persia up to the edge of India during the fourth century BC. After his death, his vast empire was divided between his three generals who declared themselves kings. The result was that the Greek language and Greek culture became the dominant language and culture all over the eastern parts of the Mediterranean world. That was the start of the Hellenistic age.

Bust of Zeus, Vatican Museum

The religious scene of the Hellenistic world was characterized by the availability of a wide range of religioms from various countries. Inhabitants of these countries often settled elsewhere and took their old religions with them. They often recruited new adherents from the locals. People could choose between the traditional Greek religion (later merged with the Roman religion after Rome had taken over the Hellenistic world), the Egyptian religion, the religion of Israel, and other religions from the East.

There were, for instance, Jews not only in Judea and Galilee, but also in Alexandria in Egypt, in Babylonia, in Greece, in Asia Minor (where the apostle Paul grew up), and even in Rome (see chapter 16 of Paul's letter to the Romans in which he sent his greetings to Jewish acquiantances in Rome).

All these religions couldn't escape the influence of the Greek culture and borrowed certain elements from it.[79] A good example was the Jewish theologian and philosopher, Philo of Alexandria, who was a contemporary of Jesus of Nazareth. He tried to combine the teachings of the Old Testament with the philosphy of Plato.[80]

Various syncretistic and secret cults emerged in this world. According to Smith, they often preached a neo-Platonic dualism between body and soul (see chapter 7). It was thought that the soul had a pre-existence before being united with the material body in the evil and corrupt world. The adherents of the cult had to be instructed about their origin and their eventual destination after death where they would be reunited with the deity.[81]

The ancient Greek oracles – especially the Oracle of Delphi – are well known. Robert Temple investigated the histories of these oracles and concluded that most of them amounted to a "pious fraud". Clients who came for information about the future or advice from the gods were often drugged before they encountered the priest(ess), sybil, or seer – which brought them into a confused state during which they were highly suggestible. Many a pronouncement of the oracles was extremely ambiguous and vague and could be interpreted in any way. Many seers also used drugs to induce an altered state of consciousness during which they experienced hallucinations, which were seen as messages from the gods. The priests or seers operating the oracles became rich since their clients paid much for the "privilege" to consult the gods and the spirits.

Ancient oracles around the Mediterranean Sea were connected by a network of carrier-pigeons, which could deliver news in the form of messages tied to their legs from far-away places – the outcomes of battles, the death of kings, *etcetera* – within a day, long

---

[79] Smith, "Helenistic Religion".
[80] Enc Brit, "Philo Judaeus:.
[81] Karoglou, "MysteryCults"; Smith, "Helenistic Religion".

before this news reached that place through conventional means, namely through official couriers and other travelers. That enabled the oracle to "predict" certain events before they became known through other, more conventional, means.[82]

Temple gave a detailed description of the very ancient Oracle of the Dead at Cuma, on the Bay of Naples in Italy. This oracle, which was closed down in the time of Emperor Augustus, consisted of a network of tunnels to simulate the Underworld or Tartarus where the souls of the dead were supposed to be kept. There was even a make-believe Styx, the river across which the souls of those who were gone had to be taken in a boat to reach their final destination.

People who consulted this oracle were kept in isolation for three days while they were being drugged, before they were led deeper into the tunnels where they encountered the sybil or pythia, as well as people playing the parts of dead spirits, who responded to their enquiries.[83]

Astrology

After Alexander the Great had conquered the Babylonian and Persian empires in the fourth century BC, the Babylonian cosmology and astrology were taken over by the Hellenistic world and later by the Roman Empire.[84] Peters constatates: "For nearly five centuries, from the mid-second century before Christ to the triumph of Christianity, the ancient world was in the almost unchallenged grip of this half-religious, half-scientific phenomenon".[85]

The Greeks knew that the earth is a globe. For them, the earth was hanging motionless at the center of the universe and the seven

---

[82] Temple, *Netherworld*.
[83] Temple, *Netherworld*, 3–162.
[84] Malina, *On the Genre and Message of Revelation*, 6.
[85] Peters, *The Harvest of Hellenism*, 438.

planets moved in circular orbits around the earth. Beyond the planets, the fixed stars were to be found. The positions of the planets in relation to the background stars and the horizon revealed to them the intentions of the gods.[86]

The city of Alexandria in Egypt with its world-famous library was the center of learning in the Mediterranean world before Christianity became the leading religion under Emperor Constantine in the fourth century AD. Taylor and Hay remark that "in this city, astral symbolism was built into its very nomen-clature". They also conclude "that astrology was one of the most important 'Chaldean' cultural imports into Alexandria".[87] The Egyptian astronomer and mathematician Ptolemy (Latin name: Claudius Ptolemaeus), who lived during the second century AD, collected all the scientific knowledge regarding the cosmos of his day and wrote the books known as the Almagest and the Tetrabiblos. He is still regarded today by the astrological fraternity as the greatest expert on astrology. His earth-centered cosmology held sway throughout the Middle Ages in Europe and the Arabian world.[88]

The Hellenistic and Roman cultures adopted the Babylonian constellations in the starry sky. We inherited their Latin names, such as Leo, Virgo, Pegasus, Centaurus, Sagittarius, Ursa Major, Taurus, Scorpius, Gemini, and others.

The Jews and the early Christians who lived in the Hellenistic world were unable to escape the influence of this ancient astrology as will be shown in later chapters. John of Patmos, the author of Revelation, based most of his visions on the starry skies with the astrological constellations.[89]

---

[86] Malina, *On the Genre and Message of Revelation*, 4.
[87] Taylor & Hay, "Astrology in Philo", 1 & 18.
[88] Jones, "Ptolemy".
[89] Scholtz, *The Prophecies of Revelation*.

INDIA

Hinduism

The traditional polytheistic religion of India, Hinduism, can trace its roots to the period between 2 000 and 1 500 BC. The foundational scriptures of this religion are the Vedas and the Upanishads.

One of the main tenets of this religion is that people can expect to be reborn after death into another being or person, depending upon their lifestyle during their previous lives. The ultimate goal is to break out of this never-ending cycle of reincarnation or death and rebirth.[90]

Buddhism

The beginning of Buddhism can be traced back to India since the sixth or fifth centuries BC and it is based mainly on the teachings of the Buddha. He was the legendary and charismatic teacher Siddhartha Gautama who gave up a life of luxury as a prince to find the key to true happiness and peace of mind.

The adherents of this religion can be found in most countries in Asia. This religion also espouses the belief in reincarnation, just as the Hindus. The Buddhist hopes to achieve nirvana, the dissolution of the soul after attaining moral perfection, after a series of deaths and rebirths.[91]

---

[90] Doniger & Smith, "Hinduism"; Mallam, "Hinduism".
[91] Enc Brit, "Buddhism"; Department of Religion and Theology, Bristol Buddhist Studies, "Death and Dying in Buddhism".

Chapter 4
PRE-EXILIC HEBREW SCRIPTURES

PRELIMINARY REMARKS

According to Alan Segal, it is remarkable that the Hebrew Scriptures – called the Old Testament by Christians – contain very little about the afterlife and the state of the souls of those who hav given up the ghost, in contrast with the Istraelites' neighboring nations, the Mesopotamians, Egyptians, Persians, Canaanites, and Greeks, who all left extensive records of their views regarding the afterlife.

Segal theorizes that the final editors of the various Old Testament books may have removed undesirable descriptions of the afterlife from the various books that may have reminded the Israelites of pagan ideas and practices in an effort to emphasize the difference between the monotheism of Israel and the polytheism of their pagan neighbors – although he provides no proof for this idea.

While these other cultures each had a separate deity for the netherworld, the abode of the dead, the Hebrew Scriptures merely mentioned that YHWH, their national God, reigned over all of his creation, including the netherworld, without providing too many details. The reason for this may have been an effort to counter the tendency of many Israelites to worship the gods of their pagan neighbors and to highlight the uniqueness of the Israelite religion.[92]

In the following paragraphs, the views regarding heaven, the netherworld, the afterlife, and the nature of the soul or spirit after death as described in pre-exilic scriptures, documents produced during the exile (586–539 BC), post-exilic literature, and apocryphal

---

[92] Segal, *Life after Death*, ch 3.

works from the period after the finalization of the Old Testament, will be pieced together from various sources. It is necessary to distinguish these periods from each other since the Israelites and later the Judeans after the end of the exile in Babylonia were influenced differently by their neighbors during these succesive periods.

It must be pointed out that scholars have been able to identify the constituent parts or elements of some books in the Hebrew Scriptures. It transpired, for instance, that the Pentateuch, the first five books of the Old Testament, the Jewish Torah, is a combination of four different texts that were written at different times. That means that the traditional view, namely that they were written by Moses, cannot be upheld any longer. The three oldest sources can be differentiated by their use of different names for God and a focus on worshiping practices. The oldest is the so-called J Document, which uses the name *YHWH* (יְהוָה) for God or "the Lord".[93] The Elohist (E) uses the name *God* (אֱלֹהִים – *Elohim*).[94] The Priestly Document or P is mainly concerned with the rituals, sacrifices, and purity laws and practices of Israel. These three sources can be dated to periods before or during the exile.[95] The book of Deuteronomy (D) is a separate document that grew in stages and was only finalized after the exile.[96]

The prophetic book of Isaiah consists of three separate parts, usually called Isaiah (ch 1–39), Deutero-Isaiah (ch 40–55), and Trito-Isaiah (ch 56–66). The books of the prophets Jeremiah, Micah, and Zechariah also consist of earlier and later parts.[97]

---

[93] Boshoff, *Geskiedenis*, 98.
[94] Boshoff, *Geskiedenis*, 116.
[95] Boshoff, *Geskiedeenis*, 176.
[96] Boshoff, *Geskiedenis*, 170.
[97] Boshoff, *Geskiedenis*, 6–8.

The pre-exilic period ended in 586 BC when the capital, Jerusalem, was ravaged by the Babylonian army, the Judean monarchy came to an end, and the elite of the country was taken away in exile to Babylonia. By that time, the northern Israelite kongdom was already destroyed by the Assyrians. The following pieces of literature can be classified as pre-exilic: The E Document, the J Document, Amos, Hosea, the books of Samuel and Kings, Micah, Isaiah, the first part of Jeremiah, Nahum, Zaphaniah, Habakuk, and certain Psalms.[98]

Books composed during the exile are as follows: Lamentations, certain Psalms, Esekiel, Obadiah, the P Document, and Deutero-Isaiah.

The post-exilic period started in 539 BC when the Persian king Cyrus conquered the Neo-Babylonian empire and allowed the Judean exiles to return to Jerusalem. Judea became a Persian province and the influence of Persian religious ideas become apparent in the Hebrew Scriptures during this time. Lirerature from this period include Trito-Isiaha, Haggai, both parts of Zechariah, Malachi, Joel, Ezra, Nehemiah, Job, Ruth, Jonah, Deuteronomy, the final edition of the Pentateuch, the final book of Psalms, and Proverbs.[99]

The Persian period ended in 333 BC when Alexander the Great conquored large pasrts of the Middle East, including Judea, Samaria, and Galilee. Greek became the principal language and the Hebrew Scriptures from this time show the influence of Greek ideas. The following books can be dated to this period: the books of Chronicles, Song of Songs, Ecclesiastes, Daniel, Esther, the books of the Makkabees, Enoch, and the Book of Jubilees.[100]

---

[98] Boshoff, *Geskiedenis,* 6–7.
[99] Boshoff, *Geskiedenis,* 7–8.
[100] Boshoff, *Geskiedenis,* 8.

GOD'S DWELLING

Segal points out that the pre-exilic literature of Israel is very vague about heaven as God's dwelling. [101] This is borne out by an inspection of the earliest literature of Israel that has been passed on to us after having been revised and edited during the period when the Old Testament was being finalized, more or less during the second century BC.

The very first words in the Bible assure us: "In the beginning God created the heavens and the earth" (Gen 1: 1). The rest of this creation myth in Gen 1: 1 – 2: 4 tells us nothing about the properties of this heaven and it only demotes the pagan gods of the sun, the moon, and the stars in the sky to mere creations of the God of Israel. Their functions were simply to provide light and act as time-keepers (Gen 1: 14 –19).

The word used for *heaven* and *sky*, (Hebrew: (שָׁמַיִם – *shamayim*), occurs five times in this creation myth. It is applied to the heaven in general, the expanse between the waters in the sky and the waters beneath the earth, the space in which the astronomical bodies were placed, and the space through which birds fly. In other words: everything above the earth's surface was regarded as "heaven". It is remarkable that the Hebrew word for heaven always appears in the plural and should, strictly speaking, be translated with "heavens", indicating all the spaces above the surface of the earth, including God's abode.

The builders of the Tower of Babel had the idea of erecting an edifice "whose top will go up as high as heaven" (Gen 11: 1–9).

Heaven was not seen as the only residence of God. Genesis 3: 8–10 mentions that God strolled during the early evening through the Garden of Eden, where he sought the first humans after they had

---

[101] Segal, *Life after Death*, ch 3.

eaten from the forbidden fruit.

The king of Salem and high priest of "God the Most High", Melchizedek, blessed Abram in the name of God, who is the "possessor of heaven and earth" (Gen 14: 18–20).

When Solomon inaugurated the temple in Jerusalem, he declared in his prayer:

Solomon's Prayer
1 Kgs 8: 27

> But will God in very deed dwell on the earth? Behold, heaven and the heaven of heavens can`t contain you; how much less this house that I have built!

Solomon's prayer shows that he thought of heaven as having more than one part – the "heaven of heavens", consisting of the different layers of the sky above the earth. The temple was supposed to be God's dwelling on earth.

Isaiah described the following vision:

Isaiah's Vision
Isa 6: 1–4

> 1. In the year that king Uzziah died I saw the Lord sitting on a throne, high and lifted up; and his train filled the temple.
> 2. Above him stood the seraphim: each one had six wings; with two he covered his face, and with two he covered his feet, and with two he did fly.
> 3. One cried to another, and said, Holy, holy, holy, is YHWH of Hosts: the whole earth is full of his glory.
> 4. The foundations of the thresholds shook at the voice of him who cried, and the house was filled with smoke".

Isaiah saw God's throne in his celestial temple or palace. His train or robe filled the whole place. He was surrounded by heavenly beings and he is called "YHWH of hosts". The word for *hosts* (צְבָאוֹת – *tsbaoth*) may be applied to an army with soldiers, a host of angels, or a cluster of stars. The smoke that he saw, may well have been the Milky Way, filled with star clouds, which he saw as surrounding God's throne in the sky. It is clear from Amos 5: 8 and Ps 148: 1–6 that the Israelites in this period thought of the stars as angels (instead of some of the gods as their pagan neighbors used to think). This host surrounded God's throne, which was situated between the stars, where Isaiah saw Him.

We read of only two men in the pre-exilic literature who were possibly taken up into heaven:

Men Taken up into Heaven
Gen 5: 24 and 2 Kgs 2: 12

- Enoch walked with God, and he was not, for God took him.
- It happened, as they still went on, and talked, that behold, [there appeared] a chariot of fire, and horses of fire, which parted them both apart; and Elijah went up by a whirlwind into heaven.

It is not quite clear what happened to Enoch and Elijah. Ancient alien enthusiasts guess that Elijah was taken away by an alien spacecraft from a far-away planet. It is impossible to determine whether something like that really happened, although it must be highly unlikely. In any case, we don't read in pre-exilic books of any other human beings who made it into God's heaven.

SOULS AND SPIRITS

An important text to understand how the pre-exilic Israelites thought about man as a creature of God is Gen 2: 7 –

Creation of Man
Gen 2: 7

> "YHWH God formed man from the dust of the ground, and breathed into his nostrils the breath of life; and man became a living soul."

The whole verse must also be quoted in Hebrew:

> וַיִּיצֶר יְהוָה אֱלֹהִים אֶת־הָאָדָם עָפָר מִן־הָאֲדָמָה וַיִּפַּח בְּאַפָּיו נִשְׁמַת חַיִּים וַיְהִי הָאָדָם לְנֶפֶשׁ חַיָּה

Some observarions about this text must be made:

- There is a clear play of words – *man* (הָאָדָם – *ha-adam*) was made from the *dust* of the ground or soil (הָאֲדָמָה – *ha-adamah*). This was to emphasize that man is a product of the earth and is made from the same sruff as other parts of creation.
- The life-giving force, given by the Creator, is נִשְׁמָה (*nishmah*), which means "breath, spirit". This point of view is understandable from the perspective of the ancients who associated the spirit or life with breathing. The sign that somebody had died was when he stopped breathing.
- This life-giving breath caused man to become a *living soul*. The expression used is נֶפֶשׁ חַיָּה (*nephesh chayah*). The word "nephesh", that occurs often in the Bible, has a rich meaning, namely: "soul, self, life, creature, person, appetite, mind, living being, desire, emotion, passion, that which breathes, the breathing substance or being, the inner being of man". These concepts may be regarded as synonyms in Hebrew.
- In other words: the soul or spirit of man was deemed to be synonymous with his breath. The soul was, therefore, not a non-material, supranatural entity, but simply the whole human being as a living organism who was breathing.

According to Segal, the Hebrews did not think of themselves as having a body and a separate soul, as we tend to think nowadays; they rather simply thought of themselvs as being souls.[102]

The word "nephesh" is used with the same meaning in Ps 343: 20, Ps 42: 5, 2 Kgs 9: 15, *etcetera*.

The usual Hebrew word for *spirit* is רוּחַ (*ruach*) and it has a wide range of meanings: "wind, air, breath, mind, heart, spirit" – which may be seen as synonyms. It is also used of the "Spirit of God". It is used in the double meaning of "breath" and "spirit" in the following passage:

Breath and Spirit
Ps 104: 29–30

> You hide your face: they are troubled; You send forth your Spirit they are created. You renew the face of the ground.

By using the same word for "breath" and "spirit", the Hebrews saw these concepts as identical. A person's breath was simply the sign that his spirit was still functioning and in running order. Dead people turned into *dust* or dry earth (Hebrew: עָפָר – *'aphar*) from which man was made in the first place.

The spirit (ruach) may be seen as the seat of emotions:

Spirit and Emotions
1 Sam 1: 15 –

> Hannah answered, No, my lord, I am a woman of a sorrowful spirit: I have drunk neither wine nor strong drink, but I poured out my soul before YHWH.

This verse demonstrates that the Hebrews saw the concepts of *soul* and *spirit* also as synonyms, describing the same thing since both

---

[102] Segal, *Life after Death*, ch 3.

occur in the quoted verse. In this verse, the words *spirit* and *soul* simply mean something like "mind" or "emotional mood".

The same applies to the following verse from Isaiah:

Soul and Spirit
Isa 26: 9

> With my soul have I desired you in the night; yes, with my spirit within me will I seek you earnestly.

THE PROCESS OF DYING

The second creation myth explains in Gen 2: 15–17 and Gen 3: 17–19 that man became mortal by disobeying God's order not to touch the fruit of a certain tree. That act, presumably, condemned all of mankind to die at some or other stage.

In general, it can be said that somebody dies when he stops breathing and gives up the *soul* or the *spirit* – according to the following verses in the Old Testament. We are, for instance, told of the patriarch Jacob:

Jacob Dies
Gen 49: 33

> When Jacob made an end of charging his sons, he gathered up his feet into the bed, and yielded up the spirit, and was gathered to his people.

This verse uses the word גוע (*gava*), which means "to expire, die, perish, give up the ghost, yield up the ghost, be dead".

We read in 1 Kgs 17: 20–23 that the prophet Elijah revived a dead boy whose soul ("nephesh") had left him by lying on the body of the child and praying to God to send back his soul, which happened – although Elijah's body heat may have revived a freezing child who became unconscious. See also Gen 35:18–19 regarding Rachel's passing away in the same manner.

King David's death is described as follows:

David's Death
1 Kgs 2: 1, 2 & 10

> Now the days of David drew near that he should die; and he charged Solomon his son, saying, I am going the way of all the earth. (...) David slept with his fathers, and was buried in the city of David.

Abraham received the promise that he would die a good death:

Abraham's Death
Gen 15: 15

> But you will go to your fathers in peace. You will be buried in a good old age.

Ancient family tombs in the country of Israel

These texts show that to sleep with one's fathers or ancestors simply means to be buried in a grave – mostly in a family tomb – and not to join them somewhere in an afterlife. 1 Kings 13: 22 mentions explicitly "the tomb of your fathers".

The fully clothed remains of the dead person were usually carried on a bier or litter to the tomb, which was a cave or a tunnel carved into a hillside. Burial in a coffin, cremation, and embalming were unknown. It was usually the duty of the heirs of the deceased to organize the funeral, which usually took the form of a procession to the tomb. The Torah did not prescribe how a funeral had to be conducted and it is unknown what ceremonies and rituals were supposed to be performed.

It is presumed that a funeral occurred within a day after death on account of the hot climate in Palestine. Num 19: 16 declared that anybody who was in contact with a corpse "will be unclean for seven days" and that may also have prompted the family members to get rid of the corpse as soon as possible.

The corpse was usually laid on a shelf inside the tomb and the tomb was then closed, usually with a flat round stone. After a few months, after the corpse had decomposed, the bones of the skeleton were gathered in a box or in a corner of the tomb to make place for new burials. Literary sources from those times do not mention any grave goods – jewelry, personal possessions, food and drink, or magical objects – that were to be buried with the corpse. In this respect, the ancient Israelites differed from their pagan neighbors who provided the corpse with objects that the spirit would have needed in the afterlife. The archaelogical record seems to confirm this, although some tombs were richly decorated.[103]

It was important to be buried in a family tomb in order to "sleep with the fathers" – and not in a foreign country or in a strange place.[104]

---

[103] Finkelstein &Silberman, *The Bible Unearthed*, 245–46.
[104] Jewish Virtual Library, "Death & Bereavement".

The Israelites wished to have a good death and avoid a bad death. An example of a good death was that of Abraham. He died a natural death at an advanced age, had offspring, was surrounded by his family, and was buried in the family tomb he had bought.

An example of a bad death was that of Absalom (2 Sam 18). He was still a relatively young man who died a violent and dishonorable death as a rebel against his father, King David, and he did not receive a proper funeral.[105]

THE REALM OF THE DEAD

Exodus 20: 4 tells us that the Israelites thought that God's creation consisted of three layers on top of each other:

Layers of Creation
Ex 20: 4

> You shall not make for yourselves an idol, nor any image of anything that is in the heavens above, or that is in the earth beneath, or that is in the water under the earth.

The earth was regarded as a flat disk. The netherworld, consisting of the primal flood and the abode of the dead, was to be found beneath the earth's surface. Everything above its surface was regarded as part of the heavens.

Under the surface of the earth there was supposed to be a deep *abyss*, called תְהוֹם (*tehom* – Gen 1: 2). This word has many meanings: "deep, depths, deep places, abyss, the deep, deep of subterranean waters, primeval ocean, the grave." This abyss encompassed the whole of the underworld.

Just as the Mesopotamians, Persians, and Greeks, the ancient Israelites thought that the souls or spirits of dead people went to a

---

[105] Spronk, "Good Death and Bad Death".

place under the surface of the earth, called "Sheol" (Gen 42: 38 and 44: 31). The Hebrew word שְׁאוֹל (*sheol*), is usually translated as "underworld, grave, hell, pit, the abode of the dead".

That this part of creation was indeed seen as being below the surface of the flat earth, is best illustrated by Num 16: 31–33 –

Realm of the Dead
Num 16: 31–33

> 31. It happened, as he [Moses] made an end of speaking all these words, that the ground split apart that was under them [a group of rebels];
> 32. and the earth opened its mouth, and swallowed them up, and their households, and all the men who appertained to Korah, and all their goods.
> 33. So they, and all that appertained to them, went down alive into Sheol: and the earth closed on them, and they perished from among the assembly

This is, no doubt, a description of a sinkhole that suddenly caved in, consisting of a cave or hollow space under the earth's surface and of which the roof unexpectedly collapsed.

Amos 9: 2 tells us that it was even possible to "dig into Sheol".

That this netherworld did not have its own reigning or managing deity, as the pagans thought, is displayed by Ps 139: 8 –

God in the Netherworld
Ps 139: 8

> If I ascend up into heaven, you [YHWH] are there. If I make my bed in Sheol, behold, you are there!

Sheol was thought of as a monster with a gaping mouth, with which it swallowed the dead:

Sheol a Monster
Isa 5: 14

Therefore Sheol has enlarged its desire, and opened its mouth without measure; and their glory, and their multitude, and their pomp, and he who rejoices among them, descend [into it].

The souls of the dead in Sheol were thought to be mere shaddows or silent ghosts, as is clear from Ps 88:

Ps 88: 10

Do you show wonders to the dead? Do the dead rise up and praise you?

The word used for *the dead* in the second part of this verse, is רְפָאִים *(repha'im)*, which means "shadows" or "ghosts".

Sheol is a Place of Silence:
Ps 115: 17

The dead do not give praise to the Lord; or those who go down to the underworld.

The Hebrew word for *underworld* in this text, דּוּמָה *(dumah)*, actually means "silence". This silence results from the inability of the dead inside Sheol to speak because they are asleep with their fathers:

Ps 31: 18

Let me not be shamed, oh Lord, for I have made my prayer to you; let the sinners be shamed, and let their mouths be shut in the underworld.

Isa 31: 18–19

> 18. For the underworld is not able to give you praise, death gives you no honour: for those who go down into the underworld there is no hope in your mercy.
> 19. The living, the living man, he will give you praise, as I do this day: the father will give the story of your mercy to his children.

There is also the idea that the spirit with its thoughts and memories disappears at death:

Spritis Vanish
Ps 146: 4

> His spirit departs, and he returns to the earth. In that very day, his thoughts perish.

It was forbidden, but also impossible, for the living to make contact with the dead. Leviticus 20: 6 clearly condemned any effort in this regard:

No Contact with the Dead
Lev 20: 6

> The soul that turns to those who have familiar spirits, and to the wizards, to play the prostitute after them, I will even set my face against that soul, and will cut him off from among his people.

The Hebrew word for *necrmancers* or people with familiar spirits is הַיִּדְּעֹנִים (*hayidd`oniyim*) – strictly speaking, the persons who have (esoteric) knowledge, but also soothsayers or necromancers.

Isaiah 19: 3 condemns the pagan Egyptian "spirit" of wizardry and communication with the dead:

Isa 19: 3

> The spirit of Egypt shall fail in the midst of it; and I will destroy the counsel of it: and they shall seek to the idols, and to the charmers, and to those who have familiar spirits, and to the wizards.

The Hebrew word for "those who have familiar spirits" in this passage is הָאֹבוֹת (*ha'obot*) – meaning "those who evoke the dead".

There is, though, a famous example of a prominent Israelite who did just that. We read in 1 Sam 28 that King Saul had a consultation or a séance at night with the witch of Endor and requested her to bring the spirit of the prophet Samual up because he wanted to know what the outcome of the looming battle against the army of the Philistines would be. Samuel purportedly announced that he and his sons would join him in the netherworld the next day, which frightened Saul severely, and which could have prompted him to give up the fight and commit suicide.

One may wonder: was it really Samuel's spirit that spoke to Saul? Saul – and his two servants – did not see Samuel themselves and asked the woman what she saw in the dark. She replied that she saw a man with a cloak coming from the earth. It is more than likely that the witch imitated Samuel's voice. The superstitious Saul and his servants erroneously believed that they really had contact with the late Samuel's spirit, who predicted Saul's imminent death.

GOD'S JUDGMENT

An important stage in the journey of the soul to the afterlife, according to the Egyptian religion, was the weighing of the heart. A similar thought is found in the pre-exilic literature of Israel:

God's Judgment
Ps 26: 1–2

> Judge me, YHWH, for I have walked in my integrity. I have trusted also in YHWH without wavering. Examine me, YHWH, and prove me. Try my heart and my mind.

Job 31: 5–7

> 5. If I have walked with falsehood, and my foot has hurried to deceit
> 6. Let me be weighed in an even balance, that God may know my integrity;
> 7. if my step has turned out of the way, if my heart walked after my eyes, if any defilement has stuck to my hands,
> 8. then let me sow, and let another eat; yes, let the produce of my field be rooted out.

However, this judgment was to take place during life on earth – not during an afterlife. The Hebrew Scriptures, though, also contain the promise that "the Day of the Lord" would arive, when the nations will be judged by God. The following passage is clear about this hope:

God's Judgment

Zeph 3: 8–12

> 8. "Therefore wait for me," says YHWH, "until the day that I rise up to the prey, for my determination is to gather the nations, that I may assemble the kingdoms, to pour on them my indignation, even all my fierce anger, for all the earth will be devoured with the fire of my jealousy.
> 9. For then I will purify the lips of the peoples, that they may all call on the name of YHWH, to serve him shoulder to shoulder.

> 10. From beyond the rivers of Cush, my worshipers, even the daughter of my dispersed people, will bring my offering.
> 11. In that day you will not be put to shame for all your doings, in which you have transgressed against me; for then I will take away out of the midst of you your proudly exulting ones, and you will no more be haughty in my holy mountain.
> 12. But I will leave in the midst of you an afflicted and poor people, and they will take refuge in the name of YHWH."

A careful reading of this prophecy makes it clear that this "day of the Lord" was not supposed to happen at the end of time or in the afterlife. This day of judgment was meant to be the start of a wonderful future for the people of God on earth.

COMMENTS

One has to concur with Segal who commented that it is clear that the pre-exilic literature of Israel provide very little details about the netherworld, the abode of the dead. Sheol was not regarded as a place or situation where respectable, righteous, and right-minded people were rewarded or where the bad, base, and black-hearted people were punished. It was merely the space or condition into which the dead entered when they had breathed their last breaths.[106]

The word "Sheol" may even be regarded as a general description of all graveyards or tombs where the dead were silent, sleeping with their ancestors, and unable to have any relationships with God or the living. They only lived on in the memories of their loved ones – not as individuals, each one with an identity and memories of life on earth. They were sleeping in their tombs and, therefore, not conscious of anything. They were simply dead,

---

[106] Segak, *Life after Death,* ch 3.

deceased, and departed. All that remained of them in the end was dust.

Segal adds:

> "What is most obvious in the history of preexilic Israelite thought is that reward and punishment are certainties in this life. It is possession of the land, many offspring, length of days, and a favored life that is promised by God for obedience to his covenant. (...) Land, length of days, descendants, and a happy life is what the covenant promises to the Israelites."[107]

In other words: God's blessings were meant for life on earth, not for an afterlife.

---

[107] Segal, *Life after Death,* ch 3.

Chapter 5
POST-EXILIC HEBREW SCRIPTURES

ADOPTION OF BABYLONIAN SYSTEM

During an after the exile in Babylon, the Judeans adopted the Babylonian astrology with its celestial constellations and regarded them as real entities. In Job 9: 9 and 38: 31–32 we read of the *Zodiac* (Hebrew: מַזָּרוֹת – *Mazzarot* – a word derived from "sunrise"), the Bear (Ursa Major), Orion (the Hunter) and the Pleiades (the Seven Sisters, a star cluster inside Taurus, the Bull). The "fleeing serpent" in the heavens is mentioned in Job 26: 13, and with that the constellation of Serpens (the Serpent) is meant. Serpens was traditionally associated with the snake of Genesis 3, the serpent that lured Adam and Eve into tasting and treating themselves with the forbidden fruit.[108]

Jeremiah 44: 17–19 mentions the "queen of the sky". It is not certain what this means – it may well refer to the planet Venus, that is, Astarte or Isis of the Israelites' pagan neighbors. In 2 Kgs 17: 30 a pagan deity "Nergal" is mentioned; this was the Mesopotamian name for the constellation of Sagittarius (the Archer).[109]

The people who hid the so-called Dead Sea Scrolls in a series of caves near Qumran in Palestine during the Jewish war of AD 66–70 against the Romans definitely adopted and adapted the Babylonian astrology. They had, amongst others, an astrological calendar naming the twelve constellations in the Zodiac by their Hebrew or Aramaic names. This document was dated to the last

---

[108] Allen, *Star Names,* 375.
[109] Allen, *Star Names,* 354.

decades of the first century BC. They removed the pagan elements from the names and the descriptions of these constellations in order to avoid any form of pagan idolatry.[110]

The Beit Alpha mosaic with Hebrew names for the different constellations of the Zodiac. The seasons are depicted on the corners.

The Jews still adhered to the Babylonian Zodiac a few centuries into the Christian era. Archaeologists found mosaic floors of ancient synagogues in the country of Israel depicting the Zodiac, with Hebrew names for the different constellations. The mosaic in the Beit Alpha synagogue (sixth century AD) is the best known.[111]

The Jews thought that the planets, stars, and constellations were angels and cherubs, instead of gods – which actually amounts

---

[110] Jacobus, "The Zodiac Sign Names".
[111] Dennis, "Jewish Myth".

to more or less the same. In Job 38: 4–8 we are told that when the foundations of the earth were laid by God, "the morning stars sang together, and all the sons of God shouted for joy." These "sons of God" are, of course, the angels – and they are equated with the stars.

Ps 148: 2–3 contains this call: "Praise him, all his angels! Praise him, all his host! Praise him, sun and moon! Praise him, all you shining stars!" That means that the angels, the host of heaven, and the astrological bodies were seen to be the same entities. Nehemiah 9: 6 assures us that God created everything, including the "host" of stars and that "the host of heaven" worships God.

The Sumerian, Chaldean, and Babylonian astrologers and priests studied the skies in order to find out what the intentions of the gods in the sky were regarding the fate of kingdoms, kings, and other important people. They drew up horoscopes in which the positions of the sun and other planets against the background of the constellations of the Zodiac and the horizon were plotted. That helped important people to make decisions regarding auspicious days on which to start new ventures and how to avert potential dangers.[112]

The post-exilic Scriptures seem to hold the same view. In Job 38: 33, this question is asked: "Do you know the laws of the heavens? Can you establish the dominion of it over the earth?" This question presupposes the view of ancient pagan astrology that events on earth are being influenced by the stars in heaven. Jeremiah 31: 35 mentions "the ordinances of the moon and of the stars", which were given by God. We also read of God's "ordinances of heaven and earth" in Jer 33: 25. These expressions suggest the rules according to which astrologers interpreted the divine intentions.

---

[112] Malina, *On the Genre and Message of Revelation*, 2–20.

HEBREW VIEW OF HEAVEN AND EARTH

It has already been shown that the Hebrew word for *heaven*, שָׁמַיִם (*shamayim*), was used for everything in the skyc, containing the atmosphere, the clouds, the stars, and the dwelling place of God.

Together with the Mesopotamians, the Judeans thought of the sky or the heaven as a vault above the earth. The author of the book of Job informs us in 22: 14 that God "walks on the vault of the sky", which means that He was to be found immediately beyond the dome surrounding the earth and onto which the planets and the stars were affixed. Isaiah 40: 22 tells us that God "sits above the circle of the earth, and the inhabitants of it are as grasshoppers…" The Hebrew word for *circle* (חוּג – *chug*) may also be translated as "vault" or "dome".

Various texts contain the idea that God spread the sky or the heavens like a sheet or a curtain over the earth (Job 9: 8; Ps 104: 2; Isa 40: 22; Isa 42: 5; Isa 44: 24; Isa 45: 12–13; Zech 12: 1).

We also find the notion that God dwells between the stars: "Isn't God in the heights of heaven? See the height of the stars, how high they are!" (Job 22: 12). Ps 19: 4 calls the firmament "a tent for the sun" behind which he hides at night and comes forth in the morning "as a bridegroom coming out of his chamber". This firmament rests on pillars that are planted on earth (Job 26: 11).

The result of all this is that the heavens as abode of God are part of the same space occupied by the earth and other celestial bodies. After all, Isa 66: 1 proclaims: "Thus says YHWH, heaven is my throne, and the earth is my footstool." There is, therefore, continuity between heaven and earth and the cosmos is a single closed system, containing God's heaven and earth.

All these texts make it clear that the Judeans thought of the heaven in a very concrete way. For them, the sky, the atmosphere, the starry skies, and the heaven as the home of God were parts of one and the same setup or structure. The contemporary idea that God's heaven must be somewhere outside the universe, probably in another dimension, would have been incomprehensible to the authors and original readers of the Old Testament books.

To summarize: there was, according to ancient Israel, no real difference between the sky with its clouds, the vault onto which the stars were pasted, and the dwelling of God. For that reason they used only one word, שָׁמַיִם (*shamayim*), to name the *sky*, the *starry heavens,* and the *heaven* as God's home.

As has been pointed out already, the world was thought to be a flat disc floating upon the primeval ocean (Exod 20: 4) and as such it had boundaries or a limit (Ps 74: 17). Proverbs 30: 4 mentions "all the ends of the earth" – in other words: the world had an edge or extremity where it ended. It was thought that there was water below the earth – most probably the source of the water that flowed from fountains (Deut 4: 19). Psalm 136: 6 says that God "spread out the earth above the waters." Proverbs 8: 28 mentions "the springs of the deep".

The world rests upon pillars or foundations (Prov 8: 29; Jer 31: 37; Zech 12: 1). On the other hand, the earth was deemed to be hanging in the void and Job 26: 7 says that God "stretches out the north over empty space, and hangs the earth on nothing."

HEBREW VIEW OF THE AFTERLIFE AND UNDERWORLD

The Old Testament gave very little attention to the afterlife and it is only the late book of Daniel, dating from the second century BC, that contains a promise that the faithful will be resurrected at the end of time and inherit life everlasting with God in heaven. We read in Dan 12: 2–3 –

Resurrection of the Dead
Dan 12: 2–3

> Many of those who sleep in the dust of the earth shall awake, some to everlasting life, and some to shame and everlasting contempt. Those who are wise shall shine as the brightness of the expanse; and those who turn many to righteousness as the stars forever and ever.

In other words: Daniel expected that some of the deceased faithful would be revived and gain places in the starry skies and that others would be sent to a horrible place. The influence of the Persian religion can be detected here, although the Egyptian notions about the afterlife between the stars may also have played a role.

Trito-Isaiah seems to contain a hint that a bad fate awauted God's evil enemies after death where they would be consumed by insatiable worms and an eternal fire:

God's Enemies
Isa: 60: 24

> They [thefaithful people of Israel] shall go forth, and look on the dead bodies of the men who have transgressed against me: for their worm shall not die, neither shall their fire be quenched; and they shall be an abhorring to all flesh.

For the rest, the Israelites merely expected to go to the underworld (שְׁאוֹל – *Sheol*) after they had stopped living where they would experience a shadowy existence (Ezek 31: 15, *etc*). This realm of the dead was thought to be below the surface of the flat earth. Ps 63: 9 locates it in "the lower parts of the earth". Whenever the Old Testament mentioned Sheol, it was made clear that the dead had to "descend" into this underworld.

According to Ps 6: 5, those in Sheol have no memories of God and they are silent, unable to give thanks to God.

Below the surface of the earth there was also supposed to be a deep *abyss*, called תְהוֹם (*tehom* – Gen 1: 2; Prov 8: 27–28). This word has many meanings: "deep, depths, deep places, abyss, the deep, deep of subterranean waters, primeval ocean, the grave". This abyss encompassed the whole of the underworld.

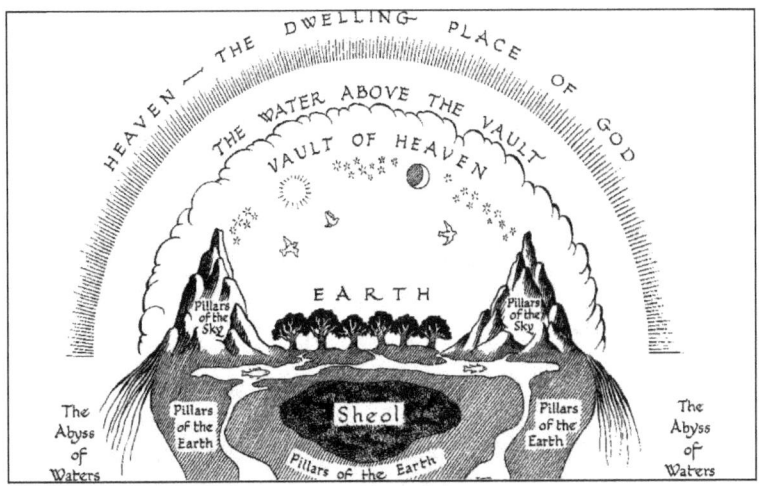

The Hebrew conception of the cosmos.

The illustration (above) provides a simplified view of how the the heavens, earth, the underworld, and the ocean under the earth were conceptualized by the authors of the Old Testament.

BURIAL OF THE DEAD

For a post-exilic Jew it was important to be buried with his ancestors – just as in pre-exilic times. We read, for instance, of Nehemiah:

Nehemiah's Forefathers
Neh 2: 5

> I said to the king," If it please the king, and if your servant have found favor in your sight, that you would send me to Judah, to the city of my fathers' tombs, that I may build it."

HEBREW VIEW OF THE SPIRIT

The Hebrew word for *spirit*, רוּחַ (*ruach*), has a wide range of meanings, as has been pointed out earlier: "wind, air, breath, mind, heart, spirit". It is also used of the "Spirit of God". In the light of our finding that the Old Testament envisaged God, heaven and angels in a very concrete way, it seems likely that all these meanings of the word *spirit* were synonyms and that the spirit was not regarded as a non-material entity, but something composed of air or wind and equated with the breath of man. An analysis of the use of this word in the post-exilic literature confirms this expectation.

The whole human being is regarded as a spiritual being (Ezek. 18: 31). God created the spirit within man (Zech 12: 1).

The following pronouncements in the Old Testament clearly use the words *spirit* and *breath* or *wind* as synonyms:

- But there is a spirit in man, and the breath of the Almighty gives them understanding (Job 32: 8).
- Thus says God Yahweh, he who created the heavens, and stretched them forth; he who spread abroad the earth and that which comes out of it; he who gives breath to the people on it, and spirit to those who walk therein (Isa 42: 5).
- Then said he to me, Prophesy to the wind, prophesy, son of man, and tell the wind, Thus says the Lord Yahweh: Come from the four winds, breath, and breathe on these slain, that they may live. So I prophesied as he commanded me, and the breath came into them, and they lived, and stood up on their feet, an exceeding great army" (Ezek 37: 9–10).
- Woe to him who says to the wood, 'Awake!' or to the mute stone, 'Arise!' Shall this teach? Behold, it is overlaid with gold and silver, and there is no breath in the midst of it (Hab 2: 19).

The human mind and heart as seat of emotions is often called *spirit*:

- A glad heart makes a cheerful face; but an aching heart breaks the spirit (Prov 15: 13)
- A cheerful heart makes good medicine, but a crushed spirit dries up the bones (Prov 17: 22).
- Nebuchadnezzar dreamed dreams; and his spirit was troubled, and his sleep went from him (Dan 2: 1).

The human spirit is also seen as the seat of the mind and thoughts:

- The spirit of my understanding answers me (Job 20: 3).
- My spirit diligently inquires: Will the Lord reject us forever? (Ps 77: 6–7).

The spirit is seen as the seat of desires:

Isa 26: 9

With my soul have I desired you in the night; yes, with my spirit within me will I seek you earnestly.

The following text says that the spirit of man somehow survives death – as in the pagan religions of Israel's neighbors and in contrast with the pre-exilic period:

The End of Man
Eccl 12: 7

And the dust returns to the earth as it was, and the spirit returns to God who gave it.

This text does not, thought, state whether the spirit survives as a separate entity, or whether it is dissolved into God. There is, though, also the idea that the spirit disappears at death – as was the case in literature from before the exile:

Ps 146: 4

> His spirit departs, and he returns to the earth. In that very day, his thoughts perish."

Eccl 3: 19–23

> 19. For that which happens to the sons of men happens to animals. Even one thing happens to them. As the one dies, so the other dies. Yes, they have all one breath; and man has no advantage over the animals: for all is vanity.
> 20. All go to one place. All are from the dust, and all turn to dust again.
> 21. Who knows the spirit of man, whether it goes upward, and the spirit of the animal, whether it goes downward to the earth?
> 22. Therefore I saw that there is nothing better, than that a man should rejoice in his works; for that is his portion: for who can bring him to see what will be after him?

From the preceding it may be concluded that the human spirit was not seen as an invisible part of man but that it often stood for the whole person, his thoughts, mind, emotions, and breath.

Ecclesiastes 3 also contains the belief that there is no fundamental difference between the deaths of people and animals and that man should enjoy and make the most of his one and only life on earth.

HEBREW VIEW OF THE SOUL

In the post-exilic parts of the Old Testament one repeatedly finds references to the *soul* of man, as was also the case before the exile. The Hebrew word, נֶפֶשׁ (*nephesh*), has multiple meanings: "soul, self, life, creature, person, appetite, mind, living being, desire, emotion, passion, throat, and breath". It could even be used for a dead body.

This word indicates the life force of a person. At times, the soul of a human is identified with his blood because a severe loss of blood leads to death (Deut. 12: 23).

The soul is also the seat of human emotions (Song 3: 1–3).

The soul is, however, never depicted as a "spiritual", supernatural, or immaterial thing or component of man. We read about a hungry soul (Ps. 107: 9) or a thirsty soul (Prov. 25: 25). The soul often represents the whole human being and for this reason, many Bible translations sometimes translate the word for *soul* with *life*.

On the other hand, Job 34: 15 describes death as final, without the survival of a soul or a spirit: "All flesh would perish together, and man would turn again to dust."

It is, therefore, safe to conclude that the Hebrew view of the soul amounted to a very concrete concept, just as in pre-exilic times. The *soul* was not regarded as something separate from the human body; it was only the less visible aspects of the human being – his mind, his emotions, his needs and desires, and his life force as represented by his blood, even his (invisible) breath.

CONCLUSIONS

From the preceding arguments and quotations from Israel's post-exilic literature, it must be clear that there was no expectation of an afterlife where the soul or spirit of the deceased could continue to exist in a conscious state, as the pagans believed. Death was seen as the final end. Although Sheol, the realm of the dead, was thought to be a physical space below the surface of the earth, it only contained sleeping shadows, silent specters, or witless ghosts – not the immaterial and conscious souls or spirits of dead people.

Heaven, containing the dwelling of God, the dome onto which the stars – actually angels – were fastened, and the sky filled with clouds, was a very concrete place for the Judeans. For them, it was part of the same space or system as the inhabited earth and the abyss or underworld. It is, therefore, not a surprise that God was sometimes described in physical or materialistic terms. Heaven and hell were not seen as the destinations of the soul or spirit after death.

The exceptions are –

- A single verse in Eccl 12 that declares that the spirit is to return to God after death – although it is not stated whether it continued to exist as an independent entity with God after death, or was dissolved into God;
- A single verse in chapter 66 of the late Trito-Isaiah that describes a hell for sinners; and
- The very late book of Daniel that contains the concept that only some of the faithful could expect some form of resurrection and an existence after death in heaven where they will shine as stars, while some evil people were condemned to a miserable afterlife. Daniel is silent about what would happen to the rest who are not to be resurrected.

These exceptions may be attributed to the influence of the pagan religions of Israel's neighboring nations after the end of the exile in Babylonia and especially an acquaintance with the Persian religion.

Kaufmann Kohler wrote as follows in the Jewish Encyclopedia about the views expressed in the Hebrew Scriptures regarding the afterlife:

"As long as the soul was conceived to be merely a breath ('nefesh'; 'neshamah'; comp. 'anima'), and inseparably connected, if not identified, with the life-blood (Gen. ix. 4, comp. iv. 11; Lev. xvii. 11….), no real substance could be ascribed to it. As soon as the spirit or breath of God ('nishmat' or 'ruaḥ'), which was believed to keep body and soul together, both in man and in beast (Gen. ii. 7, vi. 17, vii. 22; Job xxvii. 3), is taken away (Ps. cxlvi. 4) or returns to God (Eccl. xii. 7; Job xxxiv. 14), the soul goes down to Sheol or Hades, there to lead a shadowy existence without life and consciousness (Job xiv. 21; Ps. vi. 6 [A. V. 5], cxv. 17; Isa. xxxviii. 18; Eccl. ix. 5, 10)."[113]

In other words: the Judeans generally did not expect an afterlife. They would simply turn to dust and ceased to exist when they died.

---

[113] Kohler, "Immortality of the Soul".

Chapter 6
APOCRYPHAL HEBREW SCRIPTURES

BOOKS CONSIDERED

After the Jewish Bible was deemed to be completed and finalized with the inclusion of the book of Daniel during the second century BC, a number of so-called "apocryphal" or unauthorized books were written. Some of them were later incorporated into the Bible of the Roman Catholic Church and are called "deutero-canonical" books. Protestant churches chose to adhere to the Jewish canon (the list of biblical books considered to be inspired by God).

Article 6 of the Belgic Confession, one of the doctrinal creeds of Reformed Churches, for instance, states:

> "We distinguish between these holy books [of the Bible and the apocryphal ones. (…) The church may certainly read these books and learn from them as far as they agree with the canonical books. But they do not have such power and virtue that one could confirm from their testimony any point of faith or of the Christian religion. Much less can they detract from the authority of the other holy books."

The following books in this category will be investigated for their views regarding the afterlife, heaven, hell, and the human soul: The Wisdom of Ben Sira, 2 Makkabees, and the Wisdom of Solomon.

Attention will also be given to Enoch and the Book of Jubilees, books known only from Ethiopian translations. They are regarded as Scripture only by the Ethiopian Church, although the letter of Jude in the New Testament quotes a verse from Enoch as if it were Scripture. These two works were written during the second and first centuries BC and they were probably recognized by the Qumran Sect as authoritative Scripture, since scraps of these books were found amongst the Dead Sea Scrolls, the library of this sect that was hidden in caves overlooking the Dead Sea during the Jewish War against the Roman Army during 66–70 AD.[114] They are called pseudographia because they pretend to have been written by characters mentioned elsewhere in the Bible, although they were written much later.

It is important to consider these apocryphal books since some of the ideas contained in them certainly influenced the authors of the New Testament documents.

THE WISDOM OF BEN SIRA (AKA SIRACH)

The Wusdom of Ben Sira was probably written between 200 and 175 BC by Jeshua (or Jesus) Ben Sira in Hebrew. His grandson later translated it into Greek. Only parts of the Hebrew text are extant, but the whole Greek text survived and is part of the Catholic Bible. It is often referred to under its Greek name, Sirach. It is a fairly long document with 51 chapters.[115]

It contains some interesting thoughts about heaven, the afterlife, death, and the human soul. It is no surprise that this book views God's creation in the same manner as the other Hebrew Scriptures. According to Sirach, creation consists of the highest heaven as God's dwlling, the vault of heaven, the earth, and the abyss or pit below the earth. The following quotations illustrate this point of view:

Heaven
Sir 1: 3

---

[114] Rylaarsdam, "Biblical Literature"; Wikipedia, "List of the Dead Sea Scrolls".
[115] Boshoff, *Geskiedenis,* 241–42.

> Heaven's height, earth's extent, the abyss and wisdom—who can explore them?

Sir 18: 18–19

> Look, the heavens and the highest heavens, the abyss and the earth tremble at his visitation. The roots of the mountains and the earth's foundations — at his mere glance they quiver and quake.

The same thought is also found in Sir 17: 32 and 24: 3–5.

Sheol is seen as the destination of man after death, as described in Sir 21: 10 – "The path of sinners is smooth stones, but its end is the pit of Sheol." (See also Sir 14: 12, 17: 27, and 28: 21).

The soul is seen as a designation of the whole person. For instance, Sir 51: 29 says: "May your soul rejoice in God's mercy; do not be ashamed to give him praise."

Man is seen as a being purely from the earth in the following texts:

Man Made from Earth

Sir 17: 1

> The Lord created human beings from the earth, and makes them return to earth again.

Sir 17: 32

> God holds accountable the hosts of highest heaven, while all mortals are dust and ashes.

Various passages make the point that Ben Sira did not envisage a conscious and happy afterlife in Sheol or wherever for the deceased:

Sheol

Sir 17: 27–30

27. Who in Sheol can glorify the Most High in place of the living who offer their praise?
28. The dead can no more give praise than those who have never lived; they who are alive and well glorify the Lord.
29. How great is the mercy of the Lord, and his forgiveness for those who return to him!
30. For not everything is within human reach, since human beings are not immortal. ().

- Weep over the dead, for their light has gone out; weep over the fool, for sense has left him. Weep but less bitterly over the dead, for they are at rest; worse than death is the life of a fool (Sir 22: 11).
- Better is death than a wretched life, everlasting sleep than constant illness (Sir 30: 17).
- With the dead at rest, let memory cease; be consoled, once the spirit has gone (Sir 38: 23).

The only way a dead person can have an afterlife is when his children remember him and continue his work:

Offspring of the Dead
Sir 30: 47

At the father's death, he will seem not dead, for he leaves after him one like himself.

There is no reward for virtuous and upright people and no punishment for evil and wicked persons in an afterlife. Punishment consists of a bad death and a reward is connected to a good and honorable death:

Sir 11: 26

> For it is easy for the Lord on the day of death to repay mortals according to their conduct.

2 MACCABEES

Both books of the Maccabees describe the revolt of the Jews against the cruel King Antiochus IV Epiphanes of Syria, the great-grandson of one of the generals of Alexander the Great who inherited a part of his empire. Antiochus tried to eradicate the Jewish religion after robbing the Jerusalem temple of its treasures.

The first book is a factual description of the Jewish war against this tyrant and it contains very little information about the religious convictions of the Jews at that time, apart from the fact that they wished to adhere to the Law of God, the Torah. The second book, probably written after 160 BC in Greek, describes in a few instances the faith of the Jews regarding the resurrection after death, just as Dan 12 does.[116]

Chapter 7 tells the story of a mother and her seven sons who were torured and killed by the king, one after the other, because they refused to renounce their faith. The following excerpts are important:

The Mother with her Seven Sons
2 Macc 7: 9–11

> And when he [the second brother] was at his last breath, he said, "You accursed wretch, you dismiss us from this present life, but the King of the universe will raise us up to an everlasting renewal of

---

[116] Boshoff, *Geskiedenis*, 244–45.

life, because we have died for his laws." After him, the third was the victim of their sport. When it was demanded, he quickly put out his tongue and courageously stretched forth his hands, and said nobly, "I got these from Heaven, and because of his laws I disdain them, and from him I hope to get them back again".

2 Macc 7: 14

And when he [the fourth brother] was near death, he said, "One cannot but choose to die at the hands of men and to cherish the hope that God gives of being raised again by him. But for you there will be no resurrection to life!" .

The mother encouraged her remaining sons as follows:

2 Macc 7: 23 & 29

"Therefore the Creator of the world, who shaped the beginning of man and devised the origin of all things, will in his mercy give life and breath back to you again, since you now forget yourselves for the sake of his laws" (…) "Do not fear this butcher, but prove worthy of your brothers. Accept death, so that in God's mercy I may get you back again with your brothers."

These words unambigeously testify of a faith in an afterlife with God after the resurrection, during which the bodies of the demised abd departed faithful would be restored and made complete again. It must be concluded that the restored bodies were deemed to of a material nature since the faithful would become alive again – but in a perfect everlasting state on earth.

The Resurrection

Chapter 14 tells the story of a certain pious Jewish elder in Jerusalem, Razis, who was pursued by some soldiers. He preferred death by his own hand, rather than capture and torture and –

> …with his blood now completely drained from him, he tore out his entrails, took them with both hands and hurled them at the crowd, calling upon the Lord of life and spirit to give them back to him again. This was the manner of his death (2 Macc 14: 37–46).

In other words: this man – just as the mother and her seven sons – had the expectation that he would receive a completely new body during the resurrection.

THE WISDOM OF SOLOMON

Although this book claims to contain the wisdom of King Solomon, it was written centuries after his time by an unknown author in Greek. The place or origin seems to be Alexandria in Egypt and its date of compilation is uncertain – any time between the second century BC and the first part of the first century AD. The contents consist of a series of aphorisms. The character of a personified Wisdom plays an important role, just as in the canonical book of Proverbs.[117]

The traditional Israelite cosmology of the Old Testament is absent from this book. The only reference to the cosmos is found in Wis. 13: 2 where "the circle of the stars, … or the luminaries of heaven" are mentioned – a part of God's creation worshipped by pagans as gods. The "circle of stars" is likely a reference to the Zodiac as part of the astrology of those times.

There are, however, various indications that the author expressed his belief in a blessed afterlife for God-fearing people who obeyed God's laws and an unpleasant destination for the pagans

---

[117] Boshoff, *Geskiedenis,* 245–46.

and wicked people in Hades.

In this book, one finds a clear dualism regarding the human body and soul or spirit – probably due to the influence of the Greek philosopher Plato (see chapter 7). When God created man, He "inspired him with an active soul and breathed into him a living spirit" (Wis 15: 11). When man dies, he "goes to the earth from which he was taken, when he is required to return the soul that was lent him" (Wis 15: 8).

God created man with immortality to participate in his own immortality or indestructibility (Wis 12: 1). We also find –

Immortality
Wis 2: 23–24

> God created man for incorruption, and made him in the image of his own eternity, but through the devil's envy death entered the world, and those who belong to his party experience it.

The result is that the "perishable body weighs down the soul, and this earthy tent burdens the thoughtful mind" (Wis 9: 15).

Pagans and godless people argue that there is no afterlife (Wis 2: 1–5). This is, though, a mistake because they are destined for Hades (Wis 17: 14) after having been tried or tested by God (Wis 3: 5). There "with one chain of darkness they all were bound" (Wis 17: 17). Hades is thought of a city with gates (Wis 16: 13) from which no one ever returns or escapes (Wis 2: 1) and where the inmates will be tormented and haunted "by monstrous specters" (Wis 17: 15).

God "will dash them [the pagans and sinners] speechless to the ground, and shake them from the foundations; they will be left utterly dry and barren, and they will suffer anguish, and the memory of them will perish" (Wis 4: 19).

There is, on the other hand, this promise: "But the souls of the righteous are in the hand of God, and no torment will ever touch them" (Wis 3: 1). Also: "the righteous man is God's son" and God will protect him through death and keep him out of Hades (Wis 2: 18 and 16: 13)

There is also the assurance that deceased righteous men "will govern nations and rule over peoples, and the Lord will reign over them for ever" (Wis 3: 8).

The righteous will receive immortality after they have died (Wis 3: 4). Somebody who gives heed to Lady Wisdom's laws, receives "assurance of immortality, and immortality brings one near to God" (Wis 6: 18–19). It is also written that "in kinship with wisdom there is immortality" (Wis 8: 17). Those who receive immortality will be "perfected" (Wis 4: 16). The author of this book prayed to God: "For to know thee is complete righteousness, and to know thy power is the root of immortality " (Wis 15: 3).

The word used for "immortality" is ἀθανασία (*athanasia*), which means the "absence of death, eternity, immortality" – a word used in the New Testament (1 Cor 15: 53; 1 Tim 6: 16, *etetera*).

It is, therefore, clear that the author of the Wisdom of Solomon was convinced that either heaven, or hell, are the fates of the souls of dead people after they have been tried or tested by God.

THE BOOK OF ENOCH

This book purportedly contains the description of the visions and revelations received by the ancient patriarch Enoch. According to Gottheil and Littmann, this book was written to preserve legends and "Jewish folk-lore in the last pre-Christian centuries" about the patriarch Enoch, as well as ideas about the flood in Noah's time, angels, heaven, the netherworld, and hell.[118]

---

[118] Gottheil and Littmann, "Enoch".

This book was regarded by some early Christians to be part of Scripture. The biblical letter of Jude states the following:

Enoch
Jud 1: 14 –15

> To these also Enoch, the seventh from Adam, prophesied, saying, "Behold, the Lord came with ten thousands of his holy ones, to execute judgment on all, and to convict all the ungodly of all their works of ungodliness which they have done in an ungodly way, and of all the hard things which ungodly sinners have spoken against him."

This is a quotation from Enoch 1: 9. Jude clearly thought that the book was written by the very ancient Enoch himself – and not by anonymous authors many centuries later.

John of Patmos, the author of Revelation, quoted repeatedly or referred to visions found in Enoch, without naming his source.[119]

No other documents in the New Testament seems to have quoted from Enoch directly, although more than one document made use of ideas found in Enoch. Around AD 300 the church fathers openly and finally rejected Enoch as part of Scripture.[120]

The only groups at present that regard Enoch as Holy Scripture are Ethiopian sects. The only surviving complete text is in Ethiopic, which was translated from Greek, which was, in turn, translated from the original Aramaic.[121] Our knowledge about Enoch, therefore, depends upon a translation of a translation of a translation. This process of repeated translations could have caused the English translations to be less than accurate or uncertain in cer-

---

[119] Scholtz, *Revelation*, 27, 33, 47, 64, 67, 190, 281, 295.
[120] Gottheil and Littmann, "Enoch".
[121] Enc Brit, "Enoch".

tain spots.

This Ethiopic text was translated into English by respectively George Schodde and Robert Charles. The translation by Charles will be used in this chapter and the explanatory notes of Schodde will be consulted.

Some Aramaic fragments of Enoch were found in the caves at Qumran containing the Dead Sea Scrolls.[122] That means that the Qumran Sect, the Essenes, must have used it as Scripture. It will be shown in a later chapter that Jesus, who was a prominent member of this sect, was certainly influenced by ideas from Enoch.

We read the following about the ancient patriarch Enoch in Genesis:

Enoch
Gen 5: 21–22

> Enoch lived sixty-five years, and became the father of Methuselah. Enoch walked with God after he became the father of Methuselah three hundred years, and became the father of sons and daughters. all the days of Enoch were three hundred sixty-five years. Enoch walked with God, and he was not, for God took him.

Since Enoch was such a pious man who walked with God, the anonymous author(s) of the book of Enoch argued that he must have been walking in heaven with God and the angels. This book is a description of these purported heavenly visits, visions and ventures of Enoch, told in the first person singular at times, but also written about Enoch in the third person singular.

The book, as we have it, consists of five distinct parts:

- The Book of the Watchers (ch 1–36);

---

[122] Rylaarsdam, "Biblical Literature"; Wikipedia, "List of the Dead Sea Scrolls".

- The Book of Parables (ch 37–71);
- The Book of the Heavenly Luminaries (ch 72–82);
- Two visions of Enoch regarding the Flood and the history of the world (ch 83–90); and
- A speech by Enoch (ch 91–107).[123]

These parts were written at different times by different authors and were originally independent works. Only the Book of the Watchers is important for the purposes of the present book.

The Book of the Watchers, which deals with the fallen angels who were banned from heaven after having taken human wives and having taught mankind secret knowledge that led to idololatry, strife, warfare, and magic, can be dated to between 250 and 200 BC. That was during the Hellenistic period in Israel's history. Various Persian and Greek influences had been absorbed at this time.[124]

The Book of the Watchers grapples with the question: where do evil, sin, iniquity, arrogance, pride, and violence come from? To answer this question, the author took as his starting point an enigmatic passage in Genesis 6:

The Nephilim
Gen 6: 1–4

1.	It happened, when men began to multiply on the surface of the ground, and daughters were born to them,
2.	that God's sons saw that men's daughters were beautiful, and they took for themselves wives of all that they chose.
3.	YHWH said, "My spirit will not strive with man forever, because he also is flesh; yet will his days be one hundred

---

[123] Rylaarsdam, "Biblical Literature".
[124] Denova, "The Origin of Satan".

> twenty years."
> 4. The Nephilim were in the earth in those days, and also after that, when God's sons came to men's daughters. They bore children to them: the same were the mighty men who were of old, men of renown.

The Hebrew word for *the Nephilim* (הַנְּפִילִים – *hannephilim*) is usually translated as "the giants".

Although the focus in the first part of Enoch is primarily on the origin and expulsion from heaven of Satan and his demonic helpers, this book contains much material about how the afterlife in heaven and hell, as well as the human soul or spirit, was regarded.

The Book of the Watchers pre-supposes the ancient cosmology of a heaven above the earth as the residence of God and his angels, the heavens filled with stars, winds, and clouds, the flat earth with its edges, and a netherworld, the abyss. There is a void outside this system.

Heaven contains God's throne (Enoch 18: 8), God's angels (Enoch 18: 6), and the spirits of saints and martyrs, like Abel who was killed by his brother (Enoch 22: 4–7). Heaven is thought of a big city because we read of "the gates of heaven" (Enoch 9: 9–10).

There is a firmament resting on pillars, consisting of the four winds of the earth. The sun and the stars are fastened and fixed onto this firmament (Enoch 18: 2–6).

Some of the angels in heaven visited earth and lusted after human damsels. After they had made these women pregnant, who bore giants, they were apprehended by the archangels and expelled from heaven (Enoch 5: 1–9; 10: 11). Enoch provides no explanation of how it was possible that angels, who are heavenly spiritual beings, could make earthly women pregnant.

The stars in heaven are actually those angels who "have transgressed the commandment of the Lord in the beginning of their rising" and that is why they disappear to the abyss below the earth each night (Enoch 18: 5–7).

Gustave Doré: Satan thrown into the abyss by Michael

Below the earth there is a deep abyss, filled with columns of fire (Enoch 18: 11–12). This abyss contains "four hollow places, deep and wide and very smooth" (Enoch 22: 2). These separate hollow spaces were meant to keep the souls of the reighteous and the sinners apart (Enoch 22: 8–3).

These hollow spaces were filled with the spirits of dead people who waited for "the great judgement" (Enoch 22: 1–4). It must be concluded that the idea of these four hollow spaces in the abyss was copied from Zoroastrianism.

Enoch describes the void beyond the earth and the abyss as follows:

The Void
Enoch 18: 12–13

> And beyond that abyss I saw a place which had no firmament of heaven above, and no firmly founded earth beneath it: there was no water upon it, and no birds, but it was a waste and horrible place.

The archangel Michael received the following order from God:

Satan to be bound
Enoch 10: 11–14

> "Go, bind Semjaza [the original name of Satan] and his associates who have united themselves with women so as to have defiled themselves with them in all their uncleanness. And when their sons have slain one another, and they have seen the destruction of their beloved ones, bind them fast for seventy generations in the valleys of the earth, till the day of their judgement and of their consummation, till the judgement that is for ever and ever is consummated. In those days they shall be led off to the abyss of fire: and to the torment and the prison in which they shall be confined for ever."

There was, in other words, a hell waiting for Satan, his demonic helpers, and their offspring, the giants, as well as the souls of the godless and guilty dead, where they would receive their eternal punishment after Judgment Day.

From Enoch 16: 1–2 and 22: 1–4 it is evident that the words *spirit* and *soul* are used as synonyms. That was the part of a human being that survived bodily death and was held in the abyss to await Judgment Day. This is a sign that Enoch adopted the Greek Platonic dualism of body and soul as two separate components of man.

THE BOOK OF JUBILEES

The Book of Jubilees is another extra-biblical book, probably dating from the second or first century BC. It is impossible to determine who wrote it.[125]

The only extant complete manuscripts are in Ethiopic and an English translation has been made from those by Robert Charles in 1895. It seems that the Ethiopic version is a translation from Greek. Some fragments of this book in the original Hebrew were found among the Dead Sea Scrolls.[126] Other documents of this Essene library contain various quotations from the Book of Jubilees, which indicates that this Jewish sect regarded the Book of Jubilees as authoritative.[127]

There is no indication that early Christians regarded it as part of Scripture and no known quotations from it are contained in the New Testament, although some of its ideas resonated in the New Testament, especially in the book of Revelation. It is regarded as Scripture only in Ethiopia.[128]

This book contains a summary of and a commentary on parts of Genesis and Exodus. There is a great interest in angels and demons.[129] Toy and Kohler observe that the author of this book "transfers to Satan and his hosts those acts of God which seem unworthy of Him – such as the tempting of Abraham, the attempt on Moses' life, the hardening of the heart of Pharaoh, and the slaying of the first-born."[130] This tendency to blame Satan for all evil, bad,

---

[125] Boshoff, *Geskiedenis*, 253; Rylaarsdam, "Biblical Literature."
[126] Wikipedia, "List of the Dead Sea Scrolls".
[127] Enc Brit, "Jubilees, Book of"; Rylaarsdam, "Biblical Literature".
[128] Boshoff, *Geskiedenis*, 253; Toy and Kohler, "The Book of Jubilees".
[129] Toy and Kohler, "The Book of Jubilees."
[130] Toy and Kohler, "The Book of Jubilees."

and wrong things to exonerate God often occurs in the New Testament.[131]

As can be expected, the Book of Jubilees repeats the ancient Hebrew views about the composition of God's creation. In its comments on the first chapter of Genesis, it even contains some animistic traits by attributing spirits to natural phenomena, like the seasons, the winds, clouds, and snow:

Creation
Jub 2: 2

> For on the first day He created the heavens which are above and the earth and the waters and all the spirits which serve before him – the angels of the presence, and the angels of sanctification, and the angels [of the spirit of fire and the angels] of the spirit of the winds, and the angels of the spirit of the clouds, and of darkness, and of snow and of hail and of hoar frost, and the angels of the voices and of the thunder and of the lightning, and the angels of the spirits of cold and of heat, and of winter and of spring and of autumn and of summer and of all the spirits of his creatures which are in the heavens and on the earth, (He created) the abysses and the darkness, eventide and night, and the light, dawn and day, which He hath prepared in the knowledge of his heart.

There is a firmament above the earth, onto which the sun, moon, and stars are attached (Jub 2: 4 & 8; 19: 27). Heaven is described as a city with gates (Jub 5: 29; 27: 25). God's dwelling is above this firmament (Jub 19: 27).

The Book of Jubilees seems to share the ancient faith in astrology. We read that Abraham, who lived in the country of the Chaldeans before moving to Canaan, "observed the stars to find out

---

[131] Pretorius, *To Hell with the Devil*, 261–65.

what the future would hold" (Jub 12:17; see also 8: 3 and 11: 7).

Jubilees briefly repeats the same story as Enoch about how it came about that Satan and his helpers were kicked out of heaven after having had sexual intercourse with women on earth (Jub 5: 1–7). It is not explained how these angelic, spiritual beings could impregnate females of flesh and blood.

The *abyss* below the surface of the earth plays a prominent role in Jubilees. After the flood in Noah's time, all the excessive amounts of water flowed down into the abyss to leave the earth dry again (Jub 5: 29; 6: 26). The abyss also contains Sheol, the destination of the dead (Jub 5: 14; 7: 29). The archangels had to bind "all the malignant evil" fallen angels "in the place of condemnation" (Jub 10: 11).

For Jubilees, the spirits and souls of mankind are synonyms and these concepts may be regarded as other names for the human heart or mind (Jub 1: 14 & 19; 26: 26; 31:6, *etcetera*). The Greek Platonic dualism between body and soul or spirit is absent from Jubilees, as is evident from the following verse: "And do not eat any blood for it is the soul; eat no blood whatever" (Jub 21: 18).

However, the soul or spirit of man, somehow, survives death and descends down into Sheol, "into the darkness of the deep" (Jub 5: 14; 7: 29). However, there doesn't seem to be a conscious existence beyond the grave and the Book of Jubilees condemns the pagan nations who "offer their sacrifices to the dead… [and] eat over the grave" (Jub 22: 17).

On the other hand, the idols of the pagans don't have spirits and are, therefore, quite dead (Jub 12: 1–5). God will judge all the sinners and scoundrels at some point in future, when they will receive their fair punishment – a thought copied from the Egyptian and Persian religions (Jub 5: 9, 13–15).

We are informed that on "the day of judgment, on which the

Lord God shall judge them with a sword and with fire for all the unclean wickedness of their errors, wherewith they have filled the earth with transgression and uncleanness and fornication and sin" (Jub 9: 15).

This punishment would not happen in the afterlife, but during the lifetimes of these villains and vagabonds, as God did when Cain, the slayer of Abel, was killed when his house collapsed upon him (Jub 4: 31). We also read:

Punishment
Jub 23: 22 – 23

> And a great punishment shall befall the deeds of this generation from the Lord, and He will give them over to the sword and to judgment and to captivity, and to be plundered and devoured. And He will wake up against them the sinners of the Gentiles, who have neither mercy nor compassion, and who shall respect the person of none, neither old nor young, nor any one, for they are more wicked and strong to do evil than all the children of men.

This punishment will not be meted out during an afterlife, but will happen during the lifetime of those who are guilty.

After the final Judgment –

New heaven and earth
Jub 1: 28

> … the heavens and the earth shall be renewed and all their creation according to the powers of the heaven, and according to all the creation of the earth, until the sanctuary of the Lord shall be made in Jerusalem on Mount Zion, and all the luminaries be renewed for healing and for peace and for blessing for all the elect of Israel, and that thus it may be from that day and unto all the days of the earth.

The righteous and God-fearing people of Israel will be rewarded and blessed after the establishment of this new heaven and new earth – and not during an afterlife in heaven:

Israel cleansed
Jub 50: 5

> And the jubilees shall pass by, until Israel is cleansed from all guilt of fornication, and uncleanness, and pollution, and sin, and error, and dwells with confidence in all the land, and there shall be no more a Satan or any evil one, and the land shall be clean from that time for evermore.

Wonderful conditions will prevail on this new earth where people will reach a fantastic old age, just as described in the genealogical list of Adam and his descendants:

Conditions on the renewed earth
Jub 23: 26–31

> And there shall be no old man, nor one who is <not> satisfied with his days, for all shall be (as) children and youths.
> And all their days they shall complete and live in peace and in joy,
> And there shall be no Satan nor any evil destroyer;
> For all their days shall be days of blessing and healing.
> And at that time the Lord will heal His servants,
> And they shall rise up and see great peace,
> And drive out their adversaries.
> And the righteous shall see and be thankful, and rejoice with joy for ever and ever, and shall see all their judgments and all their curses on their enemies.
> And their bones shall rest in the earth, and their spirits shall have much joy, and they shall know that it is the Lord who executes

> judgment, and shows mercy to hundreds and thousands and to all that love Him.

The following words in Revelation were probably inspired by these thoughts in the Book of Jubilees:

New heaven and earth
Rev 21: 1

> I saw a new heaven and a new earth: for the first heaven and the first earth have passed away, and the sea is no more.

Chapter 7
GREEK PHILOSOPHERS

In the paragraphs that follow, the thoughts of a few important Greek philosophers and philosophical movements that had some influence on the Jewish and Christian Scriptures must be presented. Western philosophy started with the Greeks who learnt how to use rational thought and logical arguments to find answers to fundamental questions, instead of relying on religious myths to explain the world.

PYTHAGORAS AND HIS SCHOOL

The Greek philosopher Pythagoras lived during the sixth century BC in the Greek city of Kroton in Southern Italy, where he founded a school, which also operated as a secret religious society. Little is known of the life of Pythagoras and his teachings were only written down by his students long after his death. It is, therefore, impossible to disentangle the ideas of Pythagoras from those of his followers.

Theory of Numbers

Two elements of Pythagorean thought are relevant for the purposes of this book. The first is that Pythagoras and his students were competent mathematicians. They taught that the underlying principle of all of reality is to be found in numbers. They even thought that the distances between the planets could be reduced to numerical proportions, just as as the various notes on a musical stringed instrument could be produced by shortening or lengthening the strings according to certain numerical proportions. That even led to the theory of the "music of the spheres" – the idea that the planets produced harmonious musical notes during their travels in the sky.

Transmigration of Souls

The Pythagoreans believed in reincarnation or the transmigration of souls and it is not known whether they copied this idea from an Indian source. They taught that one could break the cycle of repeated rebirths by following appropriate rituals, an ascetic lifestyle, and studying mathematics and philosophy.[132]

Although the doctrine of reincarnation played almost no role in the Hebrew and Christian Scriptures or Western thought through the centuries, it is, nevertheless, necessary to take note of it as a possible way of thinking about the afterlife and an existence after death.

PLATO

Student of Socrates

Plato, the Athenian teacher and philosopher who lived during the fifth and fourth centuries BC, was a student of Socrates, an original thinker who questioned many conventional beliefs of his time. Plato was the foundee of a school in a gymnasium, called the Academy and he was the first thinker to construct a whole system of thought to cover all aspects of reality.

Theory of Ideas or Forms

The core of Plato's philosophy is his theory of Ideas. These Ideas are eternal and universal perfect templates of a huge variety of qualities, characteristics, and things in which all aspects of the world participate. The Ideas are generalizations and expressions of the universal essential elements of material objects, such as the Idea of man, horse, tree, or mountain in general. They may also be abstract concepts such as the Idea of beauty, justice, or virtue. There are Ideas

---

[132] Stace, *Greek Philosophy,* 31–39; Thesleff, "Pyhagoreanism".

of qualities such as whiteness. roundness, heavyness, or squareness. These Ideas, which may also be called Forms, exist independently of the material world and knowledge of them constitute truth – in contrast with mere opinions or perceptions, which may be false. Things and actions in the world are materializations of these eternal, perfect, and general qualities, definitions, forms, or Ideas, made by the "demiurge", a hypothetical spiritual creative being.

These Ideas exist in a realm of their own, outside time and space. They are tied together by the Idea of the One, or Being as such. Plato also calls this unifying Idea the Idea of the Good. This supreme Idea may be differentiated into the other Ideas. The common element between all the Ideas is that of perfection and, therefore, the Idea of the Good or Perfection in itself must be the supreme Idea.

Plato

Since all things participate in these perfect Ideas, the universe must be moving in the direction of greater perfection or goodness.

Plato often identifies the Idea of the Good with God, the creator and ruler of the universe. This God is, of course, an impersonal God – just as the impersonal Idea of the Good is eternal and outside of time and space.

There is a hierarchy of Ideas where separate Ideas resort under more general Ideas. The Ideas of roundness and squareness, for instance, are governed by the Idea of shape. Each Idea can only exist in a dialectical relationship with its opposite. For instance, the

Idea of light can only exist if contrasted with the absence of light, which is darkness. The highest Idea, the Idea of the One, of the Good, of Being as such, can only exist in contrast with the Ideas of the many, the bad, and non-being or nothingness.

Mathematics is an important introduction to philosophy because the numbers and geometrical figures of mathematics are just as eternal as the Ideas. This is a thought that Plato borrowed from the Pythagoreans.[133]

Doctrine of the Human Soul

According to Plato, the human rational soul has a pre-existence in the realm of IdeaS before birth into a human body. There it contemplated the Ideas. When imprisoned into a physical body, it forgets about the Ideas, but it is reminded of them when experiencing the qualities and charateristics of aspects in the world.[134]

The human soul is divided into three parts: the immortal and indestructible soul of reason, located in the head, the emotional soul, located in the upper body, and the vegetative soul, located in the lower body. Animals only have the two last-mentioned souls, which are mortal. The rational human soul also participates in the soul of the world – sometimes called God or the demiurge – the agency that impresses the qualities inherent in the eternal Ideas upon unformed matter, which is actually nothing but empty space, to create the things in the world, including the human body.

Since the human rational soul originally came from the realm of Ideas, it is destined to return thither after death if that person has led a virtuous life on earth. After a long time, that soul may again be reincarnated into another body. Evil people can be reincarnated into lower forms of life, including animals. This

---

[133] Stace, *Greek Philosophy,* 164–207; Barnes, "Plato".
[134] Stace, *Greek Philosophy,* 205–07; Barnes, "Plato".

doctrine of the transmigration of the soul was also copied from the Pythagoreans.[135]

The fundamental difference between the rational, immortal, and indestructible soul and the mortal body of man, means that man is a duality – a combination of body and soul. Plato is famous for this dualism regarding these two elements of a human being. This may be ascribed to his Greek background since the Greek mythology also thought of man as a combination of a mortal body and an immortal soul.

As has been shown in the previouys chapter, the apocryphal books of the Wisdom of Solomon and Enoch contain this dualism of body and soul, probably ultimately plagiarized from Plato.

Criticism

A weak point of Plato's philosophy is that he cannot explain how and why the Idea of the One or of the Good can differentiate itself into other less general Ideas. Neither can he explain why and how an immaterial soul, which belongs to the world of Ideas, can get combined with a material human body or how and why an immaterial Idea can become a quality or characteristic of material objects.

It must be mentioned that there is no scientific proof for the doctrine of reincarnation, as will be pointed out in a later chapter.

ARISTOTLE

Student of Plato

The most famous student of Plato was Aristotle who lived during the fourth century BC. He was, in turn, the teacher of the young prince Alexander and son of King Philip of Macedonia. When Philip

---

[135] Stace, *Greek Philosophy*, 207–27; Barnes, "Plato".

died and Alexander succeeded him, Aristotle's work ended and Alexander ventured out to conquer the Egyptian and Persian empires. When Alexander and his army ventured out on their campaign of conquest in 336 BC, Aristotle returned to Athens where he founded a school at the Lyceum.

Aristotle had admiration for Plato, but he was not blind for the weak spots in his master's thought system. For instance, he pointed out that Plato's Ideas, the ultimate reality, could not be used to explain the existence of the world. Instead of invoking a realm of Ideas to explain the essential qualities of groups and categories of beings, he posited that each being has his own inherent qualities, which it may, or may not, share with other beings.

Aritstotle did not only write about philosophy and the discipline of logics. He also wrote about astronomy, zoology, and other scientific subjects. His thoughts about God, the cosmos, and the human soul are relevant for the purposes of the present book.

Doctrine of the Soul
Although Aristotle had great respect for Plato, he did away with almost all of Plato's philophy. For instance, he got rid of Plato's realm of Ideas and the dichtomy between body and soul.

Aristotle, who was a pioneering naturalist, noted that each thing in the cosmos had its own qualities, characteristics, or organization, unique to that thing. He called these qualities the *form* of that thing, which was made of matter. Mattter without a form is unthinkable, just as forms without matter is equally impossible. He illustrated this with the example of a tablet of wax on which impressions were made. The wax and the impressions are inseperable.

The world is made up of all sorts of things and they can be classified from lower beings to higher beings, depending on how complex their forms are. The least complex is, for instance, a lump of soil. On a next level are plants, which have vegetative souls as part of their forms. They can absorb nutrients, grow, and reproduce. Above plants, animals also have vegetatitve souls, as well as sensitive souls or forms. They have the ability or faculty of absorbing nutrients, growth, resproducing, but also of locomotion and sensation.

Human beings occupy a still higher position in the ladder of beings. They posses vegetative and sensitive souls or forms, like the animals, but also the faculties of memory, recollection, imagination, thought, and reason.

When a man experiences sensations, his various senses, such as sight, hearing, touch, or smell, are combined into a whole or a single experience by a central ganglion in his soul, located in the heart. When a man, for instance, encounters a horse, he can see, hear, touch, and smell the horse, but he experiences the horse as a single thing.

Planets and stars also possess souls with reason and they may be regarded as gods – just as many ancients believed. Planets are on a lower plane that the fixed stars. All of them move in circles around the stationary earth, a circle being the perfect shape because it doesn't have a beginning or an end. The orbits of the fixed stars are at the outer edge of the universe, where space ends.

The heavenly bodies, the sun, moon, planets, and stars, are not composed of the same stuff or matter as terrestrial things, which are made of earth, water, air, and fire. The celetial beings arer made of a fifth element, the so-called quintessence.

Outside the space of the universe, as well as beyond the unending time of the universe, the realm of pure or absolute reason is to be found. This realm must not be confused with Plato's realm of Ideas. Since it is eternal and timeless, outside space and time, it permeates or penetrates the whole cosmos because everrything in the cosmos has a rational or reasonable form. The basic priniple on which the cosmos operates is that of rationality.

Aristotle

It is understandable that Aristotle regarded reason and the principle of rationality as of prime importance since he was the originator of the disciplne of logics. He formulated the rules that had to be obeyed when people were thinking and arguing logically and rationally. It is clear that Aritstotle rejected Plato's dualism of body and soul with a soul inprisoned in a body, from which it had to be liberated at death.

For him, the two are a unity. Since no thing, includsing the body of a man, can exist without a form, body and soul cannot be torn apart at death. The soul perishes together with the body when a man dies, although the rational aspect of his soul or form returns to God, the absolute or pure reason that is the basic principle on which the whole of reality rests. This rational soul that returns to absolute reason, is without a memory or recollection and, therefore, there is no possibility of reincarnation or the immortality of the individual soul.[136]

Aristotle, therefore, gave no place in his philosophy to the classical Greek fields of Elysium where happy souls reside after death or Hades and Tartarus where unfortunate souls languish.

---

[136] Stace, *Greek Philosophy,* 296–313; Kenny, "Aristotle".

Human souls are simply obliterated and exterminated when the human body dies and decays.[137]

The Doctrine of the Prime Mover

Aristotle, the observer of nature, noted that everything is constantly changing. There is growth, decay, development, movement, birth, death, and procreation. All these changes or movements are brought about by causes, which are also in motion. The current state of affairs is, therefore, the result of preceding conditions.

One may therefore ask: what caused all these movements and developments in the first place? It is not possible that there can be an infinite series or chains of causes for current conditions and, therefore, there must have been a prime unmoved mover that caused all the movement in the universe.

This unmoved initial mover may be called God and may also be equated with the eternal absolute reason that is the fundamental ground of all being.

When Aristotle declared that present conditions and changes must have been caused by preceding conditions and changes, he actually posed a fundamental principle of modern science, namely that prevailing situations have natural causes that may be identified by observation or experiments or tests. Cosmologists are convinced that there was indeed a prime mover, the so-called Big Bang, when the universe was born and set in motion.

Criticism

Chruistian and Muslim philosophers gladly and gratefully made use of Aristotle's notion of a prime mover as the cause of all movement in the universe. They equated this unmoved mover with the God

---

[137] Stace, *Greek Philosophy*, 314–30; Kenny, "Aristotle".

found in the Scriptures, the creator of creation, and they used this idea as proof for the existence of God.

However, it is unclear how Aristotle's prime mover could have remained unmoved or unchanged when causing the cosmos to move, evolve, change, and develop. It is also a mystery how an eternal principle, outside of time and space, could act upon the material and temporal and spatial world and set it in motion.

Aristotle's cosmology was, of course, part of the ancient unsophisticated and prescientific cosmology. Planets and stars were seen as living and even divine beings. He also accepted the theory of his predecessor, Empedocles, about the four elements of which the world is made, namely earth, water, air, and fire. He invented a fifth element from which the celestial bodies are composed, without explaining where this mysterious element came from.

STOICISM

One of the more influential philosophical movements after the death of Aristotle was Stoicism. The founder of this movement, Zeno of Cyprus, who worked during the third century BC, studied philosophy in Athens at the late Plato's Academy where some successors of Plato continued to teach his philosophy.

Zeno broke away from Platonism and started his own school in the Stoa Poikile ('Η ΠΟΙΚΊΛΗ ΣΤΟΆ, *hē poikílē stoá*) in Athens, the Pained Collonade, which was a popular public meeting place – hence the name of the school, namely Stoicism. The adherents of this movement were called Stoics.

Zeno was succeeded after his death by Cleanthes, who was again followed by Chrysippus. This philosophical sect exerted much influence throughout the Helenized world, and one of its most famous followers was Emperor Marcus Aurelius of the Roman Empire during the late second century AD. Since the writings of the founders are lost, our knowledge of Stoicism is gathered from the books of later philosophers. In the paragraphs that follow, a general description of Stoicism is given – not necessarily the ideas of Zeno.

The reconstructed Stoa of Attalos in Athens, a museum with busts of historical philosophers. The Stoa Poiukile of Zeno must have looked similar.

Stoicism was primariuly a philosophy of ethics, but this ethical system rested upon the discipline of logics and a theory of physics. This philosophy can be described as determinitic and materialistic. Stoics argued that since every thing and every event must have a cause, the state of affairs of the world at any moment is totally determined by the preceding conditions. Man has no free will and when he chooses to do something, it only means that he agrees with whatever he was moved or caused to do.

The universe is held together by the divine fire of reason. Reason is the cause of the existence of the world and this fire differentiates itself into air, water, and earth. After a long time, everything is again consumed by this fire. This is a continuous cycle that is repeated endlessly and each cycle is an exact repetition of previous cycles.

Since the whole of reality consists of matter – earth, water, air, and fire – there is no soul in man to survive death. His mind is merely a function of his body.

This stance causes some difficulties with the ethical doctrines of this brand of philosophy, since man has no power to break out of the cycle of cause and effect and cannot choose to behave differently. Stoic ethics boils down to the prescription that man must avoid anything that is irrational, against reason, and against nature, which is constructed rationally.[138]

NEO-PLATONISM

The Hellenistic world was characterized by many philosophical schools, drawing inspiration from Greek thinkers of previous centuries. An influential varietiy of philosophy may be branded as Neo-Platonism, although a definite Neo-Platonic school was only founded during the thrd century AD by Plotinus.[139] During the first and second centuries AD, especially two philosophical traditions that drew inspiration from the ideas of Plato deserve mention because they left their mark on Christianity: the ideas of Philo of Alexandria and Gnosticism.

Philo of Alexandria

The Jewish theologian and philosopher, Philo, who was born about a decade before the birth of Jesus of Nazareth, lived and worked in the intellectual center of the Roman Empire, Alexandria in Egypt. He was deeply influenced by Plato and he tried to demonstrate that the Greek philosophers, especially Plato, were influenced by the Torah, the purported writings of Moses. His philosophy is, therefore, an effort to merge Judaism with Platonism.

For Philo, God is ultimately unknowable, although his existence is a certainty. As the eternal source of being, he cannot be

---

[138] Stace, *Greek Philosophy,* 344–53; Saunders, "Stoicism:.
[139] Enc Brit, "Platonism".

contaminated by (evil) matter and, therefore, he created a bunch of intermediate beings between Himself and the material world – spirits, angels, demons, and so forth. The most important of these, the Logos – which may be equated with the Platonic Idea of the One or the Good and the Aristotelian reason – is the mind or thoughts of God, containing his designs for the different parts of creation.

Philo adopted Plato's dualism of body and soul. The soul, which is part of the immaterial world of God's thoughts, is imprisoned in a material body, from which it is unchained upon death, to return to higher spheres.[140]

Von Ehrenkrook writes that "in good Stoic fashion Philo posits that the human soul consists of the fifth substance, a fragment (apospasma) of the ether to which the soul will ultimately return." He adds that the souls of wise people "will enjoy immortality and a return to their original communion with the divine." [141]

Gnosticism and the Gospel of Thomas

Not much is known about the origin of Gnosticism, although one of the early leaders was Simon the Magician (or Simon Magus) of Samaria of whom we read in Acts 8 in the New Testament. This amorphous movement seems to have been influenced by various sources: Judaism, early Christianity, the Persian religion, and Platonism. The extra-biblical Gospel of Thomas is a good source for information about Gnosticism.

To recapituale: Plato taught that the visible world is the materialization of eternal Ideas, which reside in an eternal realm of Ideas. These Ideas are the templates of material objects and their qualities. A spirit, called a *demiurge*, created the material world by impressing these ideas onto unformed matter. Plato also taught a

---

[140] Stace, *Greek Philosophy*, 370–71; Enc Brit, "Philo Judaeus".
[141] Van Ehrenkrook, "The Afterlife".

dualism between body and soul. The body is part of the material world, while the soul belongs to the realm of Ideas.

The Persian religion taught that there is an eternal struggle between the forces of good and evil, personalized as a good god and an evil spirit.

The name Gnosticism is derived from the Greek word γνωσις (*gnosis*), which means "(esoteric or secret) knowledge", which a person needs to acquire to connect him to his origin and destiny in the kingdom of heaven, akin to the realm of Ideas.

Some gnostic sects or groups, such as the Egyptian group where the Gospel of Thomas originated, claimed Jesus as their own and distorted some of his teachings to fit into their thought systems.

The Gospel of Thomas is a short book, containing only 114 sayings. Most of them start with the words: "Jesus said…" This gospel, which was unearthed with some other Gnostic literature at Nag Hammadi in Egypt in 1945, was written during the second century AD in Greek, although the only known complete copy is a Coptic or old Egyptian translation. It is written in language that resembles the language of the gospels of the New Testament, but various terms are used with a new meaning.

This gospel avoids the name of God and calls him "the Father" or "the Lord". The "kingdom" is another word for the hereafter, the realm of spiritual beings and the abode of God. The human body, made of flesh or evil matter, is the prison of the immaterial and immortal human soul. Happiness and salvation can only be attained when man gains the knowledge of his soul's origin and his eventual destination after death in the kingdom of heaven, resembling the Platonic realm of Ideas.[142]

---

[142] Enc Brit, "Gnosticism" and "Simon Magus"; Pretorius, *The Gospels Explained*, 624–78.

Chapter 8
JESUS OF NAZARETH

THE RELIGIOUS SCENE DURING THE 1ST CENTURY AD

Jewish Parties or Sects

Christians regard themselves as followers of Jesus Christ, also known as Jesus of Nazareth, and they believe in him as the eternal Son of God and the redeemer of mankind. As a consequence, his thoughts are of prime importance to Christians.

Jesus spoke much about Judgment Day and eternal life after death and to understand his point of view, it is necessary to provide a brief description of the religious and political environment in Palestine and elsewhere in the Jewish world in which he operated as a Jewish rabbi during the thirties of the first century AD.

Palestine, the area occupied by the old kingdoms of Israel and Judah, was a minor Roman province in those times. Judea was governed by a Roman governor, while other parts were ruled by client kings, the sons and grandsons of Herod the Great who had ruled over the whole of Palestine and who had died in 3 BC.

There were three Jewish religious and political parties in Judea and Galilee before the destruction of Jerusalem by the Romans in AD 70:

- The party of the *Pharisees* was the most important. They were orthodox or conservative Jews who did their best to uphold the Law of God as found in the Torah, and who found inspiration in the other documents of the Old Testament, namely the books of the prophets and other writings. This is the only party that survived the disastruous Jewish War against the Romans of 66–70 AD.

- The *Sadducees* were the aristocratic priestly class, especially in Jerusalem, where they controlled the temple complex, the focal point of Jewish religious life. They accepted only the Torah as divinely inpsired and they usually cooperated with the Roman authorities.
- The *Essenes* or *Nazoreans* were ascetic Jews who held firm views about various issues and who regarded the Sadducees as corrupt and hypocritical traitors. They abhorred the opulence and luxuries of rich people and they lived simply, while practicing hospitality and generosity towards members of their own faction. Their headquarters was at Qumran near the Dead Sea and their library, consisting of the so-called Dead Sea Scrolls, was discovered in some caves in 1947, where they were hidden during the Jewish War of 66–70 AD.[143]

Jesus was a member of the sect of the Essenes or Nazoreans (Matt 2: 23; John 19: 19; Acts 24: 5) and most of his supporters seem to have belonged to this group as well. As a member of this sect, he frequently clashed with the Sadducees, but sometimes also with some Pharisees.[144]

Jewish Diaspora

Many Jews lived outside of Palestine in the diaspora. One of them was Saul or Paul of Tarsus, who grew up in a Greek-speaking city in Asia Minor. He studied theology in Jerusalem as a student of Gamaliel, a famous scholar. He received visions and revelations

---

[143] Cohn, *The Trial and Death of Jesus,* X; Pretorius, *The Gospels Explained,* X.
[144] Pretorius, *Jesus of Nazareth,* passim; Pretorius, *The Gospels Explained,* passim.

about Jesus and he became a missionary for the emerging Christian movement. He targeted Jews and Gentiles in Asia Minor and Greece with his message. We are well informed about his views because some of his letters to various churches, dating from the fifties and early sixties of the first century AD, are preserved in the New Testament.

The New Testament Writings
The oldest parts of the Gospels, the documents containing the story of Jesus, were written wintin two or three decades after Jesus' execution. The oldest is the so-called Q-Document, containing those parts in the gospels of Matthew and Luke that were clearly copied by both from an earlier source, probably dating from the forties of the first century AD. The narrative parts of the Gospel of John, which seem to contain the recollections of this apostle, probably date from the fifties or sixties of the first century AD.[145]

The Gospel of Mark and those parts of Matthew and Luke that were evidently copied from Mark, as well as some unique material in the last-mentioned two Gospels, were written after the fall of Jerusalem at the end of the Jewish War in AD 70 – a few decades after Jesus' time. The discourses, sermons, and philosophical parts of the Gospel of John were added to the narrative parts much later. The parts of the Gospels that were written after the Jewish War may be regarded as less reliable than the earlier sections. The lectures and sermons in John were certainly never delivered by Jesus, but were the compositions of some students of John, probably written in Ephesus during the nineties of the first centurt AD.[146]

In order to present the views of Jesus regarding the afterlife in heaven and hell, the oldest parts of the Gospels will be scrutini-

---

[145] Pretorius, *The Gospels Explained*, 176–86.
[146] Pretorius, *The Gospels Explained*, 536–37.

zed to find possible and probable autherntic sayings of Jesus.

Paul's thoughts, as expressed in his letters, and the views of the later parts of the Gospels of Mark, Matthew, and Luke, as well as the writings of students of the Apostle John, will be presented after that. Attention will also be given to the way John of Patmos, the author of the book of Revelation, dealt with the topic of the afterlife.

JESUS THE NAZOREAN, KING OF THE JEWS

To understand the life and message of Jesus of Nazareth, it is necessary to keep in mind that he saw himself as the legitimate king of Israel. His teachings, as preserved in the oldest parts of the Gospels, must be interpreted against this background. The following facts support this supposition:

- Jesus often called himself "the Son of God" and he called God his Father (Matt 6: 9; Matt 11: 27; Matt 16: 27–28; Matt 23: 9; Matt 27: 54; John 3: 35; John 5: 21; John 6: 46; John 8: 18; John 8: 42 *etcetera*). The title "Son of God" was used in the Old Testament for the kings from the House of David (2 Sam 7: 14; 1 Chr 17: 13; 1 Chr 22: 10; 1 Chr 28: 6; Ps 2: 6–7, 12; Ps 89: 26–28) and Jesus claimed this title since he was a descendant of David (Matt 1: 1–17; Matt 21: 9; Luke 3: 23 – 38).
- In John 1: 49–51, the titles "Son of God" and "king of Israel" were used as synonyms and applied to Jesus.
- Jesus' favorite topic in his sermons and parables was the kingdom of God or Heaven. The conventional explanation is that he meant the heavenly kiongdom of God, which his faithful followers would enter in the afterlife. That is, however, certainly not what he meant, since he often assured his audiences that this kingdom would be established very soon, during their lifetimes

and before they died (Matt 16: 27–28; Matt 24: 34; Matt 26: 29, 64; Mark 9: 1; Mark 13: 20; Luke 9: 27; Luke 21: 32).
- He taught his disciples to pray: "May your kingdom come. May your will be done, as in heaven, so on earth" (Matt 6: 10). They had, therefore, to pray for the coming of God's kingdom on earth – with Jesus on the throne as David's successor.
- His disciples and even some Pharisees had the clear expectation that he would restore the Israelite kingdom in the immediate future (Luke 17: 20; Luke 19: 11; Acts 1: 6).
- There were people who wanted to "take him by force, to make him king" (John 6: 15).
- He told his disciples, "Most assuredly I tell you, that you who have followed me, in the regeneration when the Son of Man will sit on the throne of his glory, you also will sit on twelve thrones, judging the twelve tribes of Israel" (Matt 19: 28). In other words, they would be judges or leaders of Israel and his cabinet ministers or councilors.
- We read in Matt 25: 31 that he told his disciples: "But when the Son of Man comes in his glory, and all the holy angels with him, then will he sit on the throne of his glory." John 1: 51 also reported: "He said to him, 'Most assuredly, I tell you [Nathaniel], hereafter you will see heaven opened, and the angels of God ascending and descending on the Son of Man.'" He expected an army of aggressive angels from heaven to aid him in getting rid of the Roman yoke and re-establish the Israelite monarchy.
- When Jesus entered Jerusalem on the back of a donkey a few days before his crucifixion, he was hailed by the enthusiastic crowd as the Son of David and the king of Israel. He did not contradict them, even when some Pharisees demanded that he silence them. He actually staged this event to fit a prophecy from

the Old Testament (Matt 21: 1–11, 15; Mark 11: 1–11; Luke 19: 29–44; John 12: 12–19).
- When he was tried after his arrest by the Roman governor, Pontius Pilate, he comfirmed that he was indeed the king of the Jews (Matt 27: 11; Mark 15: 2; Luke 23: 3; and John 18: 33).

- He was sentenced to death precisely because he proclaimed himself king of the Jews without the consent of the emperor in Rome, which warranted the death penalty by crucifixion. A notice mentioning his crime in three languiages was placed on the cross: "JESUS THE NAZOREAN, KING OF THE JEWS" (John 19: 19; see also Matt 27: 37; Mark 15: 26; and Luke 23: 38).

The 17th-cent painting *Christ Crucified* by Diego Velázquez

Apart from being a king-in-waiting, Jesus also saw himself as a religious reformer who wanted to lead his people back to God. He was a popular preacher and many of his sayings, stories, and sermons were recorded in the Gospels.

His perspectives on the afterlife are presented below:

HEAVEN

It does seem as if Jesus held the same views as his contemporaries about the composition of the universe, when one considers his quotation of Isa 66: 1 –

View of the Cosmos
Matt 5: 33–35

33.	Again you have heard that it was said to them of old time, "You shall not make false vows, but shall perform to the Lord your vows,'
34.	but I tell you, don't swear at all: neither by heaven, for it is the throne of God;
35.	nor by the earth, for it is the footstool of his feet; nor by Jerusalem, for it is the city of the great King".

In Matt 23: 21–22, he later repeated something similar. In other words: Jesus believed that God resided in heaven above the earth, but also on earth, and especially in the Jerusalem temple.

Jesus' condemnation of the taking of the oath is, incidently, explainable from his Essene background. One of the teachings of this sect was that all oaths were to be avoided, although the Old Testament allowed them (Num 30: 2; Deut 23: 21–23; Lev 19: 12).

He regarded his Father as the "Lord of heaven and earth" (Luke 10: 21). He also mentioned his "Father who is in heaven" (Matt 23: 16).

Jesus was adamant that the Torah may not be altered:

The Torah
Matt 23: 18

> For most assuredly, I tell you, until heaven and earth pass away, not even one smallest letter or one tiny pen stroke shall in any way pass away from the law, until all things are accomplished.

Where he mentioned the possibility that heaven may pass away, he had the heaven filled with stars and clouds in mind, not the eternal dwelling of God.

ANGELS, SATAN, AND EVIL SPIRITS

As an orthodox Jew, Jesus believed that a crowd of angels reside in heaven with God (see for instance: Luke 12: 8–9). This is an idea he got from many spots in the Hebrew Scriptures.

In the Parable of the Good Shepherd, he explained:

Joy in Heaven
Luke 15: 7 & 10

> 7. Just so, I tell you, there will be more joy in heaven over one sinner who repents than over ninety–nine righteous persons who need no repentance. (…)
> 10. There is joy in the presence of the angels of God over one sinner who repents.

Jesus was confident that a host of angels from heaven woul aid him to ascend the throne in Jerusalem and overcome all of God's enemies. He also declared:

The Coming of the Son of Man
Matt 16: 27–28

> 27. For the Son of Man will come in the glory of his Father with his angels, and then will he render to every man according to his deeds.
> 28. Most assuredly I tell you, there are some standing here, who will in no way taste of death, until they see the Son of Man coming in his kingdom.

(see also: Matt 25: 31; Mark 8: 38; Mark 14: 62; Luke 9: 26; Luke 22: 69; John 1: 51).

Temptation by the Devil
According to Matt 4: 1–11 and Luke 4: 1–13, Jesus experienced temptations by Satan in the desert, after he had been baptized by

John the Baptist. Satan purportedly promised him various favors in return for being honored by Jesus as his superior. It is probable that Jesus suffered from hallucinations after having had nothing to eat or drink for an extended period in the hot desert (see Chapter 2 in this regard). He was, though, convinced that he had an encounter with the devil and he must have told his friends about it, with the result that it was recorded in the Gospels.[147]

It has to be stressed that the figure of Satan, as God's adversary, is absent from the Old Testament. He was copied from the Persian religion through the books of Enoch and Jubilees and entered the New Testament from those sources as has been demonstrated in a prvious chapter.[148]

Jesus accepted – just as everybody in those days – that evil or unclean spirits were responsible for the bad things that happen to people, especially all sorts of diseases, disabilities, and disorders. This belief was also introduced into the Jewish religion by the books of Enoch and Jubilees, as has been shown in a previous chapter.

The Gospels are filled with stories of how Jesus healed sick people who reportedly suffered from the infestation of evil, foul, or dirty spirits or demons. A good example is the following:

Jesus Heals People
Luke 6: 17–19

> 17. He came down with them, and stood on a level place, with a crowd of his disciples, and a great number of the people from all Judea and Jerusalem, and the sea coast of Tyre and Sidon, who came to hear him, and to be healed of their diseases;

---

[147] Pretorius, *The Gospels Explained,* 82–84.
[148] Pretorius, *To Hell with the Devil,* 155–56.

> 18. also those who were troubled with unclean spirits, and they were being healed.
> 19. All the multitude sought to touch him, for power came forth from him, and healed them all.

According to Luke 11: 14–23, Jesus was accused by his opponents of driving out the evil spirits with the help of Beelzebul, the devil, but Jesus was able to point out their skewed logic:

Jesus and Beelzebul
Luke 11: 14–23

> 14. He was casting out a demon, and it was mute. It happened, when the demon had gone out, the mute man spoke; and the multitudes marvelled.
> 15. But some of them said, "He casts out demons by Beelzebul, the prince of the demons."
> 16. Others, testing him, sought from him a sign from heaven.
> 17. But he, knowing their thoughts, said to them, "Every kingdom divided against itself is brought to desolation. A house divided against itself falls.
> 18. If Satan also is divided against himself, how will his kingdom stand? Because you say that I cast out demons by Beelzebul.
> 19. But if I cast out demons by Beelzebul, by whom do your sons cast them out? Therefore will they be your judges.
> 20. But if I by the finger of God cast out demons, then is the kingdom of God come to you.
> 21. When the strong man, fully armed, guards his own dwelling, his goods are safe.

> 22. But when someone stronger comes on him, and overcomes him, he takes from him his whole amor in which he trusted, and divides his spoils.
> 23. He that is not with me is against me. He who doesn't gather with me scatters.

This is an example where Jesus was maligned and slandered when he was accused of casting out demons with the power of Beelzebul (Greek: Βεελζεβούλ – *Beelzeboul*), the prince or ruler of the demons. Jesus easily pointed out the flaw in this accusation by arguing that it is unthinkable that Satan (Beelzebul) would be willing to get rid of his helpers, the lesser little devils. Jesus also compared himself with a strong man who overpowered another strong man (Satan) by looting his armor and his treasures.

The name Beelzebul is derived from the name of a Philistine deity, mentioned in 2 Kgs 1: 2–3, 6, and 16) where he is called Beelzebub (Baal or Lord of the Flies) (Hebrew: בַּעַל זְבוּב – *Baal-Zebub*). Those who accused Jesus of using the power of Beelzebul tried to discredit him as an imposter, somebody in an alliance with Satan or a pagan god. Jesus countered by declaring that the demons were driven out "by the finger of God" and that that was a sign that God's kingdom on earth would be established soon. He added that those who did not gather (followers or helpers for his campaign to become king in Jerusalem) together with him, were against him and only scattering the people of God.

Jesus had to admit that his efforts to drive out demons were not always successful:

Returning Spirits
Luke 11: 24–26

> 24. When the unclean spirit has gone out of a person, it wanders through waterless regions looking for a resting place, but not finding any, it says, 'I will return to my house from which I came.'
> 25. When it comes, it finds it swept and put in order.
> 26. Then it goes and brings seven other spirits more evil than itself, and they enter and live there; and the last state of that person is worse than the first.

All these passages demonstrate that Jesus was certainly not a materialist. He believed in the existence of invisible spiritual beings, the angels, as well as demons, who were supposed to be fallen angels. The angels resided in heaven with God, while the demons were to be found in the *Abyss* (Luke 8: 31) – an idea taken from Enoch and the book of Jubilees – and indirectly from the Persian religion.

THE HUMAN SOUL AND SPIRIT

In Jesus' parable of the rich man, this man said to himself: "And I will say to my soul, 'Soul, you have ample goods laid up for many years; relax, eat, drink, be merry.'" However, Jesus added: "But God said to him, 'You fool! This very night your life is being demanded of you. And the things you have prepared, whose will they be?'" (Luke 12: 19–20).

The Greek word used for *soul* and *life* is ψυχή (*psyche*). In this context, it may be an indication of the whole person, but also the element of that person that survives death.

When Jesus was hanging on the cross, he cried out according to Luke: "Father, into your hands I commit my spirit!" (Luke 23: 46). The word used for *spirit* is πνεῦμα (*pneuma*). This word may also be translated as "wind" or "breath", and all these meanings may be regarded as synonyms.

It also seems that the words πνεῦμα and ψυχη may be regarded as synonyms, both signifying the invisible element of man that leaves the body at death, when the last breath has been taken. It is likely that Jesus – just as other people in those days – accepted the dualism of body and soul, as propagated by Plato.

Jesus mentioned that a tomb contains "dead men's bones" (Matt 23: 27) – all that remain of the body after death after the soul or spirit have entered heaven.

JUDGMENT DAY

The concept of a Judgment Day, as found in the Egyptian religion, the Persian religion, the Jewish Apocrypha, Enoch, and Jubilees, was taken over by Jesus.

Jesus warned that sinners would be condemned on Judgment Day: "You have heard that it was said to them of old time, 'You shall not murder;' and 'Whoever shall murder shall be in danger of the judgment'" (Matt 5: 21).

In Luke 11, Jesus advised the people of his time to repent because Judgment Day was awaiting them:

Judgment Day
Luke 11: 27–28

27. The queen of the South will rise at the judgment with the people of this generation and condemn them, because she came from the ends of the earth to listen to the wisdom of Solomon, and see, something greater than Solomon is here!
28. The people of Nineveh will rise up at the judgment with this generation and condemn it, because they repented at the pro-

> clamation of Jonah, and see, something greater than Jonah is here.

In other words: The Queen of Sheba and the people of Nineveh repented and, therefore, Judgment Day would not be so terrible and horrible for them as for some Jews in Jesus' time who rejected his message.

Jesus condemned the Galilean towns of Capernaum, Chorazin, and Bethsaide, because their inhabitants were less open to his message than the people of Tyre and Sidon in Phoenicia, who reacted positively. Jesus warned them that Judgment Day was looming and that Hades or hell was awaiting them (Luke 10: 13–15).

The parable of the sheep and the goats (Matt 25: 31–46) is mostly interpreted as a depiction of Judgment Day. It is, however, the way Jesus envisaged his reign as king of Israel where he would judge his opponents in Jerusalem. After all, this parable begins with these words: "But when the Son of Man comes in his glory, and all the holy angels with him, then will he sit on the throne of his glory." This throne was meant to be his royal throne in Jerusalem, possibly in the palace built by Herod the Great.

ETERNAL LIFE AND RESURRECTION

Jesus repeatedly told people how to inherit eternal life in heaven. He advised an unnamed man to obey all of the Ten Commandments, to practice charity, and follow Jesus "and you will have a treasure in heaven" (Mark 10: 17–21).

We read in Luke 10 of the following episode:

How to Inherit Eternal Life
Luke 10: 25–28

> 25. Behold, a certain lawyer stood up and tested him, saying, "Teacher, what will I do to inherit eternal life?"
> 26. He said to him, "What is written in the law? How do you read it?"
> 27. He answered, "You shall love the Lord your God with all your heart, with all your soul, with all your strength, and with all your mind; and your neighbor as yourself."
> 28. He said to him, "You have answered correctly. Do this, and you will live."

In other words: a pious and charitable life, while obeying the law of God, will ensure eternal life in heaven.

According to Luke 12: 33–34, Jesus advised his followers to sell all their possessions and donate the proceeds to charity with the aim of gaining "an unfailing treasure in heaven, where no thief comes near and no moth destroys."

A Reward in Heaven
Luke 6: 22–23

> 22. Blessed are you when people hate you, and when they exclude you, revile you, and defame you on account of the Son of Man.
> 23. Rejoice in that day and leap for joy, for surely your reward is great in heaven; for that is what their ancestors did to the prophets.

Jesus consoled his followers who experienced rejection and discrimination by the religious authorities of the day that they would receive a reward in heaven.

Lazarus and the rich man
Luke 16: 19–31

19.	Now there was a certain rich man, and he was clothed in purple and fine linen, living in luxury every day.
20.	A certain beggar, named Lazarus, was laid at his gate, full of sores,
21.	and desiring to be fed with the crumbs that fell from the rich man's table. Yes, even the dogs came and licked his sores.
22.	It happened that the beggar died, and that he was carried away by the angels to Abraham's bosom. The rich man also died, and was buried.
23.	In Hades, he lifted up his eyes, being in torment, and saw Abraham far off, and Lazarus at his bosom.
24.	He cried and said, "Father Abraham, have mercy on me, and send Lazarus, that he may dip the tip of his finger in water, and cool my tongue! For I am in anguish in this flame."
25.	But Abraham said, "Son, remember that you, in your lifetime, received your good things, and Lazarus, in like manner, bad things. But now here he is comforted and you are in anguish.
26.	Besides all this, between us and you there is a great gulf fixed, that those who want to pass from here to you are not able, and that none may cross over from there to us."
27.	He said, "I ask you therefore, father, that you would send him to my father's house;
28.	for I have five brothers, that he may testify to them, lest they also come into this place of torment."
29.	But Abraham said to him, "They have Moses and the prophets. Let them listen to them."

> 30. He said, "No, father Abraham, but if one goes to them from the dead, they will repent."
> 31. He said to him, "If they don't listen to Moses and the prophets, neither will they be persuaded if one rises from the dead."

This well-known parable of Jesus tells the story of the beggar Lazarus who sat at the gate of a rich man, wishing to eat the crumbs that fell from his table. Both of them died. Lazarus was carried by the angels to Abraham's bosom in heaven, while the rich man ended up in Hades or hell, where he experienced horrible torments.

This story gives the impression that both of them reached their eternal destinations directly after they had died. Jesus also made it clear that no contact between those in heaven and in hell is possible and that contact between those in in the afterlife and the living on earth is out of the question. The rich man in hell retained his memories because he remembered that he had brothers who were still living on earth.

Jesus made the point that one has to take the messages of "Moses and the prophets" to heart to avoid hell and gain eternal life at "Abraham's bosom".

The body in hell

Jesus also warned his listeners:

Matt 10: 28

> Don't be afraid of those who kill the body, but are not able to kill the soul. Rather, fear him who is able to destroy both soul and body in Gehenna.

In this passage, Jesus uses the name of Gehenna (Greek: γέεννα – also used in Matt 18: 9, Matt 23: 33, and Luke 12: 50 for the hell).

According tio this saying, Jesus was convinced that the whole human being, body and soul, ended up in hell, although his physical remains were kept in a tomb. It is not clear with what type of resurrected body one would arrive in heaven or in hell. He regarded the soul as being immortal, since it could not be killed by men, although it could be destroyed by God.

The Greek word Jesus used for *destroy* in this saying is ἀπόλλυμι (*apollumi*), which may also mean "to put out of the way entirely, abolish, put an end to ruin". That may be an indication the Jesdus may have thought that those in Gehenna or hell would be totally destroyed and cease to exist. That would mean that hell would eventually be empty. This idea is contradicted by other sayings of Jesus where he taught that there will be no end to the tortures and tribulations in the eternal flames of hell.

Jesus' Resurrection
According to John 19: 38–42 and John 20: 1–10, the earliest and probably most accurate report of the aftermath of Jesus' crucifixion, his friends Joseph of Arimathea and Nicodemus nursed him back to life with copious amounts of an expensive medicinal and antiseptic mixture of an aloe extract and myrrh. After his recovery, Jesus had several meetings with his disciples and even had breakfast with them on the shore of the Lake of Galilee (John 21).

The conventional explanation of Jesus' appearances is that he was really dead, but was resurrected miraculously, probably with a spiritual body (1 Cor 15: 40–44). John's account provides enough details so that we can conclude that Jesus did not really die. Jesus' survival after having been crucified cannot, therefore, be regarded as a case of a resurrection from the dead.

Jesus also promised his followers that he would return, presumably to restart his campaign of gaining the throne in Jerusalem (John 21: 23) – which never happened.

Jesus' announcement that he would come back was interpreted in the later parts of the gospels as a return at the end of time, on Judgment Day. When the later parts of the Gospels were compiled after the Jewish War, during the last decades of the first century AD, there was, of course, no possibility that Jesus would reappear and ever become king in Jerusalem. Therefore, his promised comeback was postponed to Judgment Day in the unknown future.[149]

HELL AND DAMNATION

Jesus told his audiences much about the afterlife in hell, which is the fate of the godless and those who refused to believe in him and to support him. Two Greek words were used in the gospels when Jesus spoke about hell:

- Hades (Greek: ᾅδης) – for instance, in Luke 10: 15. This concept was taken from Greek mythology and was used for the netherworld, the abode of the dead, the place where the gods incarcerated their foes. This word was used in the Greek translation of the Old Testament when the Hebrew word *sheol* was encountered.
- Gehenna (Greek: γέεννα) – used in Matt 10: 28; 18: 9, and 23: 33, Mark 9: 43–48; and Luke 12: 5. This name is name derived from the Hebrew/Aramaic name for the Valley of Hinnom, the place where Jerusalem's garbage was dumped and burnt and which was a symbolic depiction of hell: גֵּיא־הִנֹּם (*Gē'-Hīnnōmm*).

Jesus described *hell* as a big and eternal fire or flame (Matt 18: 8–9, Matt 25: 41; Mark 9: 43–50; Luke 16: 24). On the other hand, the

---

[149] Pretorius, *The Gospels Explained*, 238–49; 263–73.

unbelievers will be thrown "into the outer darkness; there is where the weeping and grinding of teeth will be" (Matt 22: 13; see also Matt 8: 12). It is diffecult to reconcile an eternal fire with total darkness, unless it is understood that these descriptions are only meant as figures of speech.

Jesus also told his opponents: "There will be weeping and gnashing of teeth when you see Abraham and Isaac and Jacob and all the prophets in the kingdom of God, and you yourselves thrown out" (Luke 13: 28). That meant that Jesus believed that the souls of the ancient patriarchs and the prophets of the Old Testament were already in heaven at that time.

The parable of Lazarus and the rich man made the point that it is impossible to escape from of Hades and that no contact between the inhabitants of hell and the living is possible (Luke 16: 19–31).

CRITICAL REMARKS

There seem to be some unclear and even contradictory elements in Jesus' teachings about the afterlife.

On the one hand, he taught that the deceased would arrive at their eternal destinations directly after their dreary deathbeds and fancy funerals. On the other hand, he told his followers that the dead would only be sent to either heaven, or hell, on Judgment Day, somewhere in the unknown future. It is difficult to reconcile these ideas with each other.

Jesus' teaching that hell would consist of an eternal fire with the endless torment and torture of those unfortuante souls who got there, seems to be contradicted by his remark that the sinners' bodies and souls woud be uttrerly destroyed in hell.

Of course, these contradictory remarks may be the result of incoorect recollections of what Jesus had said by those who provided information to the authors of the Godspels. These authors may also have misunderstood their informants. It must be remebered that Jesus spoke Aramaic, while the gospels were written in Greek, with the result that the translation of his words may have been wrong in some cases.

Gregory Jenks provided a useful summary of the teachings of Jesus about the afterlife.[150] These findings are quoted below and those ideas that cannot be substantiated are printed in italics, with critical remarks in brackets:

- *"Death will be followed—at the end of time—by a day of judgment.* (Jesus sometimes taught that one would reach his eternal destination directly after death.)
- "The final judgment would involve the separation of righteous from the evil.
- "Wealth acquired during our earthly life cannot be taken into the world to come.
- "A deceased person's status in the next life reflects not the possessions acquired during this life, but the wealth given away and shared with others less fortunate than themselves.
- "Generosity to the outcasts will be repaid at the resurrection of the just.
- "God has power not only to bring death but also to consign a person to Gehenna.
- "Fear of eternal punishment encourages moral discipline in the present life.
- "Those who are consigned to eternal punishment will experience a radical reversal of their previous privilege, retribution for their wrong deeds, and no opportunity for respite or early release.
- "Some believers might escape death should the End come be-

---

[150] Jenks, "Jesus and the Afterlife."

fore they die.
- "All believers will share the experience of Jesus in coming from and returning to the Father.
- "Faithful disciples will be rewarded with a share of the life of the world to come in addition to any tangible rewards they experience in this life.
- *"Human futures after death derive from the character, power, and grace of God and do not result from any inherent immortality.* (It will be shown in a later chapter, dealing with the later parts of the gospels, that Jesus purportedly held the idea that the human body or flesh is supposed to be the prison of the immortal soul or spirit, which had to be liberated at death).
- "While sometimes imagined as an experience of 'spiritual embodiment,' life in the next world is qualitatively different from life in this world and involves no familial or sexual relationships.
- *"For some people the transition from this life to the next can be immediate,* and the metaphor of access to Paradise suggests consolation and comfort." (This conclusion of Jenks is contradicted by his earlier statement that the afterlife only starts after the day of judgment, somewhere in the future).

Most of the conclusions of Jenks can be accepted. A weakness of his investigation is that he did not distinguish enough between the earlier and the later parts of the gospels, although he conceded: "The discourses reflect the creative hand of the Gospel's author, and the Johannine Jesus has a very different 'voice' from the Jesus we meet in the Synoptics." In spite of this, he treated all the pronouncements attributed to Jesus as equally authentic.

Chapter 9
PAUL OF TARSUS

VISIONS AND REVELATIONS

Saul – or Paul as he was mostly called – grew up in the Greek city of Tarsus in Asia Minor and he wrote his letters to various churches in good Greek, a sign of a good Hellenistic education. He also studied Jewish theology in Jerusalem. He was initially an opponent of the Jesus movement that continued to exist in Jerusalem and elsewhere after Jesus' crucifixion and disappearance, but a traumatic experience on the Damascus Road caused him to become one of Jesus' followers (Acts 9: 1–7,; 22: 5–11; and 26: 12–18).

The Apostle Paul (ceiling mosaic, Archiepiscopal Chapel of St. Andrew, Ravenna, Italy)

He claimed to have received various visions and revelations about Jesus, who appeared to him as a heavenly being (Gal 1: 11–19; 1 Cor 2: 10; 11: 23; 15: 1–9; 2 Cor 12: 1–5; Eph 3: 3; Col 1: 26–27). He developed his own interpretation of the life and message of Jesus, which differed from that of Jesus' followers in Jerusalem, including Jesus' apostles, whom he accused of hypocrisy and being false apostles (Acts 15; Gal 2: 4, 11–14; 2 Cor 11).

The main differnece between Paul and the apostles in Jerusalem was that the apostles followed Jesus'example and worshipped God according to the guidelines of the Torah and required of all Gentile followers of Jesus to be circumcized as Jews (Acts 15: 1–2). They regarded themselves only as Jews, not as Christians, and they merely belonged to the Jesus party.

Paul, on the other hand, taught that the laws of the Torah were fulfilled in Jesus Christ when he died on the cross and that they did not apply anymore to his mostly Gentile converts, who became to be known as Christians (Acts 11: 26; Acts 26: 28; 1 Pet 4: 16).

He interpreted Jesus' title of Son of God as an indication that Jesus was, in fact, a divine person in heaven, the equal of his heavenly Father, who adopted a human form during his life on earth. He was a co-creator, with his Father, of the universe (1 Cor 8: 6; Eph 3: 9; Col 1: 16–17). With that, Paul transformed Jesus Christ into a Greek mythological figure, on par with the many sons of Zeus, the chief Greek deity and father of the gods.[151]

The different aspects of Paul's thoughts about the afterlife are presented in the paragraphs that follow:

HEAVEN

Paul subscribed to the cosmology found in the Old Testament, as well as that of the ancient pagan world, namely a cosmos consisting of a stationary earth, a heaven above, and an underwordl below the earth's surface. In Phil 2: 9–11 he wrote that "at the name of Jesus every knee would bow, of those in heaven, those on earth, and those under the earth."

In accordance with this ancient world-view, Paul asserts that the heaven is "above" (Col 3: 1–2). According to Eph 4: 10, Christ "ascended far above all the heavens". These other heavens are, of course, the heavens filled with clouds and stars. He reported that he

---

[151] Pretorius, *Jesus of Nazareth,* 122–23.

was "caught up into the third heaven" during one of his visions. This third heaven must be the dwelling of God, above the two lower chunks of the heavens (2 Cor 12: 2).

Heaven is the residence of God, as well as of the exalted Jesus Christ and of God's angels (Rom 1: 18; Rom 8: 34; Gal 1: 8; Eph 1: 20; Eph 2: 6; Eph 4: 9–10; 1 Thess 4: 16).

Heaven is often called "the kingdom of God" (1 Cor 6: 10; Gal 5: 21; Eph 5: 5). It is on account of Paul's usage of this expression that Jesus' references to the kingdom of God are usually interpreted in a spiritual sense – and not as the resurrected earthly kingdom of Israel with Jesus on the throne in Jerusalem. Paul must have changed the meaning of this expression since the kingdom that Jesus envisaged never materialized.

HELL AND UNDERWORLD

Paul calls the underworld the A*byss* (Greek: ἄβυσσος – *abussos*), the place where the dead are being kept and where Christ stayed after his deadly crucifixion and before his resurrection (Rom 10: 7). This word means "bottomless pit" and this idea was copied from the book of Enoch and Greek mythology. Likewise, Eph 4: 9 informs us that Christ "descended into the lower parts of the earth" after his execution.

People who are guilty of a long list of misconducts and misbehaviors would not be allowed to enter heaven, the kingdom of God (1 Cor 6: 9–10; Gal 5: 19–21). Paul is silent about their fate after death in these passages, apart from his view that they would be denied admission into this kingdom.

BODY, SOUL, AND SPIRIT

Paul thought of the human body and soul in the same way as Plato did. For him, they were two fundamentally different parts, brought together in a human being.

The human body, which is the seat of sin and lusts, is perishable after death (Rom 6: 12) – in contrast with the immortal spirit or soul.

Paul wrote a long passage in Gal 5 to point out the corruption and tendency of the human body, the *flesh,* to slide into vice and villainy, and the possibility to have a saintly *spirit* when allowing Christ into one's life:

Spirit and Flesh
Gal 5: 16–26

16.	But I say, walk by the spirit, and you won't fulfil the lust of the flesh.
17.	For the flesh lusts against the spirit, and the spirit against the flesh; for these are contrary the one to the other, that you may not do the things that you desire.
18.	But if you are led by the spirit, you are not under the law.
19.	Now the works of the flesh are obvious, which are: adultery, sexual immorality, uncleanness, lustfulness,
20.	idolatry, sorcery, hatred, strife, jealousies, outbursts of anger, rivalries, divisions, heresies,
21.	envy, murders, drunkenness, orgies, and things like these; of which I forewarn you, even as I did forewarn you, that those who practice such things will not inherit the kingdom of God.
22.	But the fruit of the spirit is love, joy, peace, patience, kindness, goodness, faithfulness,
23.	gentleness, and self-control. Against such things there is no law.

> 24. Those who belong to Christ Jesus have crucified the flesh with its passions and lusts.
> 25. If we live by the spirit, let's also walk by the spirit.
> 26. Let's not become conceited, provoking one another, and envying one another.

Where Paul mentions the *spirit* in this passage, it was often thought that he referred to the Holy Spirit. Where he mentions the *spirit* here, he nowhere calls it the Holy Spirit, the third divine Person. It is, though, clear from the context that he thought of the human body, the *flesh*, as the source of lust and licentiousness. In contrast, the immortal spirit, which is the part of a human being that is redeemed by Christ, may be transformed into a source of all the admirable virtues.

As a good Platonist, Paul more than once uttered the wish to be liberated from his earthly and sinful body, the flesh, and be with Christ in heaven, as is evident from the following quotations:

Death Wish

2 Cor 5: 8

> We are of good courage, I say, and are willing rather to be absent from the body, and to be at home with the Lord.

Phil 1: 21–24

> 21. For to me to live is Christ, and to die is gain.
> 22. But if to live in the flesh, this will bring fruit from my work; then I don't make known what I will choose.
> 23. But I am in a dilemma between the two, having the desire to depart and be with Christ, for that is very far better.
> 24. Yet, to remain in the flesh is more needful for your sake.

Paul also uttered the following wish:

Spirit, Soul, and Body
1 Thess 5: 23

> May the God of peace himself sanctify you completely. May your whole spirit, soul, and body be preserved blameless at the coming of our Lord Jesus Christ.

It must be pointed out that when Paul refers to the *body* in this verse, he uses the Greek word σῶμα (*soma*) and not σάρξ (*sarx*), which he used in Gal 5 for the foul and filthy source of sin. When he uses the word *body* in this verse, it denotes the sanctified or transformed body that will be resurrected at Christ's return on Judgment Day.

ANGELS, SATAN, AND DEMONS

Paul did not write much about the angels of God. The most important fact about them is that they reside in heaven with God – as has been noted above.

He expected that Judgment Day will happen when God descends onto the earth "with the voice of the archangel, and with God's trumpet" (1 Thess 4: 16). He also wrote that "mighty angels in flaming fire" would descend from heaven on Judgment Day (2 Thess 1: 7). The idea of archangels or chief angels was introduced into the Jewish religious thought by Daniel and Enoch.

In Eph 3: 10 he calls the angels "the principalities and the powers in the heavenly places".

Paul had much more to say about Satan and evil spirits.

He seemed to have suffered from some painful or unpleasant ailment or medical condition, which he ascribed to an evil spirit, sent by the devil:

Angel of Satan
2 Cor 12: 7

> By reason of the exceeding greatness of the revelations, that I should not be exalted excessively, there was given to me a thorn in the flesh, an angel of Satan to buffet me, that I should not be exalted excessively.

Paul warns his readers:

Spiritual Warfre
Eph 6: 12

> For our wrestling is not against flesh and blood, but against the principalities, against the powers, against the world's rulers of the darkness of this age, and against the spiritual hosts of wickedness in the heavenly places.

Paul's word for "heavenly places" (ἐπουράνιος – *epouranios*) may also be translated with "sky". He envisaged these "powers" and "hosts" to be composed of invisible matter since they occupied the sky above. The "rulers of darkness" can only be the stars shining at night and the astrological constellations – deemed to be angels or demons.

When Christ was resurrected from the dead, he conquored all evil forces, as explained in the following passage.

Christ the Conquoror
Eph 1: 20–22

> [When God] raised him from the dead, and made him to sit at his right hand in the heavenly places, far above all rule, and authority, and power, and dominion, and every name that is named, not only in this world, but also in that which is to come. He put all things in subjection under his feet, and gave him to be head over all things ....

Paul added that Christ also rules over –

Col 1: 16

> ... all things created, in the heavens and on the earth, things visible and things invisible, whether thrones or dominions or principalities or powers; all things have been created...

All these entities include Satan and his evil spirits.

THE RESURRECTED BODY

Paul had a firm conviction that those who had faith in Jesus Christ could expect to be raised from the dead when Christ returns. He expresse the hope that "I may attain to the resurrection from the dead" on account of Jesus who was raised from the dead (Phil 3: 10–11).

In what is probably his earliest letter extant, he wrote:

The Lord's Return
1 Thess 4: 16–17

> 16. For the Lord himself will descend from heaven with a shout, with the voice of the archangel, and with God's trumpet. The dead in Christ will rise first,
> 17. then we who are alive, who are left, will be caught up together with them in the clouds, to meet the Lord in the air. So we will be with the Lord forever ().

A similar thought is found in Philippians:

Heavenly Citizenship
Phil 3: 20–21

> 20. For our citizenship is in heaven, from where we also wait for a Savior, the Lord, Jesus Christ;
> 21. who will change the body of our humiliation to be conformed to the body of his glory, according to the working whereby he is able even to subject all things to himself.

When Paul mentions "the body of our humiliation", he has the evil *flesh* in mind. This body would be transformed into the same glorious type of body with which Christ rose from the tomb.

Paul gave a detailed description of his views regarding the resurrected body in 1 Cor 15, expanding upon his other descriptions. It is necessary to look at the most important thoughts in this chapter.

First of all, Paul argues that Christ would not have been raised from the dead if there is no such thing as the resurrection of the body in general. If there were no resurrection, then our faith in Christ would be useless. That there really is a resurrection was proved by Christ who was raised and, therefore, we may also expect to be resurrected (vs 13–20).

The question is, though: "How are the dead raised?" and, "With what kind of body do they come?" (vs 35). He uses the (false) example of a seed that must die in the soil before it can grow and develop into a plant to demonstrate that we must die before we are ready to be taken into heaven after death (vs 36–38).

To illustrate the idea that the resurrected body differs from the earthly body, he mentions that "there is one flesh of men, another flesh of animals, another of fish, and another of birds" (vs 39). He continues with this illustartion to state:

The Resurrected Body
1 Cor 15: 40–44

> 40. There are also celestial bodies, and terrestrial bodies; but the glory of the celestial differs from that of the terrestrial.
> 41. There is one glory of the sun, another glory of the moon, and another glory of the stars; for one star differs from another star in glory.
> 42. So also is the resurrection of the dead. It is sown in corruption; it is raised in incorruption.
> 43. It is sown in dishonor; it is raised in glory. It is sown in weakness; it is raised in power.
> 44. It is sown a natural body; it is raised a spiritual body. If there is a natural body, there is also a spiritual body.

Paul's argument about the nature of the resurrected body, which he describes as a "spiritual body" and a "celestial body", is explained by contrasting the stuff from wich the earth is made with the stuff from which the glorious celestial bodies, the sun, the moon, and the stars, are made. The mortal human body is perishable and can be corrupted and is sown in dishonor at death, while the spiritual body is eternal, incorruptable, and has glory.

It is impossible to avoid the impression that Paul thought of the *spiritual body* as being composed of the same stuff as the heavenly bodies, the *sun, moon, and stars* – just as Aristotle taught that these celestial bodies were made from a fifth element, the "quintessence", which differs from the dust or soil, water, air, and fire found on earth. Paul may have picked up this idea as a youth in the Greek city of Tarsus where he grew up. Since the Jews believed the stars to be angels or demons, it follows that Paul's "spiritual body" was simply a spirit. It is also possible that Paul followed Philo of Alexandria who taught that the immortal soul of man was made from a fifth element, the ether.

Paul adds: "Now I say this, brothers, that flesh and blood can't inherit the kingdom of God; neither does corruption inherit incorruption" (vs 50). That means simply that the resurrected body, with which the faithful will inherit eternal life in heaven, cannot be made of ordinary matter, flesh and blood, but must be made from something indestructible – such as Aristotle's "quintessence".

If it is so that Paul's *spiritual body* is made of the same stuff as the sun, moon, and stars – which are actually angels or spiritual beings, according to the Old Testament – it follows that this *spiritual body* is none other than the *spirit* or *soul* of man, which is liberated from the body at death.

The last sentence in the quoted passage is important: "If there is a natural body, there is also a spiritual body." In Greek, it reads: "εἰ ἔστιν σῶμα ψυχικόν, ἔστιν καὶ πνευματικόν" (*ei estin soma psychikon, estin kai pneumatikon*). The term used for *natural body* actuslly means a "breathing body" or a "living body with a soul" (psyche). This is contrasted with the *spiritual body* – the part of man that survives death, according to Plato's dualism of body and spirit. Therefore, the *spiritual body* is merely the immortal spirit that goes to heaven after death.

Paul ends his description of the resurrected body with the following words:

The Resurrected Body
1 Cor 15: 51–57

51.	Behold, I tell you a mystery. We will not all sleep, but we will all be changed,
52.	in a moment, in the twinkling of an eye, at the last trumpet. For the trumpet will sound, and the dead will be raised incorruptible, and we will be changed.

> 53. For this corruptible must put on incorruption, and this mortal must put on immortality.
> 54. But when this corruptible will have put on incorruption, and this mortal will have put on immortality, then what is written will happen: "Death is swallowed up in victory."
> 55. "Death, where is your sting? Hades, where is your victory?"
> 56. The sting of death is sin, and the power of sin is the law.
> 57. But thanks be to God, who gives us the victory through our Lord Jesus Christ.

Paul's message is that Hades or hell has lost its victory, its ability to frighten believers. Death will also not be something to fear, because it amounts to a liberation of the indestructible spirit from the mortal body. When the last trumpet is blown – presumably by an archangel – those who are still alive will be changed into the same spiritual and immortal bodies of those who will be raised from their graves and tombs.

JUDGMENT DAY

Paul concurred with Jesus – and with the religions of Egypt and Persia, as well as Enoch – that a day of judgment awaits all those who have died, as well as all evil forces in the universe. Judgment Day will lead to eternal life for believers, an existence without any evils.

For instance, he wrote to the Christians in Thessalonica:

Destruction
1 Thess 5: 3

> When they are saying, "Peace and safety," then sudden destruction will come on them, like birth pains on a pregnant woman; and they will in no way escape.

This verse is part of a passage dealing with the unexpected "day of the Lord". That day will bring about the "sudden destruction" of godless sinners. The Greek word he uses is ὄλεθρος (*Olethros*), which means "destruction, annihilation, ruin, death". This expression implies the annihilation of unrepentent sinners on Judgment Day.

He wrote to the Romans:

God's Wrath
Romans 1: 18–20

18.	For the wrath of God is revealed from heaven against all ungodliness and unrighteousness of men, who hinder the truth in unrighteousness,
19.	because that which is known by God is revealed in them, for God revealed it to them.
20.	For the invisible things of him since the creation of the world are clearly seen, being perceived through the things that are made, even his everlasting power and divinity; that they may be without excuse.

Ungodly men don't have any excuse for not worshipping God, because he revealed his omnipotence and divine majesty adequately in his creation. This failure to worship Him awakens God's wrath and judgment.

Faithful believers are promised in 2 Thess 1: 6–10 that God will reward and repay them on Judgment Day for the "afflictions" they have suffered at the hands of unbelievers "when the Lord Jesus is revealed from heaven with his mighty angels in flaming fire". The unbelievers will be punished with "eternal destruction". The Greek word translated with "destruction" is ὄλεθρος (*olethros*) which was also used in 1 Thess 5: 3, and which may also mean "annihilation, ruin, death".

A similar thought is found in Gal 6: 8 – "For he who sows to his own flesh will from the flesh reap corruption". The Greek word for *corruption* is φθορά (*phthora*), which must be translated as "destruction, perishing, corruption".

Likewise, in Phil 1: 28 Paul writes thst the adversaries of the gospel will be condemned on Judgment Day "which is for them a proof of destruction". In Phil 3: 19, he condemns the enemies of Christ "whose end is destruction". In both these cases, he uses another strong Greek word, namely ἀπώλεια (*apoleia),* which means "utter destruction, laying waste".

It does seem as if Paul envisaged the total elimination, eradication, extinction, and extermination of the evil enemies of Christ and that hell will eventually prove to be empty.

This idea is at odds with Jesus who taught that hell consists of an eternal fire where the roasted and toasted souls of the doomed dead retain their memories of their evil earthly lives.

Paul also gave us a hint of how he envisaged the aftermath of Judgment Day for the faithful believers:

Aftermath of Judgment Day
1 Cor 15: 26 – 28

26.	The last enemy that will be abolished is death.
27.	For, "He put all things in subjection under his feet." But when he says, "All things are put in subjection," it is evident that he is excepted who subjected all things to him.
28.	When all things have been subjected to him, then the Son will also himself be subjected to him who subjected all things to him, that God may be all in all.

Some remarks about this remarkable passage are necessary. When Paul writes that death will be abolished after Judgment Day, it is usually interpreted as a state where nobody will die anymore, because everybody will, in any case, already be dead and their immortal souls will have been transported to their eternal destinations.

However, the word used for *death*, θάνατος (*thanatos*), may mean more than simply physical death. It has a rich variety of meanings, and it may also be used for eternal death or hell. If that is what Paul had in mind, it may mean that eternal death, the never-ending punishment of the wicked in hell, will be abolished or abrogated and that hell will just vanish or evaporate.

In verse 35 of the same chapter, Paul remarks: "Death, where is your sting? Hades, where is your victory?" With this remark, it is clear, Paul regards *death* and *Hades* as synonyms. In other words, if eternal death is being abolished or terminated after Judgment Day, then it also means that Hades or hell is to be scrapped and closed down, because there will be no place in the renewed creation for a spot where a sinful Satan and shameless sinners are being kept.

Paul also wrote that Christ would subject himself to God, his Father, after he had vanquished and eliminagted all evil forces. The result will be "that God may be all in all". This can only mean one thing: the whole of creation will be dissolved into God. Nothing will remain after Judgment Day, except for God Himself.

Karl Barth

The great German-Swiss theologian, Karl Barth, made the same conclusion regarding Paul's thoughts in 1 Cor 15. He wrote that those who will be resurrected will be "participating in the eternal life of God."[152]

Perhaps Paul thought that the situation that existed before God created the world and where God was totally on his own, would return after Judgment Day at the end of time.

Rom 11: 36 has something similar: "For of him [the Lord], and through him, and to him, are all things. To him be the glory for ever! Amen."

We also read in Eph 4: 6 – "[There is] one God and Father of all, who is over all, and through all, and in us all."

It is possible that Paul got this idea from The Wisdom of Somon (12: 1) – "For thy immortal spirit is in all things."

The idea that all things will eventually be contained within God, boils down to the philosophical theory of pantheism. The expression "all in all" in 1 Cor 15: 28 (Greek: πάντα ἐν πᾶσιν – *panta en pasin*) could easily have been taken from the pantheism of the Greek school of Stoicism. Pantheism can be described as "the doctrine that the universe conceived of as a whole is God and, conversely, that there is no God but the combined substance, forces, and laws that are manifested in the existing universe."[153] Pantheism teaches the eventual identity of God and his creation.

Paul's utterances certainly means that he thought that everything will eventually be absorbed into God – except for all the evil forces and wicked spirits that will be eradicated, will vanish, and will disappear into nothingness.

The Stoics believed that the universe was the creation of a primeordial fire, the fire of reason, and that all things will again be dissolved into this fire at the end of time – just as Paul thought that

---

[152] Barth, *Church Dogmatics*, III.2, 624.
[153] Reese, "Pantheism".

God would be "all in all" after Judgment Day, which means that the spirits of the faithful in heaven will be dissolved or absorbed into God.

It is quite possible that Paul was also influenced by the determinism of the Stoics. They believed that all events are predestined, that everything is caused by something else, and that man doesn't have free will. Paul taught something similar. According to him, all events were "foreordained" by God (1 Cor 2: 7). God "also predestined [us] to be conformed to the image of his Son, that he might be the firstborn among many brothers." That means that those who are saved, are "foreordained" by God (Rom 8: 29–30). The same thought is also to be found in Eph 1: 4–5 and 11; Eph 2: 4–9; and 2 Tim 1: 9, namely that God had decided from his eternity which people would be given eternal life.

EVERLASTING LIFE

For Paul, the destination of faithful believers after death is guaranteed: they will receive eternal life in heaven with God and Christ. Paul describes his thoughts about the blessed afterlife in the following ways:

That which is complete
1 Cor 13: 9–12

9.	For we know in part, and we prophesy in part;
10.	but when that which is complete has come, then that which is partial will be done away with.
11.	When I was a child, I spoke as a child, I felt as a child, I thought as a child. Now that I have become a man, I have put away childish things.

> 12. For now we see in a mirror, dimly, but then face to face. Now I know in part, but then I will know fully, even as I was also fully known.

Paul foresaw a condition after death where everything would be complete and perfect, in contrast with life on earth where things are imperfect. All imperfect and wicked elements of creation will disappear. He uses the simile of the way a child speaks and an adult speaks to illustrate how these two states will differ. He also says that our knowledge on earth is incomplete, but in the afterlife, we will have perfect knowledge, while God will also know us perfectly. That implies a unity with God.

In 2 Cor 5: 1, he notes: "For we know that if the earthly house of our tent is dissolved, we have a building from God, a house not made with hands, eternal, in the heavens." In verse 8 of the same chapter, he sighs: "We are of good courage, I say, and are willing rather to be absent from the body, and to be at home with the Lord." According to 1 Thess 4: 17, the resurrected saints will "meet the Lord in the air. So we will be with the Lord forever."

He promised the believers in Philippi: "For our citizenship is in heaven, from where we also wait for a Savior, the Lord, Jesus Christ" (Phil 3: 20).

Paul assured the Christians in Rome of the following:

Eternal Life
Rom 6: 22–23

> 22. But now, being made free from sin, and having become servants of God, you have your fruit of sanctification, and the result of eternal life.
> 23. For the wages of sin is death, but the free gift of God is eternal life in Christ Jesus our Lord.

Paul also wrote to the church in Rome,: "For I consider that the sufferings of this present time are not worthy to be compared with the glory which will be revealed toward us" (Rom 8: 18). To his friend Timothy, he wrote: "Therefore I endure all things for the elect's sake, that they also may obtain the salvation which is in Christ Jesus with eternal glory" (2 Tim 2: 10).

It must be pointed out that Paul didn't provide his readers with any descriptions of conditions in heaven. The only detail that he provides is that the spritis – or resurrected spiritual bodies – of the deceased faithful will be with God and Christ forever.

CONCLUSION

One must conclude in the light of Paul's pantheistic leanings, that he thought that the blessed souls would be transformed from temporal beings with physical bodies into eternal beings with spiritual bodies and merged with God. Since only God is really eternal (Rom 1: 20; 1 Tim 1: 17), these blessed souls must be amalgamated with the eternal God in order to enter eternity, a state of being without beginning and end.

It appears from the discussion of Paul's ideas regarding the relationship between body and soul, the nature of the resurrected body, Judgment Day, and the eventual fate of the spirits of redeemed Christians, that Paul absorbed many a philosophical and religious concept from the Hellenistic world in which he grew up.

Paul's dualism regarding the relationship between body and soul, ultimately comes from Plato. His presentation of the transformed resurrected body was propably influenced by Aristotle's fifth element from which the astronomical celestial bodies were supposed to have been made.

His pantheistic idea that God will be "all in all" after Judgment Day, may reveal the influence of Stoicism that taught the

the universe will be dissolved into the fire of reason at the end of the world.

His deification of Jesus Christ, the eternal Son of God, reminds one of the pagan religions of his time, especially the Greek mythology with the many sons of Zeus. His idea of Judgment Day – which was shared by Jesus – originally came from Egypt and Persia and entered Jewish religious thought through Enoch.

Although Paul often referred to the Hebrew Scriptures in his arguments, it is, nevertheless, apparent that his views regarding the afterlife differ fundamentally from those found in the Old Testament, as well as from the notions held by Jesus of Nazareth.

Chapter 10
THE LATER GOSPELS

LATER PARTS OF THE GOSPELS

As has been shown, the Gospels of Matthew, Luke, and John have grown in stages, which stages can easily be distinguished from each other. The earliest stages were analysed in a previous chapter to explore the views of Jesus of Nazareth regarding the afterlife. The later parts of the gospels, composed at least five decades after Jesus' time, often contain the views of some early Christians, although they are presented as accurate accounts of the words and actions of Jesus.

The following elements of the gospels display, though, all the hallmarks of legendary and mythological speculations.[154] These later additions to the gospels may be classified as –

- The incompatible nativity stories of Matthew and Luke;
- The conflicting stories of Matthew and Luke about the events after Jesus' crucifixion;
- Accounts of some of Jesus' sayings and parables (which may be accepted as mainly historical); and
- The parts of John containing philosophical arguments and purported speeches, dialogues, lectures, and sermons of Jesus.

The nativity stories can be ignored because they don't tell us anything of value regarding the subject matter of this book. Those sayings and parables of Jesus that appear only in one of the synoptic gospels, may be genuine and they were already discussed in a previous chapter. The other parts will be discussed separately here.

---

[154] Pretorius, *The Gospels Explained,* 84–90, 536–85.

THE SYNOPTIC GOSPELS

The Gospel of Mark is the oldest complete gospel and most of it was later incorporated into Matthew and Luke, who added parts of the Q Document and parts of their own. Mark contains, for the most part, a description of Jesus' actions, travels, and crucifixion. Most of the reported saying of Jesus deal with the kingdom that Jesus wanted to reestablish. There are only two passages that deal with the subject matter of this book:

The Resurrection

Jesus was a supporter of the doctrine of the resurrection of the dead, as found in Daniel and some of the apocryphal books. He got involved in a debate with some Sadducees on this topic. Since the Sadducees only accepted the Torah as authoritative, they rejected the notion of the resurrection of the dead since it is nowhere mentioned in the Torah. It is worthwhile to quote the whole passage in Mark:

Mark 12: 18–27

18.	There came to him Sadducees, who say that there is no resurrection. They asked him, saying,
19.	"Teacher, Moses wrote to us, `If a man`s brother dies, and leaves a wife behind him, and leaves no child, that his brother should take his wife, and raise up children to his brother.`
20.	"There were seven brothers. The first took a wife, and dying left no children.
21.	""The second took her, and died, leaving no children behind him. The third likewise;

22.	and the seven took her and left no children. Last of all the woman also died.
23.	"In the resurrection, when they rise, whose wife will she be of them? For the seven had her as a wife."
24.	Jesus answered them, "Isn't this because you are mistaken, not knowing the scriptures, nor the power of God?
25.	"For when they will rise from the dead, they neither marry, nor are given in marriage, but are like angels in heaven.
26.	"But about the dead, that they are raised; haven't you read in the book of Moses, at the Bush, how God spoke to him, saying, 'I am the God of Abraham, the God of Isaac, and the God of Jacob?'
27.	He is not the God of the dead, but of the living. You are therefore badly mistaken."

Jesus managed to refute the silly and absurd argument of the Sadducees by quoting specifically from the Torah, the only part of the Old Testament that they accepted. It must be concluded that the type of resurrection that Jesus envisaged, was simply the delivery to heaven of the deceased by the angels, directly after death. They will be sexless and spiritual beings, just like the angels, withoutt ransformed or glorified material bodies.

The Body in Hell
Mark 9: 43–48

43.	If your hand causes you to stumble, cut it off. It is better for you to enter into life maimed, rather than having your two hands to go into Gehenna, into the unquenchable fire,
44.	'where their worm doesn't die, and the fire is not quenched.'

> 45. If your foot causes you to stumble, cut it off. It is better for you to enter into life lame, rather than having your two feet to be cast into Gehenna, into the fire that will never be quenched
> 46. 'where their worm doesn't die, and the fire is not quenched.'
> 47. If your eye causes you to stumble, cast it out. It is better for you to enter into the kingdom of God with one eye, rather than having two eyes to be cast into the Gehenna of fire,
> 48. 'where their worm doesn't die, and the fire is not quenched.'

The conventional explanation of this passage is that one ought to be wary of anything that could cause one to stumble into committing sins and to reach hell after death because it would be better to arrive maimed and crippled in the heavenly kingdom than to have a whole body and to descend into hell "where their worm doesn't die, and the fire is not quenched."

This explanation does not satisfy, because Jesus nowhere taught that one reaches the afterlife with his earthly body – either intact or with missing body parts. The gospels rather explain that the *soul* or *spirit* of the faithful will reach heavenly bliss after death (Luke 12: 20 and Matt16: 26)

Jesus also said explicitly that is would be better "to enter into life maimed". This "life" clearly refers to life of earth – not eternal life in heaven after death.

The kingdom mentioned in this passage must, therefore, be the earthly kingdom Jesus wished to establish and it is equated with "life" on earth. When he mentioned the "kingdom" in other contexts he always meant the Israelite monarchy that he wanted to restore. The only exception in the Synoptic Gospels is Matt 23: 34 – "Then the King will say to those on his right, 'Come, you who are blessed by my Father; take your inheritance, the kingdom prepared for you since the creation of the world.'"

It is clear that Jesus contrasted "life" and his earthly kingdom with "Gehenna", the garbish dump of Jerusalem that served as a symbol of hell. This expression is usually used in the sense of the eternal hell that awaits all godless people after death (Matt 5: 22; 23: 15; Luke 12: 5), but it must be seen in this case as the opposite of Jesus' Israelite kingdom, namely the "hell" of the Roman domination and suppression of the Jews.

This saying of Jesus must have gone through a process of transformation during the four decades between Jesus' time and the recording thereof by Mark. The source from which Mark gathered this saying, clearly thought that Jesus' reference to "Gehenna" must have meant the eternal hell and he added the words "where their worm doesn't die, and the fire is not quenched" (quoted from Isa 66: 24) for greater clarity. This rendering of Jesus' saying is clearly a distortion of Jesus' original words.

Jesus warned his followers not to "stumble", that is, not to have doubts about him as the Messiah. One should remove everything from one's life that could lead to this stumbling, even if it may cause some hardship, but that is preferable above living as in the past and enduring the "hell" of the pagan occupiers of their country.

The Parable of the Weeds
Matt 13: 24–30

24.	He set another parable before them, saying, "The Kingdom of Heaven is like a man who sowed good seed in his field,
25.	but while people slept, his enemy came and sowed darnel also among the wheat, and went away.
26.	But when the blade sprang up and brought forth fruit, then the darnel appeared also.

27.	The servants of the householder came and said to him, 'Sir, didn't you sow good seed in your field? Where did this darnel come from?'
28.	He said to them, 'An enemy has done this.' The servants asked him, 'Do you want us to go and gather them up?'
29.	But he said, 'No, lest perhaps while you gather up the darnel, you root up the wheat with them.
30.	Let both grow together until the harvest, and in the harvest time I will tell the reapers, "First, gather up the darnel, and bind them in bundles to burn them; but gather the wheat into my barn."'"

This parable to explain the kingdom appears only in Matthew, but may be a genuine story told by Jesus.

The farmer in this story represents Jesus and his enemies are the Pharisees and teachers of the Law who contradicted his message, the good seed. They sowed weeds, their false messages. When it is time for the harvest, the time when the Israelite kingdom is to be re-established, the works of these enemies will be exposed and condemned.

That Jesus regarded the Pharisees as his enemies is evident, for instance, from Mark 8: 15 where he explicitly warned his followers against the "yeast" of the Pharisees.

Matt 13: 36–43

36.	Then Jesus sent the multitudes away, and went into the house. His disciples came to him, saying, "Explain to us the parable of the darnel of the field."
37.	He answered them, "He who sows the good seed is the Son of Man,

> 38. the field is the world; and the good seed, these are the sons of the kingdom; and the darnel are the sons of the evil one.
> 39. The enemy who sowed them is the devil. The harvest is the end of the age, and the reapers are angels.
> 40. As therefore the darnel is gathered up and burned with fire; so will it be in the end of this age.
> 41. The Son of Man will send forth his angels, and they will gather out of his kingdom all things that cause stumbling, and those who do iniquity,
> 42. and will cast them into the furnace of fire. There will be weeping and the gnashing of teeth.
> 43. Then the righteous will shine forth as the sun in the kingdom of their Father. He who has ears to hear, let him hear.

The explanation of the Parable of the Weeds given by Matthew is evidently his own invention, which does not agree with the parable as he recorded it from an old tradition in the previous passage.

Matthew's explanation changed Jesus' enemies from the Pharisees and teachers of the Law into the devil. The harvest is to take place on Judgment Day – not when the Israelite kingdom is restored – and the angels will gather the souls of those who belong to the spiritual Kingdom of Heaven. The sinners will be banished to the eternal fires of hell, where they will weep and gnash their teeth and they perpetually blame themselves for their fate.

RESURRECTION STORIES OF MATTHEW AND LUKE

The accounts of Matthew and Luke about Jesus' appearances to his disciples and friends after disappearing from his tomb, contain little information about heaven and hell. It must, though, be pointed out that Jesus was moving around with his physical body, after having been nursed back to life by his friends, Nicodemus and Josph of Arimathea (John 19: 38–40). He told his disciples that he was not a spirit or a ghost but a man of flesh and blood (Luke 24: 39). Later, he invited them to inspect his wounds and he enjoyed breakfast with them (Luke 24: 39–43). This amounts to a contradiction of Paul's idea that the resurrection from the dead involves a transformation of the corpse or the physical remains of the deceased into a spiritual or heavenly body (1 Cor 15).

Only Luke reports Jesus' ascension into heaven in Luke *24: 50–53* and Acts 1: 6–11. The two reports don't tell exactly the same story. According the story in Luke, Jesus levitated into heaven from Bethany, while the report in Acts tells us that it happened in Jerusalem. These reports also don't agree with the other gospels, which claim that Jesus had his last meetings with his disciples in Galilee after his resurrection – far from Jerusalem or Bethany. Tthe story of Jesus' ascension must be an invention of Luke because he didn't know what happened to Jesus after he had disappeared after his horrific ordeal on the cross and his disappointment that no crowd of angels sped to his aid, which made him cry out: "My God, my God, why have you forsaken me?" (Mark 15: 34).

Luke probably tried to provide an explanation for Paul's repeated insistence that the divine Jesus was in heaven, from where he appeared to him in various visions.[155]

JOHN'S DISCOURSES AND DIALOGUES

Two Elements of the Gospel

The Gospel of John can easily be divided into two elements: the narrative part, which probably contains the memories of the Apostle John, and some philosophical and theological parts, containg

---

[155] Pretorius, *The Gospels Explained,* 523.

purported sermons and conversations of Jesus. The last-mentioned parts were woven into the proto-gospel and they were probably composed during the nineties of the first century AD by disciples or students of John in Ephesus, where John settled after leaving Jerusalem, probably with Mary, Jesus' mother.[156]

Heaven and Hell

Heaven is mentioned numerous times in these parts of the gospel. It is merely presented as the dwelling of God (John 3: 27; 17: 1), the place from where the Holy Spirit descended upon Jesus at his baptism (John 1: 32), and the place from where the divine Jesus came before being born as a human being (John 3: 12–13; 3: 31; 6: 32–33, 38, 41–42 & 50–51; 17: 3, 5 & 8).

There are two oblique reference to hell in these parts of John. Chapter 6: 36 assures us that if somebody disobeys God's Son "the wrath of God remains on him." In chapter 17: 12, Jesus mentions Judas who betrayed him and whom he calls the "son of perdition".

Body, Soul, and Spirit

The word *soul* (ψυχή – *psyche*) is only mentioned once and it may be interpreted as "mind" (John 12: 27).

Spirit (πνεῦμα – *pneuma*) is encountered often – mostly in the context of the Holy Spirit, but also of the human immortal spirit. John 4: 24 declares: "God is a Spirit, and those who worship him must worship in spirit and truth." The human spirit mentioned here must be contrasted with the human body, called the *flesh* elsewhere (Greek: σάρξ – *sarx,* meaning "flesh, body, rotting meat"). In other words: those who worship God must deny their bodily desires and needs and purify their spirits of all evil thoughts, wishes. and urges. This presupposes the Platonic dualism of body and spirit.

---

[156] Pretorius, *The Gospels Explained,* 177–80.

John 6: 63 doesn't seem to make sense: "It is the spirit who gives life. The flesh profits nothing. The words that I speak to you are spirit, and are life." The only way to make sense of this syaing is to propose that the human *spirit* and the human *flesh* are again contrasted. The flesh is worthless, while it is the spirit that inherits eternal life.

The bodily existence of man is typified as *flesh* in a pejorative manner – just as Platonists thought of the human body as the seat of evil desires and as a prison of the soul or spirit. John 1: 14 says that the "Word" (Greek: λόγος – λ*ogos*) became *flesh*. That means that the Word, Jesus Christ, became a human being with a body and became part of this wicked world with all its evils and woes.

The Platonic dualistic nature of man, consisting of two elements, body, and spirit, is explicitly taught in John 3: 6 and 6: 63 – "That which is born of the flesh is flesh. That which is born of the spirit is spirit."

Eternal Life
The resurrection of the dead is encountered in John 6: 40, where we are informed "that everyone who sees the Son, and believes in him, should have eternal life; and I will raise him up at the last day" (see also John 6: 47). We are also told: "For as the Father raises the dead and gives them life, even so the Son also gives life to whom he desires" (John 5: 21).

Eternal life is given to those who believe in Jesus Christ (John 3: 15–16; 5: 24; 6: 40 & 47; 17: 3). This part of the Gospel is very vague about what extatcly faith in the Son of God entails; it is perhaps merely the acceptance of the idea that Jesus is the Son of God or the Messiah.

Eternal life means to "enter into the kingdom of God" (John 3: 5).

John 12: 25 warns us: "He who loves his life will lose it. He who hates his life in this world will keep it to eternal life." This is a warning against selfishness and also an invitation to surrender one's life to God and Christ. This may, perhaps, remind one of the asceticism that is typical of Neo-Platonism, which regarded the human body and life on earth as essentially wicked and wretched and thought that the spirit had to be liberated from the fetid and foul flesh at death.

Chapter 11
JOHN OF PATMOS

THE AUTHOR OF REVELATION

There is certainly no other book in the Bible that has sparked so much confusion and controversy as the book of Revelation. Many commentators see this book as a collection of prophecies pertaining to our own time and the future of the world until Christ's return on Judgment Day. However, the book pertinently declares that it deals with the situation of the Christian church at the time of writing, as well as the immediate future – not the far future. The very beginning of Revelation informs the reader:

Rev 1: 1 & 3

> 1. This is the Revelation of Jesus Christ, which God gave him to show to his servants the things which *must happen soon*, which he sent and made known by his angel to his servant, John.
> 2. (…)
> 3. Blessed is he who reads and those who hear the words of the prophecy, and keep the things that are written in it, for *the time is at hand* (own emphasis).

The same idea is also expressed in Rev 4: 1; 11: 10; and 22: 6.

It does indeed seem as if two independent scholars, Bruce Malina and Adelbert Scholtz,[157] have been able to find the key to unlock the mysteries and riddles of Revelation. They demonstrated that the author used his observations of certain astrological constel-

---

[157] Malina, *On the Genre and Message of Revelation*; Scholtz, *Revelation*.

lations and planets on certain indentifiable dates as the background of his visions and messages to his fellow-Christians, apart from descriptions of certain natural phenomena, such as a volcano, thunder storms, and a swarm of locusts. Scholtz was able to reconstruct the starry heavens on certain dates with the help of a computerized astromical program to determine exactly what John was seeing and describing in his book. The analysis of Scholtz will be used as a guide in this chapter.

Many commentators thought that the author of Revelation was the aged disciple and apostle of Jesus, John, who was also seen as the author of the gospel bearing his name and the three letters attributed to him. This is, though, an untenable position since the style of writing in Revelation differs greatly from that found in the gospel and the three epistles. Everything points to another author, as has been shown in a previous chapter.[158]

Most commentators agree that this book was written during the nineties of the first century AD. By that time, the Apostle John would have been very, very old, if he was still alive. It would have been too much for an old man in his nineties to survive the rigors and hardships of exile on a barren island and to write a book about his visions afterwards.

Scholtz has demonstrated convincingly, using ancient extra-biblical sources, that John of Patmos – as he is often called – was a priest at the Jerusalem temple who fled to Ephesus after the outbreak of the Jewish War against Rome in AD 66. He became a leader of the Christian churches in Asia Minor. His age – he was likely in his seventies at that stage – and social standing may have been mitigating factors when he was sentenced and banished to the island of Parmos, not too far from the harbor city of Ephesus, due to his refusal as a Christian to worship the Roman Emperor Domitian as a

---

[158] Scholtz, *Revelation,* 9–12.

divine figure.[159]

John reglularly made use of thoughts from the Old Testament, as well as from Enoch and the Book of Jubilees, without naming his sources. It is only possible to understand Revelation against this background.

An analysis of this book reveals that the author based most of his thoughts and visions on a series of symbolic numbers to characterize various elements of his faith – especially 3, 3½, 4, 6, 7, 10, 12, 42, 666, 1 000, and 144 000. These numbers told him something about God, the heavens, the earth, Satan, and the netherworld or the Abyss. It is not impossible that John could have picked up something about the Pythagorean theory of numbers while living in Ephesus, an important cultural and academic center at that time.[160]

HEAVEN

Most of John's visions deal directly or indirectly with heaven, the dwelling place of God, the angels, and the souls of the saintly martyrs. John mostly described the stars and constellations he saw in the sky – and therefore also God's heaven from his point of view.

He often saw God's throne in heaven – for instance, in Rev 4: 1–11. The computerized reconstruction of the night sky shows that his description of the throne and its environment places the throne at the northern celestial pole – the point around which all the stars in the northern sky revolve. This was in line with the ideas of the ancient Mesopotanians. Christ, in the image of a slaughtered lamb, was also occupying God's throne, from where he ruled his

---

[159] Scholtz, *Revelation*, 17–19.
[160] Scholtz, *Revelation*, 44–49..

church (Rev 1: 9–20).[161]

The throne was surrounded by four living creatures, a lion, a bull, an eagle, and a man (Rev 4: 1–11) – the constellations of Leo, Taurus, Aquila, and Boötes. These firgures were placed more or less at the equinoxes and solstices and symbolized all living creatures in God's creation.[162]

There were also twenty-four elders surrounding the throne (Rev 4: 1–11) – one for each hour of the day. The number of twenty-four elders symbolized the twelve Israelite patrarchs and the twelve apostles of Christ and they must be seen as representatives of the faithful of the Old Testament and the New Testament.[163]

Chapter 19: 1–4 describes a great crowd, singing God's praise, consisting of the souls of the martyrs. This crowd was to be found in the star clouds of the Milky Way.[164]

All these scenes contained the message that God is in control of his creation and that all parts of creation worship and honor Him.

THE ABYSS, HADES , AND HELL

Hades or hell is encountered at the beginning of the book, where John had a vision of Christ, sitting on the throne at the celestial north pole:

John's First Vision
Rev 1: 12–18

12. I turned to see the voice that spoke with me. Having turned, I saw seven golden lampstands.

---

[161] Scholtz, *Revelation*, 62–67.
[162] Scholtz, *Revelation*, 102–11.
[163] Scholtz, *Revelation*, 101–11.
[164] Scholtz, *Revelation*, 255–56.

> 13. And in the midst of the lampstands was one like a son of man, clothed with a robe reaching down to his feet, and with a golden sash around his chest.
> 14. His head and his hair were white as white wool, like snow. His eyes were like a flame of fire.
> 15. His feet were like burnished brass, as if it had been refined in a furnace. His voice was like the voice of many waters.
> 16. He had seven stars in his right hand. Out of his mouth proceeded a sharp two-edged sword. His face was like the sun shining at its brightest.
> 17. When I saw him, I fell at his feet like a dead man. He laid his right hand on me, saying, "Don't be afraid. I am the first and the last,
> 18. and the Living one. I was dead, and behold, I am alive forevermore. I have the keys of Death and of Hades."

The computerized recreation of this scene on Sunday, 30 January AD 96, shows the deified Christ in his glory, with seven lamps in front of him – the seven stars of the tail of the constellation of Draco. He held seven stars in his hand, the stars of Ursa Minor, the Little Bear – the angels of the seven churches in Asia Minor. He assured John that he held the keys to Death and Hades – a sign that he would be the judge on Judgment Day who will decide who will be sent to eternal death in hell.

Hell is described in Rev 19: 20 as "the lake of fire that burns with sulphur." It is the fate of Satan, his allies, and all unbelievers to be thrown into this place of pain and perdition.

Revelation contains graphic descriptions of the Abyss, the prison in which Satan and his demons are locked up in anticipation of Judgment Day. The most important is to be found in chapters 6 and 9:

The Abyss
Rev 6: 12–17

> 1. I saw when he opened the sixth seal, and there was a great earthquake. The sun became black as sackcloth made of hair, and the whole moon became as blood.
> 2. The stars of the sky fell to the earth, as a fig tree drops its unripe figs when it is shaken by a great wind.
> 3. The sky was removed as a scroll when it is rolled up. Every mountain and island were moved out of their places.
> 4. The kings of the earth, the princes, the commanding officers, the rich, the strong, and every slave and freeman, hid themselves in the caves and in the rocks of the mountains.
> 5. They told the mountains and the rocks, "Fall on us, and hide us from the face of him who sits on the throne, and from the wrath of the Lamb,
> 6. for the great day of his wrath has come; and who is able to stand?"

Rev 9: 1–2

> 1. The fifth angel sounded, and I saw a star from the sky fallen to the earth. The key to the pit of the abyss was given to him.
> 2. He opened the pit of the abyss, and smoke went up out of the pit, like the smoke from a great furnace. The sun and the air were darkened because of the smoke from the pit.

There can be no doubt that John described a real event – the outburst of a volcano and the accompanying earthquake. The Mediterranean world is renowned for its seismic activity as the continent of Africa is slowly sliding towards Europe and Asia Minor. Earthquakes and volcanic activity occur regularly where two parts of the earth's crust clash and crumble.

The most likely candidate for John's experience is the volcanic island of Nisyros, to the south of Patmos – in the opposite direction from God's throne at the northern celestial pole. He saw blobs of glowing lava being shot up into the air and falling back onto the earth and the sea, while clouds filled with smoke, steam, and ash obscured the sun and the moon. The red-hot chunks of glowing lava at night were seen as falling stars. Terrified inhabitants of Patmos sought refuge in caves – possibly also in the cave where John was living according to tradition.

An aerial photo of the Greek island of Nisyros with its volcanic crater – Rev 6: 12–17; 8: 8)

John interpreted this volcano as a sign that the pit of the Abyss, as well as hell, broke through the surface of the earth, due to the display of fireworks that could be seen clearly, especially during the night. The Greek word for *Abyss* is ἄβυσσος (*abyssos*), and the English word is clearly derived from that. It has the following meanings: "the abyss, underworld, abode of the dead, the pit."

John got the idea of the Abyss and the flames of hell from Enoch – especially Enoch 21: 1–10. That was the space where Satan was supposed to have been incarcerated after having been kicked out of heaven and where he was bound, awaiting his never-ending punishment after Judgment Day.[165]

In the following chapters, John described the horrors that were felt on Patmos due to all the ash and debris from the volcano that made life difficult and polluted drinking water supplies.[166]

Satan thrown out of Heaven
Rev 12: 7–9

7.	There was war in the sky. Michael and his angels made war on the dragon. The dragon and his angels made war.
8.	They didn't prevail, neither was a place found for him any more in heaven.
9.	The great dragon was thrown down, the old serpent, he who is called the Devil and Satan, the deceiver of the whole world. He was thrown down to the earth, and his angels were thrown down with him.

John saw this scene on 17 June AD 96. Michael, the archangel, was to be found in the constellation of Ophiuchus, the Snake Catcher, while Satan was represented by the constellation of Scorpius, the Scorpion – which was regarded by the ancient Jews to be a snake. Scorpius is situated directly below Ophiuchus and it seems as if the Snake Catcher is trampling upon the Scorpion. This scene is another

---

[165] Scholtz, *Revelation*, 129–37; Pretorius, *To Hell with the Devil*, 145–47.
[166] Scholtz, *Revelation*, 148 – 65.

perspective on the banishment of Satan from heaven, as described earlier. Although this passage says that he was thrown onto the earth, the implication is that he landed in the Abyss. The computerized reconstruction of the scene shows that Scorpius was hovering just above the horizon, as seen from Patmos, and that it disappeared behind the earth's horizon during the night.[167]

Satan is Bound
Rev 20: 1–3

> 1. I saw an angel coming down out of heaven, having the key of the abyss and a great chain in his hand.
> 2. He seized the dragon, the old serpent, which is the Devil and Satan, and bound him for one thousand years,
> 3. and cast him into the abyss, and shut it, and sealed it over him, that he should deceive the nations no more, until the thousand years were finished. After this, he must be freed for a short time.

The angel that John saw was Michael, whom he also mentioned in Rev 12: 7–9. The computerized reconstruction of the night sky during the begiining of September AD 96, shows Ophiuchus, the Serpent Catcher, with a serpent in his hands, which must have looked like the chain of the Abyss to John. At that time, Scorpius was to be seen just above the south-western horizon and during the rest of the night it disappeared into the earth, as seen from John's vantage point on Patmos. John must have interpreted that as a symbol of the Abyss, into which Satan was dropped after having been ousted from heaven.[168]

---

[167] Scholtz, *Revelation*, 184–93.
[168] Scholtz, *Revelation*, 266–72.

ANGELS AND DEMONS

John's book contains many allusions to angels and demons – God's messengers or Satan's spirit followers. In line with the primitive world view of his time he equates these beings with the stars and celestial constellations. They play an active role in his narrative, either as heavenly guides or as evil spirits and Satan's assistants.

Angels reside in heaven and perform the tasks given to them by God. A good example of an angel taking part in the heavenly drama, is to be found in Rev 5: 1–3:

The Book and the Lamb
Rev 5: 1–3

1.	I saw, in the right hand of him who sat on the throne, a book written within and on the back, sealed shut with seven seals.
2.	I saw a mighty angel proclaiming with a loud voice, "Who is worthy to open the book, and to break its seals?"
3.	No one in heaven, or on the earth, or under the earth, was able to open the book, or to look in it.

The angel described in this passage played the part of a commentator or announcer of important events.

Demons are often encountered. Perhaps the best description of demons can be found *in Rev 9: 1–11 –*

The Locust Plague

1.	The fifth angel sounded, and I saw a star from the sky fallen to the earth. The key to the pit of the abyss was given to him.
2.	He opened the pit of the abyss, and smoke went up out of the pit, like the smoke from a great furnace. The sun and the air were darkened because of the smoke from the pit.
3.	Then out of the smoke came forth locusts on the earth, and

> power was given to them, as the scorpions of the earth have power.
> 4. They were told that they should not hurt the grass of the earth, neither any green thing, neither any tree, but only those men who don't have God's seal on their foreheads.
> 5. They were given power not to kill them, but to torment them for five months. Their torment was like the torment of a scorpion, when it strikes a man.
> 6. In those days men will seek death, and will in no way find it. They will desire to die, and death will flee from them.
> 7. The shapes of the locusts were like horses prepared for war. On their heads were something like gold crowns, and their faces were like men's faces.
> 8. They had hair like women's hair, and their teeth were like those of lions.
> 9. They had breastplates, like breastplates of iron. The sound of their wings was like the sound of chariots, or of many horses rushing to war.
> 10. They have tails like those of scorpions, and stings. In their tails is their power to harm men for five months.
> 11. They have over them as king the angel of the abyss. His name in Hebrew is "Abaddon," but in Greek, he has the name "Apollyon."

John saw a star falling from the sky – most probably another huge lump of glowing lava from the volcano on the island of Nisyros in the southeast. Then the Abyss was opened by the key of an angel.

It is clear that John thought that the world consists of three stories or layers – just as other people in antiquity: heaven above, the disc of the earth in the middle, and the netherworld below.

John must have believed that the volcano he saw from afar must be the entrance to this Abyss, the abode of the dead, or Hades. From this volcano lots of smoke poured forth and obscured the sun during the day.

Then a plague of locusts appeared, seemingly out of the smoke from the abyss, but most likely from northern Afica. John found these insects so terrifying that he ascribed all sorts of characteristics to them that ordinary locusts do not possess: tails like scorpions, teeth like lions, human faces, golden crowns on their heads, hair like women's hair, and armoured breastplates. They reminded John of war horses and chariots. The sound of their flapping wings was horrifying. It is possible that John remembered the description of a disastrous invasion of locusts as described in Joel 1: 4 and 2: 25.

John wrote that the king of the locusts was called *Abaddon* (Greek: Ἀβαδδών). This is the Greek rendering of a Hebrew name (אֲבַדּוֹן – *Abaddon*), which is encountered in Job 26: 6; Job 28: 22; Prov 15: 11; and Ps 87: 12. It denotes the ruling angel of the underworld, the abode of the dead, and it means "destroyer". John translated this Hebrew word with *Apollyon*, with which he meant the angel of the bottomless pit. The Greek word also means "destroyer" or "killer". In other words: John was under the impression that the locusts came forth from the Abyss (the volcano) and that they were demons, evil spirits under the direction of Satan. The constellation that most likely represented Apollyon was Scorpius, the Scorpion, on the southern horizon. This constellation was later identified as the "dragon" or Satan (Rev 12: 3 & 9).

These demons had the task of tormenting humanity and to serve as a warning to pagans and unbelievers that they should repent and turn to God.[169]

---

[169] Scholtz, *Revelation*, 156–65.

John added the following in Rev 9: 20 –

> 20. The rest of mankind, who were not killed with these plagues, didn't repent of the works of their hands, that they wouldn't worship demons, and the idols of gold, and of silver, and of brass, and of stone, and of wood; which can neither see, nor hear, nor walk.

This means that John thought that the pagan deities and idols made of expensive and inexpensive materials were, in fact, demons.

THE HUMAN SOUL

John accepted the idea of Plato that man is composed of two separate substances: a material body and an immaterial soul. The souls of the matyrs survive physical death and are taken up into heaven. That is, for instance, apparent from the following passages:

Souls in Heaven
Rev 6: 9–11

> 9. When he [Christ] opened the fifth seal, I saw underneath the altar the souls of those who had been killed for the word of God, and for the testimony which they held.
> 10. They cried with a loud voice, saying, "How long, Master, the holy and true, do you not judge and avenge our blood on those who dwell on the earth?"
> 11. There was given to each one of them a white robe. It was said to them that they should rest yet for a little time, until their fellow servants and their brothers, who would also be killed even as they were, had been fulfilled.

These souls of the deceased martyrs in heaven were given white robes, to symbolize their innocence and that their sins were forgivenm, while they were waiting to be avenged. They were seen under the altar – a symbol of having been sacrificed. They got the promise that God would avenge their violent deaths but that they had to wait for their number to be completed at the arrival of Judgment Day before God would finally avenge them.[170]

The Souls of the Martyrs
Rev 20: 4 – 6

4.	I saw thrones, and they sat on them, and judgment was given to them. I saw the souls of those who had been beheaded for the testimony of Jesus, and for the word of God, and such as didn't worship the beast nor his image, and didn't receive the mark on their forehead and on their hand. They lived, and reigned with Christ one thousand years.
5.	The rest of the dead didn't live until the thousand years were finished. This is the first resurrection.
6.	Blessed and holy is he who has part in the first resurrection. Over these, the second death has no power, but they will be priests of God and of Christ, and will reign with him one thousand years.

The symbolic number of thousand years is a description of the long

period between Jesus' ascension into heaven and his return on Judgment Day. During this time, the souls of the dead martyrs were already in heaven as a result of the *first resurrection.*

This resurrection into heavenly glory is contrasted with the *second death*, the fate of all evil forces. It would be wrong to conclude that there is a second resurrection and a first death. These

---
[170] Scholtz, *Revelation*, 120–29.

concepts are neither mentioned, nor implied. The resurrection to glory is placed first in order of preference, while the eternal death in hell is placed on second place in orfder of desirability.

Part of a mosaic depicting a procession of 26 saints or martyrs, clothed in white and carrying crowns, in the basilica of San Apollinare Nuovo, Ravenna, Italy (6th century)

John thought that these fallen martyrs will assist Christ during Judgment Day and, therefore, they were already seated on thrones.[171]

That the faithful are promised heavenly bliss directly after having died, is also mentioned in *Rev 14: 13* –

> I heard the voice from heaven saying, Write, "Blessed are the dead who die in the Lord from now on." "Yes," says the Spirit, "that they may rest from their labours; for their works follow with them."

---

[171] Scholtz, *Revelation*, 273–76.

JUDGMENT DAY

We find promises in Revelation that Judgment Day would arrive when all godless and evil powers would be judged and condemned.

Judgment Day is described in Rev 14: 14–20 as a wheat harvest and a grape harvest where the pagans and godless people would be gathered for the wine press and the thressing floor – symbols of Judgment Day and perdition in hell. This scene, which can be dated to the end of July AD 96, contain the constellations of Hercules and Boötes next to each other in the middle of the sky. Hercules represented Jesus Christ, who directed the harvest. The angel who helped him, Boötes, the Ploughman, is traditionally depicted with a sickle in his hand.

The idea that Judgment Day could be compared with a harvest comes from Jer 51: 33 – "For thus says YHWH of hosts, the God of Israel: The daughter of Babylon is like a threshing floor at the time when it is trodden; yet a little while, and the time of harvest shall come for her."[172]

The Rider on the White Horse
Rev 19: 11–21

11.	I saw the heaven opened, and behold, a white horse, and he who sat on it is called Faithful and True. In righteousness he judges and makes war.
12.	His eyes are a flame of fire, and on his head are many crowns. He has names written and a name written which no one knows but he himself.
13.	He is clothed in a garment sprinkled with blood. His name is called "The Word of God."

---

[172] Scholtz, *Revelation*, 216–21.

14. The armies which are in heaven followed him on white horses, clothed in white, pure, fine linen.
15. Out of his mouth proceeds a sharp, two-edged sword, that with it he should strike the nations. He will rule them with a rod of iron. He treads the winepress of the fierceness of the wrath of God, the Almighty.
16. He has on his garment and on his thigh a name written, "KING OF KINGS, AND LORD OF LORDS."
17. I saw an angel standing in the sun. He cried with a loud voice, saying to all the birds that fly in the sky, "Come! Be gathered together to the great supper of God,
18. that you may eat the flesh of kings, the flesh of captains, the flesh of mighty men, and the flesh of horses and of those who sit on them, and the flesh of all men, both free and slave, and small and great."
19. I saw the beast, and the kings of the earth, and their armies, gathered together to make war against him who sat on the horse, and against his army.
20. The beast was taken, and with him the false prophet who worked the signs in his sight, with which he deceived those who had received the mark of the beast and those who worshipped his image. They two were thrown alive into the lake of fire that burns with sulphur.
21. The rest were killed with the sword of him who sat on the horse, the sword which came forth out of his mouth. All the birds were filled with their flesh.

We are told of a white horse whose rider had a sword. He was followed by an army on horseback and clothed in white. John often incorporated war horses (Rev 6: 1–11; 9: 17–19; 18:13), and swords into his visions (Rev 2: 16; 6: 8; 13: 10; 19: 15).

It is clear that this figure on the white horse represented Christ as a conqueror. He is, after all, called "the Word of God" (see John 1: 1–14) and his title, "KING OF KINGS, AND LORD OF LORDS", was also given to the Lamb (Christ) in Rev 17: 14. Moreover, he is characterised as a righteous judge (see Rev 20: 11–15). It was also stated that his garment was splattered with blood – either the blood that flowed when he was crucified, or the blood of his vanquished foes.

The white horse was evidently the constellation of Sagittarius, the Archer, which was clearly visible in the south-eastern sky towards the end of August AD 96. John perceived the arrow in his bow to be a sword protruding from his mouth. The crown on his head must be sought in the constellation of Corona Australis, the Southern Crown, directly next to Sagittarius. This constellation also symbolized Jesus Christ in Rev 6: 2 – the first horseman of the four horsemen sighted on that occasion.

The army with white clothing that followed the knight on the horse must be the heavenly angels, in other words: the starry clouds of the Milky Way, directly next to Sagittarius. We often read in the Old Testament that God or the angels assisted the Israelites in their battles against their enemies – for instance, with the fall of Jericho (Josh 6) or when Gideon and his band of 300 men overpowered the hordes of the Amalekites (Judg 7).

The "winepress of the fierceness of the wrath of God" that was treaded (Rev 19: 15) may be sought in the constellation of Scutum, the Shield, directly next to Sagittarius. A shield and an ancient winepress both have a round shape. The fact that John mentions a winepress may be due to the fact that the grape harvest on Patmos was still in progress during late summer, in August AD

96, and that he thought that it would be a fitting metaphor for God's judgment on a sinful world.

An ancient winepress found in Israel. The grapes were gathered in the pit with a diameter of 5m where they were crushed by the feet of the harvesters. The juice flowed into the hole in the bottom and from there through pipes into receptacles. John would have encountered a similar winepress on Patmos.

The angel standing on the sun that invited the birds in the sky to devour the flesh of God's enemies was the brightest object in the sky that night, the planet Venus on the western horizon. The last rays of the sun were still visible behind Venus.

The beast that tried to attack the knight on the white horse, namely the Antichrist in the form of Cetus, the Sea Monster, was only to be seen the next morning. His ally, the False Prophet in the guise of Capricornus, the Goat, was visible directly behind the knight. They were allied to the kings of the earth and prepared for war against the rider on the white horse.

The two beasts were thrown into the lake of fire that burns with sulphur, which happened when they disappeared behind the western horizon as dawn approached. There must, in addition, have been a sulphurous smell hanging around, blown over from the volcano in the south.

A similar fate for the sea monster is to be found in Isaiah: "In that day YHWH with his hard and great and strong sword will punish leviathan the swift serpent, and leviathan the crooked serpent; and he will kill the monster that is in the sea" (Isa 27: 1). Isaiah (24: 21–22) also proclaims: "It shall happen in that day, that YHWH will punish the host of the high ones on high, and the kings of the earth on the earth. They shall be gathered together, as prisoners are gathered in the pit, and shall be shut up in the prison; and after many days shall they be visited."

The same fate awaited the dragon later on (Rev 20: 10).

The birds that were filled with the flesh of the kings, merchants, and shipmasters – allies of the monsters – were evidently the constellations of Aquila, the Eagle, and Cygnus, the Swan, situated directly to the north of Sagittarius. There were enough constellations around to represent the victims of these birds, including Hercules, Orion, Auriga, Perseus and Gemini.

The threat posed by the monsters was removed, though, by the intervention of the knight on the white horse or Christ, and when dawn approached when the light of the sun – the pool of fire and sulphur – blotted the stars out.

This passage describes Judgment Day when God's enemies, including the Antichrist and the False Prophet, will be vanquished by the return of Jesus Christ, together with his army of angels. The final destination of God's enemies is the lake of fire and sulphur – in other words: eternal damnation in hell.

The idea of a double-edged sword emanating from Christ's mouth is also to be found in Rev 1: 16. That means that Christ's words are incisive, that nobody is able to contradict him and that one is obliged to heed his words.

John repeated the image of Christ ruling over his enemies with a rod of iron. This idea also occurs in Rev 2: 27 and 12: 5. In the last-mentioned text, Christ is the male child born from the woman who was attacked by the dragon, but who was taken up into heaven and was destined to rule all the nations with his rod of iron. The rod of iron conveys the message that nobody is able to withstand Christ's rule and judgment. The idea of an iron rod originally came from Ps 2: 9 – "You shall break them with a rod of iron. You shall dash them in pieces like a potter's vessel".

The image of the winepress, that occurs in Rev 14: 19–20, is repeated here. It serves to emphasize how thoroughly Christ's vengeance against his enemies will be – just as all the juice is completely pressed out of the grapes in a winepress, so he will vanquish his foes totally.[173]

Another description of Judgment Day is given in the next chapter as seen from a different perspective.

Judgment Day
Rev 20: 11–15

11.	I saw a great white throne, and him who sat on it, from whose face the earth and the heaven fled away. There was found no place for them.
12.	I saw the dead, the great and the small, standing before the throne. Books were opened. Another book was opened, which is the book of life. The dead were judged out of the

---

[173] Scholtz, *Revelation*, 260–66.

> things which were written in the books, according to their works.
> 13. The sea gave up the dead who were in it. Death and Hades gave up the dead who were in them. They were judged, each one according to his works.
> 14. Death and Hades were thrown into the lake of fire. This is the second death, the lake of fire.
> 15. If anyone was not found written in the book of life, he was cast into the lake of fire.

John looked north, just before the day was breaking in early September AD 96. He again located the throne of God at the north celestial pole. It has to be pointed out that he gave no detailed description of the celestial Judge and he merely remarked in Rev 20: 11: "I saw a great white throne, and him who sat on it, from whose face the earth and the heaven fled away." John experienced the sight of the Judge to be overpowering in its majesty while the rest of creation disappeared.

One may wonder how John's description of this scene may have been influenced by his personal circumstances. It is very likely that he was dragged before a powerful judge or magistrate in Ephesus who sentenced him to be banished to Patmos for refusing to worship Emperor Domitian as a divine being. That could not have been a pleasant experience and that must have colored his description of Judgment Day with an all-powerful heavenly Judge on a white throne, before whom the heaven and the earth fled in horror.

Where he was standing, he could see parts of the Aegean Sea. All the people who had lived on earth and had died, including those who had drowned in the sea, were assembled before God's throne. This multitude must have been found in the Milky Way, spanning the whole sky from the northwest to the southeast. The bright starlight must have been reflected upon the tranquil waters of the sea in one of the many bays on the irregular coastline of Patmos and, therefore, John could state that the sea had also surrendered all the people who had drowned in its waters.

The books containing the criminal records of all sinners were opened. These books were possibly to be found in the stars of Ursa Major, the Great Bear, to the right of the northern celestial pole where the throne of Christ was situated.

Mosaic of Christ in his glory as heavenly judge, holding the book of life (Rev 3: 5), in the Hagia Sophia Cathedral in Istanbul (Constantinople) from the 13th century.

The book of life was opened – probably the constellation of Ursa Minor, the Small Bear, next to the throne. All those whose names were not written in this book were thrown into the lake of fire – the sun behind the eastern horizon whose first rays were becoming visible as dawn approached.

Death and Hades were thrown in the lake of fire and sulphur. In other words: death was abolished and Hades was emptied of its inhabitants and occupants. Paul had the same idea: "The last enemy that will be abolished is death" (1 Cor 15: 26).

In Rev 6: 8 John mentioned "a pale horse. He who sat on him, his name was Death. Hades followed with him." This pale horse was identified as the constellation of Equuleus, the foal of Pegasus. During the early morning of 9 September AD 96, Equuleus was situated on the western horizon, ready to disappear from sight – together with Pegasus, the Winged Horse. From John's perspective, Death and Hades were to be annihilated by the rays of the rising sun in the east.

It is possible that the volcano in the south had died down by this time and that John could also declare that Hades, the Abyss, was no more.

This description of Judgment Day reminds one of the descriptions of the event found in Matt 25: 31–46 and 1 Thess 4: 13–17. These parts of Scripture teach that all people will have to appear before the divine throne where a review of each one's life will take place. Those who belong to Jesus Christ – those whose names are recorded in the book of life – will be granted life everlasting, while those who continued with their sinful and shameful lives will receive their due, which is eternal damnation in hell. The exalted Christ was the one who said in the opening scene: "I have the keys of Death and of Hades" (Rev 1: 18).

The book of life was first mentioned in Rev 3: 5 – "He who overcomes will be arrayed like this in white garments, and I will in no way blot his name out of the book of life." We are assured that "only those who are written in the Lamb's book of life" will be permitted to reside in the New Jerusalem (Rev 21: 27). This book or scroll existed "from the foundation of the earth" (Rev 13: 8 and 17: 8). That means that God knew already when He created the world who the people would be who would belong to Him.[174]

ETERNAL LIFE

In the last two chapters of his book (ch 21 and 22), John describes eternal life in a new heavcen and a new earth. It is necessary to

---

[174] Scholtz, *Revelation*, 281–86.

quote at length from this part of Revelation because it is the most detailed description of heaven in the Bible:

A New Heaven and a New Earth
Rev 21: 1–27

1.	I saw a new heaven and a new earth: for the first heaven and the first earth have passed away, and the sea is no more.
2.	I saw the holy city, New Jerusalem, coming down out of heaven from God, made ready as a bride adorned for her husband.
3.	I heard a loud voice out of heaven saying, "Behold, God's tent is with men, and he will dwell with them, and they will be his people, and God himself will be with them as their God.
4.	He will wipe away every tear from their eyes. Death will be no more; neither will there be mourning, nor crying, nor pain, any more. The first things have passed away.
5.	He who sits on the throne said, "Behold, I make all things new." He said, "Write, for these words are faithful and true."
6.	He said to me, "It is done! I am the Alpha and the Omega, the Beginning and the End. I will give freely to him who is thirsty from the spring of the water of life.
7.	He who overcomes, I will give him these things. I will be his God, and he will be my son.
8.	But for the cowardly, unbelieving, sinners, abominable, murderers, sexually immoral, sorcerers, idolaters, and all liars, their part is in the lake that burns with fire and sulfur, which is the second death."
9.	One of the seven angels who had the seven bowls, who were laden with the seven last plagues came, and he spoke with

me, saying, "Come here. I will show you the wife, the Lamb's bride."

10. He carried me away in the Spirit to a great and high mountain, and showed me the holy city, Jerusalem, coming down out of heaven from God,

11. having the glory of God. Her light was like a most precious stone, as if it was a jasper stone, clear as crystal;

12. having a great and high wall; having twelve gates, and at the gates twelve angels; and names written on them, which are the names of the twelve tribes of the children of Israel.

13. On the east were three gates; and on the north three gates; and on the south three gates; and on the west three gates.

14. The wall of the city had twelve foundations, and on them twelve names of the twelve Apostles of the Lamb.

15. He who spoke with me had for a measure a golden reed to measure the city, its gates, and its walls.

16. The city lies foursquare, and its length is as great as its breadth. He measured the city with the reed, twelve thousand stadia. Its length, breadth, and height are equal.

17. He measured its wall, one hundred forty-four cubits, by the measure of a man, that is, of an angel.

18. The construction of its wall was jasper. The city was pure gold, like pure glass.

19. The foundations of the city's wall were adorned with all kinds of precious stones. The first foundation was jasper; the second, sapphire; the third, chalcedony; the fourth, emerald;

20. the fifth, sardonyx; the sixth, sardius; the seventh, chrysolite; the eighth, beryl; the ninth, topaz; the tenth, chrysoprasus; the eleventh, jacinth; and the twelfth, amethyst.

> 21. The twelve gates were twelve pearls. Each one of the gates was made of one pearl. The street of the city was pure gold, like transparent glass.
> 22. I saw no temple in it, for the Lord God, the Almighty, and the Lamb, are its temple.
> 23. The city has no need for the sun, neither of the moon, to shine, for the very glory of God illuminated it, and its lamp is the Lamb.
> 24. The nations will walk in its light. The kings of the earth bring their glory into it.
> 25. Its gates will in no way be shut by day (for there will be no night there),
> 26. and they will bring the glory and the honor of the nations into it.
> 27. There will in no way enter into it anything profane, or one who causes an abomination or a lie, but only those who are written in the Lamb's book of life.

When John mentioned that he was seeing a new heaven and a new earth and that the sea had disappeared, one may assume that he was no longer on Patmos. The scene had changed and he could no longer see the Aegean Sea. His exile as a religious and political undesirable must have been lifted and he was allowed to return to Ephesus. This must have happened after the assasination of Emperor Domitian on 18 September AD 96, after which political and religious exiles were pardoned by the Roman Senate.

The most likely date for John's vision of the New Jerusalem must have been 20 December if one applies all his details about what he saw in the heavens and coordinate that with a computerized reconstruction of the skies above Ephesus towards the end of AD 96.

The idea of a new heaven and new earth was taken by John from Isa 65: 17–18 –

> "For, behold, I create new heavens and a new earth; and the former things shall not be remembered, nor come into mind. But be you glad and rejoice forever in that which I create; for, behold, I create Jerusalem a rejoicing, and her people a joy."

The Book of Jubilees also says in 1: 28 that " the heavens and the earth shall be renewed."

John had this vision after having been taken by an angel to a "high mountain" and having been "in the Spirit".

Ephesus lies in a valley between steep hills and John most probably ascended one of these one dark night in December AD 96 and experienced an altered state of consciousness – in other words: a light trance or state of hypnosis – while admiring the starry skies and enjoying his new-found freedom. In comparison with the small island of Patmos with no real hills, the hills surrounding Ephesus must have looked like sizable mountains. From the top of one these hills, he would have had a good vantage point from which to observe the clear starry skies.

When John says that "the first things have passed away," he was thinking of the scenes of celestial warfare and the trials and tribulations that the faithful had to endure as described in the previous chapters of his book. He also had in mind the "old" Jerusalem that had been destroyed a few decades ago during the Jewish War with the Romans.

The promise that all tears would be wiped away and that mourning and pain would disappear in the New Jerusalem may be connected to the fact that John was back at home, that his suffering had ended and that he was free to proclaim the message of the gospel of Jesus Christ once again. If John sometimes felt depressed while on Patmos, that was something of the past and he rather felt the joy of being free and looking forward to heavenly bliss.

Six categories of people would be condemned to the *second death*, the lake of fire and sulphur, namely chicken-headed cowards, soulless sinners, miserable murderers, shameless sexually immorals, stupid sorcerers, insolent idolaters, and all lousy liars (Rev 21: 8). It is no coincidence that he mentioned six categories since six is the symbolic number of sinful man. Man was, after all, created on the sixth day of creation.

In chapter 19: 7–8, the bride of the Lamb was briefly mentioned. Chapter 21 provides a detailed description of this bride, the heavenly Jerusalem, also called the "beloved city". John must have had his vision on a moonless night since he wrote that the New Jerusalem didn't need a sun or a moon.

This city had twelve gates, each of them made from a shiny pearl and guarded by an angel. The fact that John equated angels with stars must lead one to the conclusion that each of these gates with its accompanying angel must have been a prominent star. On each of these gates the name of one of the twelve tribes of Israel was written. There were three gates in each wind direction.

John took this idea from Ezekiel who also had a vision of (the New) Jerusalem (Ezek 40–48). After having described the temple complex, the city itself is also described and in Ezek 48: 32–35, the very last few verses of his book, the gates of the city are mentioned:

> "And the gates of the city shall be after the names of the tribes of Israel, three gates northward: the gate of Reuben, one; the gate of Judah, one; the gate of Levi, one. At the east side four thousand and five hundred [reeds], and three gates: even the gate of Joseph, one; the gate of Benjamin, one; the

gate of Dan, one. At the south side four thousand and five hundred [reeds] by measure, and three gates: the gate of Simeon, one; the gate of Issachar, one; the gate of Zebulun, one. At the west side four thousand and five hundred [reeds], with their three gates: the gate of Gad, one; the gate of Asher, one; the gate of Naphtali, one. It shall be eighteen thousand [reeds] round about: and the name of the city from that day shall be, YHWH is there."

John's description of the New Jerusalem also reminds one of the camps of the wandering Israelites during the exodus on their way to the Promised Land. The twelve tribes were required to camp in a large square with three tribes occupying each of the four points of the compass. The tribe of Levi with the Tabernacle was to be protected in the center (Num 2).

There were also twelve foundation stones, each with a name of an apostle of the Lamb on it and made from a shiny jewel. The main street of the city was made of pure gold. John found the sight so breath-taking that he concluded that the heavenly city must be immensely huge. According to him, the four walls, enclosing the city, were each twelve thousand stadia or Roman miles long.

It is noteworthy that the names of the precious stones mentioned in Rev 21: 19–20 correspond to a great degree with the twelve gems on the breastplate of the high priest as described in Ex 28: 15–21 – with each of the stones representing one of the twelve tribes of Israel. Eight of the jewels mentioned by Exodus appear also in John's list. Uncertainty about the translation of ancient names for the stones may account for the four differences and they may perhaps, after all, be the same stones. John scrambled the order of the jewels as mentioned in Exodus but that may be attributed to the fact that he named them from memory without consulting the original list.

The twelve gates, with their guardian angels, together with the twelve foundation stones, are to be found in the constellations of Orion (the Hunter or Nimrod, as the Jews called this constellation), Cetus (the Sea Monster), Aquila (the Eagle), and the tail of Ursa Major (the Large Bear). In each of these constellations, which occupied one of the four wind directions, there are three prominent stars in a row.

Because night was abolished there was no need ever to close these gates.

This configuration of the constellations is only visible from the latitude where John found himself during December AD 96. Any observer further north or south or during another century would not have been able to see the New Jerusalem as John described it.

The water from the spring of life, which was to be given to those who are thirsty, is to be found in the constellation of Aquarius (the Water Carrier) in the south-western sky at that time. The Jews knew this constellation as "the bucket" from which water poured since they often eliminated the figure of the Water Carrier, in their view a pagan deity. At that stage, the planet Venus as the evening star and brightest object in the sky was inside Aquarius, which would have emphasized the importance of the spring of life.

John must have had Ps 36: 8–9 in mind with this description:

> "They shall be abundantly satisfied with the abundance of your [*i e* God's] house. You will make them drink of the river of your pleasures. For with you is the spring of life."

John mentioned that "the city has no need for the sun, neither of the moon, to shine, for the very glory of God illuminated it, and its lamp is the Lamb" (Rev 21: 23). Venus, as "bringer of light" and with a magnitude of -4.43 at that stage, was by far the brightest object in the sky and John could not have missed it. As an additional symbol for Christ, as in 2 Pet 1: 19, it would have been the heavenly "lamp" for him.

The Milky Way, which stretched from east to west across the middle of the sky, was the main street of the city, as well as the river that irrigated the orchard. Due to its brightness, the Milky Way suggested to John that the main street in the heavenly Jerusalem would be paved with gold.

When examining the reconstructed New Jerusalem, it is apparent that the constellation connected to both Satan and Hades, namely Scorpius (the Scorpion), was below the horizon at that stage. That gave John the conviction that death was to be abolished and that all evil was to disappear.

Death was expected to be absent because the immortal souls of the redeemed would exclude such a possibility. In addition, John also thought that eternal death and Hades would disappear since it was unthinkable that any part of God's renewed creation, the New Jerusalem, the new heaven and earth, could contain a region where a sacriligious Satan, a detachment of dirty demons, and the souls of perverted pagans were being housed. Hell just had to disappear and be disbanded.

The Abyss and Hades, filled with evil devils and scandalous sinners would not fit into this perfectly restored creation and would, therefore, be erased, eradicated, and extuinguished. Hell would simply vanish with all its contents in a cloud of smoke. It will be consumed by its own flames and get burnt out – the *second death* or final end.

The Bible often gives the promise that the old sinful earth will be supplanted by something infinitely better, a creation restored to its original state of perfection before it was spoilt by the fall of man. It will be in the shape of the New Jerusalem. The old Jerusalem was destroyed 27 years before John wrote his prophetic book and

God promised that this ruined city will be exchanged for something that would be a more fitting abode for his children.

By declaring, "It is done!" (alternatively: "It happened!"), the Lamb affirmed that God's plans for a godless world had been fulfilled.

The wedding of the Lamb has already been briefly mentioned in Rev 19: 5. Here the bride is shown in all her glory, dressed for this momentous occasion. Believers may be assured that there will be a never-ending feast in heaven. Enoch 25: 6 promised: "And in their days shall no sorrow or plague or torment or calamity touch them."

John specifically described the new world as being without a sea. The reason for this is that the sea was seen in the Old Testament as continuously producing chaos. The sea was the dwelling of Rahab, a mythical and dangerous sea monster (Job 9: 13; Ps 87: 4). Likewise, Ps 89: 9–10 tells us: "You [God] rule the pride of the sea. When its waves rise up, you calm them. You have broken Rahab in pieces, like one of the slain."

In this New Jerusalem, God will reside with his people – He will no longer be hidden in a far-away heaven but will be in direct contact with mankind. John uses the simile of the tent or tabernacle that accompanied the Israelites through their wanderings in the desert in which God was seen to be housed in the tabernacle (Ex 25: 8 and Ex 26).

The New Jerusalem had gigantic proportions. It was a cube of which each side was 12 000 stadia or Roman miles long – the equivalent of more than 22 000 kilometers. Such a place could never exist on earth and, therefore, it had to be sought in the sky (Rev 21: 10). John gave these dimensions since the starry skies above Ephesus appeared immense to him. The number of 12 000 also has symbolic value. Twelve is the number that symbolizes the twelve patriarchs of Israel, as well as the twelve apostles of Jesus. The number 1 000 tells us that it is immeasurably large, but this number may also be represented as 10 X 10 X 10 or 10^3. This suggests the holy Trinity. The sides of the cube of this heavenly city pointed in three directions: length, width and height. That is another pointer to the divine Trinity – Father, Son, and Holy Spirit. In other words: The New Jerusalem is a very large place with space for all true believers from Israel and from the time after the ascension of Jesus Christ, but it is also the abode of the Triune God.

We are also told: "There will in no way enter into it anything profane, or one who causes an abomination or a lie, but only those who are written in the Lamb's book of life" (Rev 21: 27). In this regard, John may have kept the promise of Isa 52: 1 in mind – "Zion; put on your beautiful garments, Jerusalem, the holy city: for henceforth there shall no more come into you the uncircumcised and the unclean."

God and the Lamb were to be the sources of light for the city and, therefore, the sun and the moon were absent. God and Christ are often seen as sources of light in the Bible (Ex 3: 2; Ex 13: 21; 2 Sam 22: 9; 1 Kings 18: 1-38; Job 36: 30; Ps 4: 7; Ps 104: 2; Isa 2: 5; John 1: 4–9; John 8: 12; 1 John 1: 5). The idea that the glory of God was the source of Light and the Lamb was the lamp was taken from Isa 60: 19 –

> "The sun shall be no more your light by day; neither for brightness shall the moon give light to you: but YHWH will be to you an everlasting light, and your God your glory."

This light is often contrasted with darkness, the symbol of evil, sin, and godlessness. In other words: evil cannot exist where God is present because He is the source of light, of that which is right and that which is good.

Jupiter, the brightest planet at that time, rose the following morning as the Morning Star – symbolizing Christ.[175]

The River of Life
Rev 22: 1–5

1.	He showed me a river of water of life, clear as crystal, proceeding out of the throne of God and of the Lamb,
2.	in the midst of its street. On this side of the river and on that was the tree of life, bearing twelve kinds of fruits, yielding its fruit every month. The leaves of the tree were for the healing of the nations.
3.	There will be no curse any more. The throne of God and of the Lamb will be in it, and his servants will serve him.
4.	They will see his face, and his name will be on their foreheads.
5.	There will be no more night, and they need no lamp light, neither sunlight; for the Lord God will give them light. They will reign forever and ever.

John continued to describe his vision of the New Jerusalem where the throne of God and of the Lamb (Christ) lay at the north celestial pole. The main feature of this passage is the river of life – clearly the Milky Way, which stretched from east to west across the middle of the sky at that time. John reported that this river was flowing in the middle of the main street of this heavenly city.

It is not possible to identify the tree (or orchard) of life which lay on both sides of the river. Its fruit, though, may be found in the various bright stars in the sky, including the planets Venus and Mars.

It is also possible that John had the twelve signs of the zodiac

---

[175] Scholtz, *Revelation*, 287–98.

in mind when mentioning that the tree/orchard of life delivered a crop of fruit every month of the year. This orchard is an echo of the trees in the Garden of Eden (Gen 2: 8–9) and the river is a memory of the rivers that irrigated the Garden of Eden (Gen 2: 10–14).

The inhabitants of this celestial city will all have God's name on their foreheads to declare that they belong to Him.

Genesis 3 contains the report of the Garden of Eden that was lost after the first humans ate from the forbidden fruit. John assured us, though, that this garden will be restored. It will be a orchard with the most wonderful fruit; there will be twelve crops per year. The original Garden of Eden was irrigated by four rivers (Gen 2: 10–14); the restored Garden of Eden would be watered by the "river of water of life, clear as crystal, proceeding out of the throne of God and of the Lamb" (Rev 22: 1).

This is an indication of the wonderful abundance and happiness that the faithful would experience when they are admitted to the heavenly Jerusalem with its water of life and its abundance of fresh fruit.

An important thought of John is that the inhabitants of the New Jerusalem will be able to see the face of God. While John was writing, God was still invisible behind the vault of heaven, but that would change. God's children in heaven will be in direct contact with Him and his Name will be written on their foreheads as a sign that they are his property.[176] Something similar was to be found in the Persian religion where the happy souls in the highest of the fourth sections of House of Song were in direct contact with God, called Ahura-Mazda.

To summarize: John was convinced of an afterlife in heaven for the faithful, but that Satam, demons, and pagans would be wiped out at Judgment Day and that Hades or hell would be demolished.

---

[176] Scholtz, *Revelation*, 298–301.

Chapter 12
THE QUR'AN

MUHAMMAD

Muhammad and some Christians

The founder of the religion of Islam, the prophet Muhammad (AD 570–632), left an indelible mark on the world's history because his followers, the Muslims, form the second largest religious group in the world, second only to Christianity.

Muhammad lost his father before he was born and his mother died when he was six years old. Family members then took care of the orphan. He could trace his ancestry back to Ishmael, the son of Abraham. He married a wealthy woman, 15 years his senior, and she bore him two sons (who died young) and four daughters.

He was a religious man who initially adhered to the traditional pagan religion of the Arabs. He often retreated to the desert for prayer and meditation. When he was 40 he had his first vision when the Archangel Gabriel appeared to him and commanded him to "recite". Muhammad was reluctant to recite anything, but then the first verses of the Qur'an started to flow from his lips.

A bewildered Muhammad told his wife about this experience and she called upon a cousin, a Christian, to guide her husband through this spiritual event. He regarded this episode as his calling to become Gods messenger. For the next 23 years Muhammad received many more revelations and visions when the archangel appeared to him or when God spoke directly to him.

He recited the revelations to his family and friends who learnt them by heart because none of them could read or write. These revelations were later written down and became the Qur'an.

Muhammad often had contact with Jews and Christians during his travels as a merchant, whom he described as the "People of the Book" (the Bible). There were Jewish and Christian communities in Arabia and Syria from whom Muhammad heard stories from the Bible, which convinced him that there is only one God, called Allah in Arabian.

After the death of his first wife, he married other women, including a slave girl Mary, a Christian. There is evidence that he visited the monastery of Saint Catherine in the Sinai Peninsula and guaranteed its security and safety.[177] It is reasonable to suppose that he also heard some Bible stories from the monks in this monastery.

Epilepsy

These are some researchers who assert that Muhammad's visions and revelations were the result of temporal lobe epilepsy. Whether this was really the case cannot be determined with any degree of certainty today. However, he does seem to have displayed the typical symptoms of the so-called Geschwind Syndrome, a variety of a temporal lobe epilepsy, including hyper-religiosity, hallucinations or visions, a quick temper, and verbosity.[178] The Apostle Paul also seemed to have suffered from this condition.[179]

THE QUR'AN

Origin

The revelations of Muhammad were collected after his death into a single document, called the Qur'an. It is the holy book of Islam and

---

[177] Anon., " Mohammed and the Holy Monastery of Sinai".
[178] Aziz, "Did Prophet Mohammad (PBUH) have epilepsy?"; Freemon, "A Differential Diagnosis of the Inspirational Spells of Muhammad"; Veronelli et al., "Geschwind Syndrome".
[179] Pretorius, *Jesus of Nazareth,* 132–37.

it is regarded as the Word of God, dictated by the Archangel Gabriel or God himself to Muhammed and, therefore, perfect and without any flaw or mistake.

The Qur'an only got its final form several decades after the death of Muhammad. There were several versions, which were suppressed in favor of the final one we have today. It is much shorter than the New Testament and contains 114 Chapters or surahs of unequal length. They are arranged haphazardly with no rational order or sequence.[180]

Stories from the Bible

It is only possible to understand the Qur'an adequately with a knowledge of the Bible since this sacred text repeatedly mentions characters from the Bible and their deeds and words. One encounters, for instance, Adam, Abraham, Jacob, Moses, Aaron, David, Solomon, Mary, and especially Jesus. It is clear that Muhammad did not always remember the stories from the Bible told to him correctly and he made mistakes in this regard. For instance, he mistook Jesus' mother Mary for Aaron and Moses' sister, Miriam (Surah 3: 35–36; 19: 28).

HEAVEN

The Qur'an describes heaven as a physical place above the clouds and that is where God's throne is situated (Surah 2: 210 and 255; 8: 8; 11: 12). God's throne is also described as a couch on earth with the clouds as a canopy (Surah 2: 22). It is, in addition, situated over the waters (Surah 11: 7) – presumably the source of rain water in the sky. Angels are hovering around the throne (Surah 39: 75), while

---

[180] Jones. *The Koran;* Schimmel. "Islam".

they also carry the throne (Surah 69: 17). The heavens are kept in place by invisible pillars, planted on earth (Surah 13: 2).

God also created seven heavens or firmaments above the earth, which are layered one above the other (Surah 2: 29; 17: 44; 23: 86; 65: 12; 67: 3; 71: 16–17). It is possible that these seven heavens can be equated with the orbits of the seven planets, although the Qur'an nowhere mentions any planets, except for the sun and the moon. These seven heavens are, however, also characterized as "seven pathways" (Surah 23: 17), which may be interpreted as the orbits of the planets.

ETERNAL LIFE

After death, resurrected true believers will be transported by angels to heaven (Surah 6: 61), which is described as a beautiful garden that is irrigated by a river (Surah 3: 15, 31; 7: 42). This garden is "as wide as the heavens and the earth" (Surah 3: 133). Heaven has gates or doors, which will be opened on Judgment Day by the angels for the souls of the faithful to enter (Surah 7: 40).

HELL

Hell, the destination of the godless unbelievers and infidels after death, is somewhere below the earth and is also called the *Abyss* (Surah 4: 121–122; 7: 41; 8: 11; 101: 9). The resurrected unbelievers are transported thither by the angels of hell after they have died and after Judgement Day (Surah 8: 50; 10: 109; 37: 20).

Satan, who refused to bow before Adam (Surah 2: 34), was banished to hell, although he still exerts power over the earth by tempting people (Surah 2: 36, 268). Hell is descibed as a never-ending fire (Surah 2: 167; 3: 131; 8: 14) and it is clear that the Qur'an describes it in physical terms.

RESURRECTION OF THE DEAD

On Judgment Day, believers and sinners will all be resurrected: "And on the Day of Resurrection, they [the unbelievers] will be assigned to the most severe torment. God is not unaware of what you do" (Surah 2: 85; see also 2: 113 and 3: 55).

When the Qur'an mentions the word "soul" it is usually meant to denote the whole human being. On occasion, it also describes the condition of a person after death. In Surah 3: 161 we read for instance: "Whoever acts dishonestly will bring his dishonesty on the Day of Resurrection. Then every soul will be paid in full for what it has earned, and they will not be wronged."

The concept of "spirit" is used exclusively for God, who is often called the "Holy Spirit" (Surah 2: 87; 5: 110;16: 102).

COCLUSION

One must conclude that the Qur'an contains a much simplified and less sophisticated doctrine about the afterlife than the Christian Bible, which is understanbdable since the Qur'an is much shorter than the Bible. The afterlife is described in concrete and materiualistic terms and it seems to be merely a copy of an idealized and perfect earthly life, extended into eternity or infinity.

The Qur'an is furthermore silent about the condition of the souls of dead people before Judgment Day, which will arrive in the unknown future. These souls are due to appear before God on Judgment Day, but it is unclear what happens to them after death and before Judgment Day.

Chapter 13
SCIENTIFIC PERSPECTIVES

THE AGE OF SCIENCE

It was argued in Chapter 2 that we have entered the age of science and that sophisticated societies on earth, where a substantial number of people have received tertiary education, have left the ages of magic and religion behind them.

During this age of science, people are seeking rational explanations for all phenomena. They want to make sense of the world and find meaning in their lives and for that they employ the laws of logics and seek scientific explanations for everything. They even believe that there is a rational reason or cause for everything, although our knowledge about the universe is far from complete at this stage. Nevertheless, they trust science due to all the medical, agricultural, and technological marvels we take for granted in our time.

Perhaps the most visible sign that especially the developed parts of the world have entered the age of science is the decline in the numbers of people who belong to a Christian church. The position of America is typical. The proportion of Americans who consider themselves to be Christians has been declining steadily. Back in 1990, 86% of all Americans called themselves Christians. By 2008, that number has dropped to 76%. In a survey by the Pew Research Center during 2020, only 63% of adults in the United States still identified themselves as Christians.[181] It may be assumed that this downward trend will continue.

A survey done amongst members with e-mail addresses of

---

[181] Pew Research Center, "Measuring Religion".

the Royal Society, the most prestigious body of scientists in the English-speaking world, revealed that 78,8% of the members did not believe that a personal God exists.

The 517 members of the US National Academy of Sciences disclosed in a survey that only 7% of these scientists reported that they believed in a personal God. Of the rest, 72.2% were atheists and 20,8% called themselves agnostics.[182]

A meta-analysis done in 2002 found that there is a strong correlation between unbelief and IQ or educational level. That means that more intelligent people and better educated people tend not to believe in God.[183]

It is, therefore, necessary to investigate whether scientific investigations can tell us anything about heaven, hell, the process of dying, the human soul, and the possibility of an afterlife.

THE UNIVERSE

For people living in ancient civilizations, including the ancient Israelites, the early Christians, and the original Muslims, heaven as the dwelling of God and the angels was a part of their universe. It was seen as a region beyond the stars and the sky filled with clouds, winds, and birds. The abode of the dead, including hell, was thought to be somewhere in an abyss below the surface of the earth.

Nobody with some education in our time can accept this ancient cosmology anymore.

Sophisticated believers of our time explain heaven and hell in terms of a scientific paradigm. They argue that God cannot be part of his creation and that heaven cannot be part of the detectable universe, consisting of millions of galaxies, each one containing billions

---

[182] Stenger, *The New Atheism*, 75.
[183] Dawkins, *The God Delusion*, 102.

of stars and planets. For them, heaven must be in another dimension – transcending the dimensions of space and time with which we are familiar. This seems to a plausible explanation, although there is not the slightest scientific evidence for such a position.

Scientists are gathering information and knowledge about the universe all the time with their advanced telescopes and other instruments. Although other dimensions, apart from the spatial and temporal dimensions with which we are familiar exist in theory, there is at present no way for us to find them anywhere or to gather knowledge about them. We asre totally stuck in a three-dimensional space and in one temporal dimension.

Contemporary science has adopted the position that the universe exists of only four elements or ingredients:

- Matter and energy, including dark matter and dark energy;
- Space;
- Time; and
- Information embedded in all objects, processes, relationshipos, and events in the universe, which makes it possible to say something meaningful about all those objects, processes, relationships and events.[184]

Astronomers and physicist are convinced that the universe came into being between 13 and 14 billion years ago by means of a gigantic explosion, popularly known as the "Big Bang", during which all matter, time, and space were created. The whole process developed according to knowable natural laws, which are part of the information embedded in all objects, processes, and events.

We must, therefore, conclude that science can't tell us anything about heaven or hell. Of course, absense of evidence does not

---

[184] Pretorius, *Who, Where, and What is God?* 149–57.

necessarily amount to evidence of absense. However, until positive evidence about a heaven and hell in other dimensions are obtained, somehow or other, science is obliged to stay silent in this regard. Nothing meaningful or definite can be said at this stage.

Science can, though, tell us much about man. When scientists try to understand phenomena such as the mind, consciousness, attention, memory, intelligence, and thoughts, they investigate the central nervous systems in man and in animals. It is necessary to give an overview of the human brain to describe what type of knowledfge has been unearthed about mental abilities in man, in order to determine whether anything of importance has been found about a purported immortal soul or spirit in man.

Therefore, a simplified description of the human brain will be given, detailing the most important insights of the disciplines of neurology and neuropsychology.

THE HUMAN BRAIN

Neurons and Neurotransmitters
Composition of the brain and the nervous system
The person who wishes to understand human behavior and processes and phenomena such as consciousness, thought, self-identity, emotions, instincts, and relationships between people better, needs a basic knowledge of the human brain.[185] After all, the human brain

---

[185] The information about the brain in this chapter was taken from the following publications:
- Carter, *The Brain Book*.
- Holford and Burne, *Food is Better Medicine than Drugs*.
- Kolb and Wishaw, *Fundamentals of Human Neuropsychology*.
- Lezak *et al.*, *Neuropsychological Assessment*.
- Swaab, *Wij zijn ons Brein*.
- Zilmer *et al.*, *Principles of Neuropsychology*.

is the center or organ where all thoughts, ideas, plans, impulses, urges, and emotions are generated. The brain controls all actions, including communication – that is, sending and receiving messages or information of all sorts.

The human brain is the most complicated system that we know of in the universe, although it is small enough to fit into a human hand.

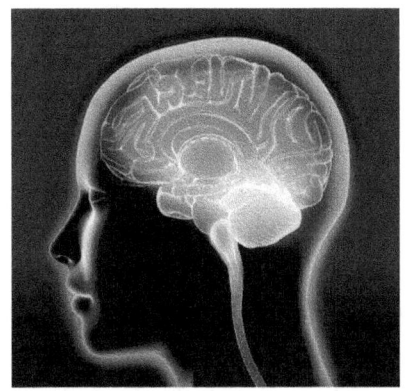
The human brain fits snugly within the skull and is protected by the skull

The brain contains ±85 billion neurons, apart from the glial cells, namely astrocytes and oligodendrocytes. All these make our human activities and processes possible: speech, emotions, thoughts, hearing, sight, smell, touch, the sense of balance, the registration of movement, the registration of temperature, the registration of pain, the contraction and relaxation of muscles, sleep *etcetera*. The brain is the most important part of the body's nervous system.

This system contains the following subsystems:

- *The central nervous system:* this consists of the brain and the spinal cord. Nerves that transmit impulses or messages from the brain to the rest of the body follow the spinal cord, along with the nerves that carry impulses and messages from the rest of the body to the brain.
- *The peripheral nervous system*: This system consists of 31 pairs of nerve branches from the spinal cord and 12 pairs of nerve branches in the head; these nerves transmit messages between

the spinal cord on the one hand and the organs, the skin and body members on the other hand.
- *The autonomous or para-sympathetic nervous system*: This system is the involuntary and unconscious part of the nervous system, controlling the automatic functions of the body, such as the heartbeat, breathing, digestion, excretion, the narrowing and widening of the eye pupils, *etcetera*.

Networks

Precisely how information is stored in the brain and how consciousness emerges from the brain is still largely unknown – and will probably remain that way since the *ego* or *mind* as the center of self-consciousness is not accessible for investigation. What *is* known, is that there are more than 100 trillion connections between the various neurons, with trillions of networks. Every time someone learns something, new connections and new networks are created.

Practice and repetition cause these networks to be strengthened, with the result that they will seldom, if ever, become undone if there were enough repetitions. It seems that memories are stored in the connections between brain cells, known as synapses. Every brain cell can establish dozens – even hundreds – of such connections. This means that there are many more synapses than brain cells. A memory is not stored in a single synapse – there are clear indications that a single memory is stored in various locations throughout the brain. It is estimated that each synapse can store more than 4 bits of information by means of chemical processes.[186]

What is clear, though, is that the storage of memories is partly a chemical process. Recent research has found that certain protein molecules in the synapses are involved in the depositing of memories, namely KIBRA (kidney and brain expressed adaptor

---

[186]Cooke, "The Brain can Store".

protein), which works in concert with another protein, called PKMzeta (protein kinase Mzeta), to target and then strengthen synapses. It's now clear that while PKMzeta is crucial to memory storage, there is no single "memory molecule."

It is the continual interaction between PKMzeta and the targeting molecule, KIBRA that is involved in memory. If KIBRA is blocked from PKMzeta, a fixed memory may be erased.[187]

Neurons can, to a certain degree, be compared with the transistors in computers and other electronic gadgets. They receive messages, process these messages, and in turn transmit these messages to other neurons. These messages, in the form of tiny electrical impulses, can travel only in one direction – away from the cell body and along a long branch, called the axon.

Since these messages tend to follow established networks, it happens that many routine activities and processes occur automatically and unconsciously – for instance, eating, walking, writing, driving a vehicle, brushing teeth, *etcetera*.

The result of psychotherapy or psychological counseling – of whatever modality – is usually that new networks are being established in the human brain and thereby altering or erasing bad habits, fears, spurious beliefs, or the effects of psychological trauma.

Since neurons are extremely small and a brain may contain ±85 billion of them, it is evident that every network must consist of millions of neurons that work together to produce a visual image, a sound, other sensations, an emotion, a thought, or an activity.

A neuron consists basically of a cell body with a nucleus and a long "branch", the axon. On the cell body there are, furthermore, dozens, or even hundreds, of smaller branches, known as dendrites. The message in the form of an electrical impulse is always carried

---

[187] Makin, "Brain Scientists Finally Discover the Glue that Makes Memories Stick".

in one direction, away from the cell body and along the axon to its end. There, it "jumps" over the synapse, the tiny gap between the neurons, to a dendrite of a next neuron and in this manner the message or impulse is carried further. The membrane of the axon consists of a stuff called myelin. The most important building blocks for this are omega-3 and -6 fatty acids. The brain consists mostly of fats and water.

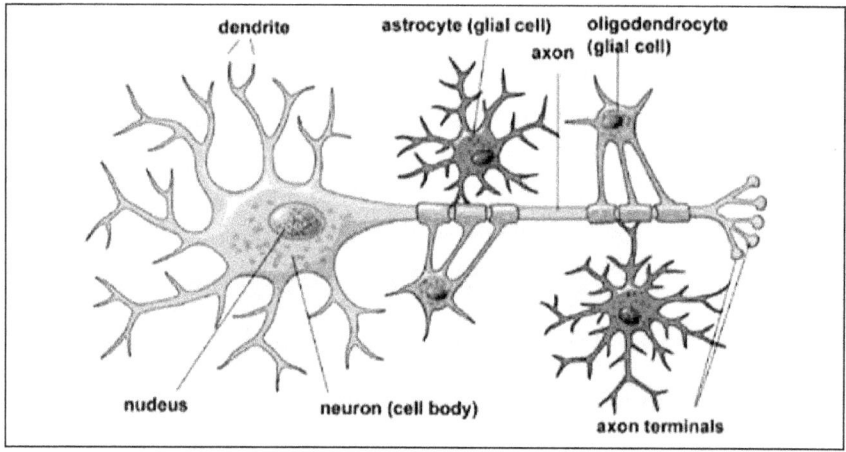

A neuron, supported by glial cells – astrocytes that connect the neuron to the blood supply and oligodendrocytes that provide the myelin sheath for the neuron's axon and keep the neuron in position.

There are other brain cells, apart from neurons. The function of astrocytes is to provide water, oxygen, and nutrients from the blood stream to the neuron. Oligodendrocytes provide structural support to the neurons.

Functions of Neurotransmitters

The transmission of impulses between neurons takes place by means of complicated chemical processes. Together with its other activities and processes, the brain is also a chemical factory in which certain transmitting chemicals – called neurotransmitters – are produced.

An inactive neuron has a negative electrical charge. The liquid on its outside, the cerebro-spinal fluid, has a positive charge. When a neuron is activated or "fires", an electrical impulse is generated. The negative charge inside the neuron and the positive charge outside neutralize each other for a brief moment and this creates a wave motion – also known as an action potential – that is always carried in one direction to the end of the axon.

The end point of the axon, the axon terminal, consists of a small bulge. Inside it, a few sacks (vesicles) contain the neurotransmitters. When the electrical impulse reaches the axon terminal, some of these vesicles are pushed through the cell membrane and the neurotransmitters are released. There are various types of transmitters, which are manufactured and secreted by different kinds of neurons in different parts of the brain or the body.

After the neurotransmitters are released, the electrical charge inside the neuron recovers and it is ready to transmit another impulse. This process happens very quickly and the speed with which an impulse travels inside the neuron is between 100 and 300 kilometers per second. Although it is very fast, it is still much slower than the speed of light, which is $\pm 300\,000$ kilometers per second.

The molecules of the neurotransmitters, which are released from the axon terminal, flow across the synapse, the tiny gap between the axon terminal and the dendrite of the next neuron. The molecules of the neurotransmitter attach to receptors on the dendrite of the next neuron. These receptors are spots or molecules on the dendrites that react chemically to the molecules of the neurotransmitter, and this creates a new electrical impulse in the next neuron.

Every type of receptor reacts to a certain type of neurotransmitter only – just as a lock can only be unlocked with the correct key. When the receptor sends a new electrical impulse along its way, the neurotransmitter molecule is again released from its binding spot. After that, one of two things can happen to that molecule: it may be neutralized by an enzyme in the fluid surrounding the neuron or it may be reabsorbed by the axon terminal for further use.

After the neurotransmitter has bound with the receptor or reacted chemically with it and a new impulse is sent along a fixed route, the impulse reaches its final destination – either a muscle, a gland, an organ, or a certain center in the brain. This then causes a movement, an involuntary reaction, a sensation, a feeling, or a thought. Muscles, glands, and other organs also contain receptors for the binding of neurotransmitters. As soon as such a receptor is activated by a neurotransmitter, a muscle contracts or relaxes, a gland secretes a hormone or an organ performs a function.

A neurotransmitter may have either an inhibitory or stimulatory/excitatory influence on the receptors of the receiving neuron. It may, therefore, either suppress or incite the generation of an action potential. The activity of the receiving neuron largely depends on its relationship with the inhibitive or stimulatory neurotransmitter.

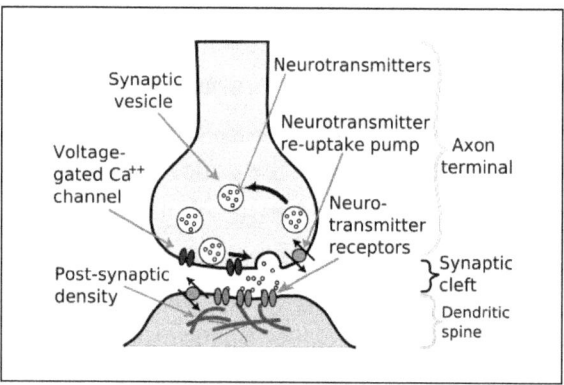

A synapse is a junction or connection that permits a neuron to pass an electrical or chemical signal to another cell (neural or otherwise).

It has already been mentioned that there are various types of neurotransmitters and neuroscientists suspect that there may be about a hundred types of which many have not yet been discovered. Every type performs a unique function. The most important types are discussed below, together with pathological states that may result on account of a deficiency or an over-production of these neurotransmitters:

Acetylcholine
This neurotransmitter has the following functions:

- It is responsible for the contraction of certain muscles, amongst which are the muscles of the digestive system.
- It is also present in the autonomous nervous system and in the sensory neurons – the neurons in sense organs.
- It plays an important role in memory and helps to cause dreams during rapid eye movement (REM) sleep.

The part of the brain where acetylcholine is most plentiful is mainly connected with memory. Damage to these parts – which blocks the action of acetylcholine – may lead to conditions such as Alzheimer's disease. This is a condition in which the patient's brain degenerates, the memory falls apart, and the personality disintegrates.

Norepinephrine (also known as noradrenalin)
Norepinephrine has the task of getting the nervous system into a state of readiness and is known as an excitatory neurotransmitter.

It is mainly present in the sympathetic nervous system and it causes blood pressure to rise and the heartbeat to accelerate. It is being secreted by the adrenal glands into the blood stream, together with the related adrenaline, which enables people to perform super-human feats in an emergency. It also plays a role in the formation of memories and in concentration.

Stress causes a depletion in adrenaline levels, while exercise stimulates the production thereof.

Drugs called amphetamines work by stimulating the secretion of norepinephrine and causing euphoria. Since the presence of the drugs and the increased production of norepinephrine overwhelm the receptors on the receiving neurons it leads to a decreased production of this neurotransmitter and this causes the abuser of these drugs to increase his doses to experience the same effect.

When the drugs are discontinued it takes a long time – often weeks – before the normal production of this neurotransmitter is resumed by the body. This causes the person to experience extremely unpleasant withdrawal symptoms due to the deficiency of norepinephrine.

Because the cessation of the drug causes such unpleasant effects, and because the person needs increasingly larger doses, it explains why dependency results. In order to feel and function as "normally" as possible, the abuser feels compelled to continue taking the drug.

Dopamine

A neurotransmitter that is related to norepinephrine is dopamine. This neurotransmitter blocks the receptors on the axons of neurons and inhibits them from firing. It is also connected with the reward mechanisms in the brain and is responsible for pleasant feelings.

Drugs such as nicotine, cocaine, opium, heroin, and alcohol initially increase the levels of dopamine artificially. Addiction to these drugs work on the same principle as with amphetamines, which replace norepinephrine and so cause dependency.

Certain varieties of the mental illness of schizophrenia may be attributed to an overabundance of dopamine in the brain. A dopamine deficiency is connected with Parkinson's disease.

GABA

Gamma aminobutyric acid (GABA) is an amino acid that also serves as a neurotransmitter. It also has an inhibitive action in that it limits the influence of excitatory neurotransmitters that may lead to anxiety attacks. People with a GABA deficiency often suffer from anxiety disorders. If GABA is absent in certain brain centers, epilepsy may result.

Glutamate

This is an excitatory neurotransmitter that is related to GABA. This neurotransmitter is the most plentiful neurotransmitter in the central nerve system ($\pm 50\%$) and it plays an important role in memory.

Too much glutamate is toxic for neurons. Several neurological disorders may be attributed to an excess of this neurotransmitter. Strokes often lead to an overproduction of glutamate and that may lead to the destruction of more brain cells than the stroke itself.

Serotonin

Serotonin plays an important role regarding emotions, moods, and perception. It is also involved in sleep, blood pressure, body temperature, and the secretion of hormones.

It is a substance that occurs throughout the body – especially in the digestive system – and only about 2% of the total amount in the body is present in the brain. It is produced from the amino acid L-tryptophane.

Serotonin deficiency often leads to depression, little control over outbursts of anger, obsessive-compulsive disorders, eating disorders, and even suicide. A deficiency may also cause the person to crave carbohydrates and to experience sleeping disorders.

Hallucinogenic drugs, such as LSD, bind with receptors for serotonin. Because serotonin plays a role in perception the use of these drugs may lead to hallucinations and euphoria. Because the presence of LSD inhibits the production of serotonin, dependency on LSD rapidly follows.

Endorphin
The name of this neurotransmitter is a contraction of "endogenous morphine".

- It is chemically related to pain killers such as morphine, opium, heroin *etcetera* and it is the body's own natural pain killer.
- It also is a neurotransmitter connected with feelings of pleasure, and it slows down the heartbeat, breathing, and digestion.

Drugs such as opium, morphine, or heroin also bind with the receptors for endorphin and that stops the production of endorphin by the body – just as these drugs also interfere with the production of dopamine. This leads to a dependency on these drugs.

Oxytocin
This neurotransmitter, produced by the hypothalamus in the brain and stored in the adrenal gland, also acts as a hormone. As a hormone, it leads to the contractions of the uterus during childbirth, as well as the production of mother's milk in the breasts.
   As a neurotransmitter, it has a profound influence on human emotions. It leads to sexual arousal, romantic attachment, and parent-infant bonding.

Poisoning
Many toxic substances influence the autonomous or central nervous system, causing paralysis, smothering, or pain. The reason is that some of these substances interfere with the effect of neurotransmitters – with the result that messages to and from the brain cannot be transmitted. Other substances imitate and strengthen the

workings of neurotransmitters – and that may cause abnormal reactions.

The Architecture of the Brain

When describing the architecture of the brain and explaining the functions of the different parts and elements, it must be kept in mind that this description is very superficial. Thick books have been written on this subject.

It must also be remembered that no two brains function in exactly the same way. For instance: a musician who plays the piano uses more of the brain parts connected to bodily movement for the operation of his fingers than a non-musician.

Another example: The parts of the brain connected to the left hand are bigger than the parts connected to the right hand in a musician who plays the violin or the guitar because he has to manipulate the strings of the instrument with the fingers of his left hand. The parts controlling the left hand are bigger than in people who don't play the violin or the guitar.

Neuroscientists call this phenomenon the plasticity of the brain. That is the ability of some parts of the brain to adapt to the person's behaviour and the demands of daily life.

The most noticeable feature of the brain is that it is divided into two halves or hemispheres. Each hemisphere is the seat of different abilities and functions.

It may be said in general that the left part of the brain performs the following functions: logical thinking, analysis, organisation, calculating, administration, recollection of facts, and focus on detail.

The right hemisphere is the part where intuitive abilities are situated, together with the expression of emotion, interpersonal skills, beliefs and moral attitudes, music appreciation, artistic expression, and concentrating on the bigger picture.

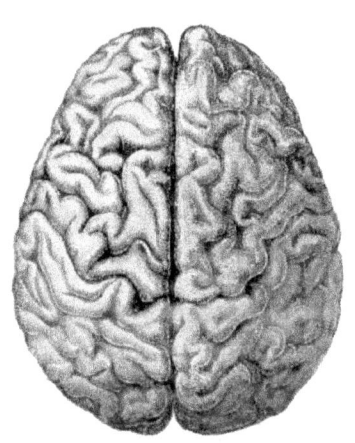

The right side of the body is controlled by the left hemisphere of the brain and vice versa. A noticeable feature is that the surface of the brain is wrinkled and folded. This results in more surface area for the outer layers of the brain, called the cortex. This Latin word means the "bark of a tree". The cell bodies of a large number of neurons are situated in the cortex and this is called the "grey matter".

The "white matter", more to the inside of the brain, consists mainly of the axons of the neurons, connecting the various parts of the cortex.

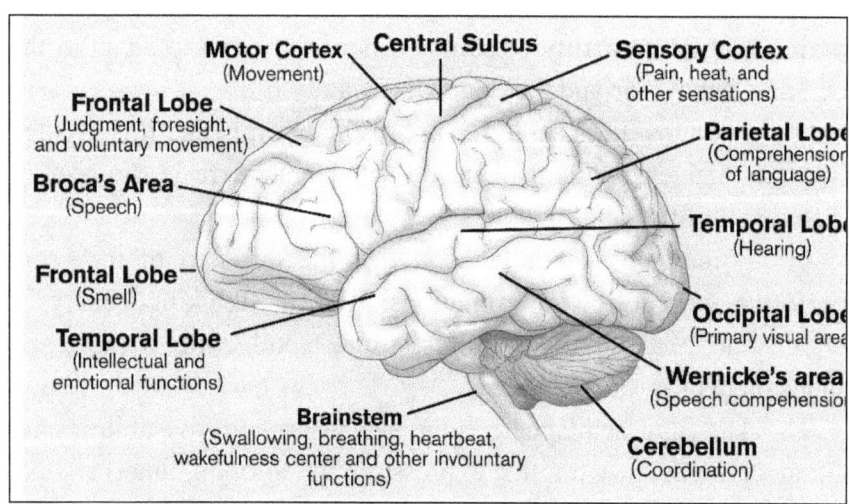

The different lobes of the cerebrum, together with the cerebellum and the brainstem, with a short description of the functions of each part

The grooves between the wrinckles are called sulci (singular: sulcus) and the ridges between them are called gyri (singular: gyrus).

The main part of the brain, the cerebrum, can be divided into certain lobes. In addition, there is the cerebellum on the bottom of the brain, as well as the pons and the brain stem, the "bridge" between the cerebrum and the spinal cord – as shown on the illustrations above and on the next page.

When the brain is viewed from the inside, it becomes clear that there are various structures hidden inside. The main set of structures, in the center of the brain, is called the limbic system[188], consisting mainly of the thalamus, hypothalamus, amygdala, and hippocampus. This is a more primitive part of the brain and is connected to emotions and instincts. The amygdala, for instance, is the alarm system of the brain and it deals with the fight or fright response of the individual whenever a danger or threat is looming.

By means of summary, the following functions can be connected to the different parts of the brain:

- Cerebrum, the top part of the brain and the biggest structure: sensory, motor and the higher mental functions.
- Cerebral cortex, the layer of grey matter on the outer surface of the cerebrum and folded into gyri: it contains $\pm 75\%$ of the cell bodies of the neurons.
- Frontal lobes on both sides of the brain: concentration, problem solving, planning, cognition, and movement.
- Parietal lobes, directly behind the frontal lobe: understanding speech, using grammar and organising words.

---

[188] The term "limbic" is derived from the Latin word, "limbus", which means "border or edge."

- Occipital lobes, on the back side of the brain: recognizing visual images from the eyes.
- Corpus callosum: connecting the hemispheres of the cerebrum.

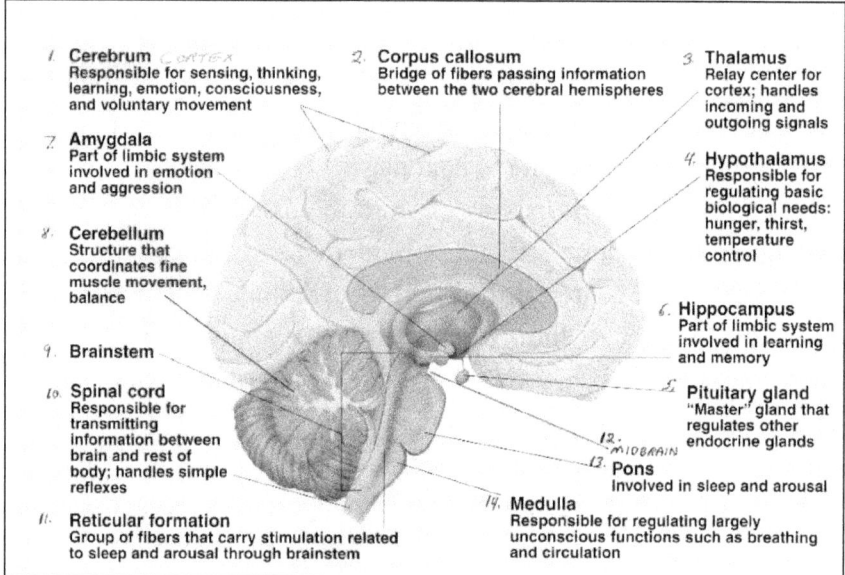

Structures and areas of the human brain, seen from the inside, together with a short description of the function of each structure

- Temporal lobes, on the bottom of the cerebrum, next to the temples on the skull: interpretation of sensory input, hearing, interpretation of speech, and long-term memory.
- Broca's area, deep into the frontal lobe: organisation of speech.
- Wernicke's area, usually on the left temporal lobe: processing of language and perception.
- Cerebellum, at the back and bottom of the cerebrum: coordinating movement, keeping balance, and reflexes.
- Spinal cord: the connection between the brain and the rest of the body.
- Pons, on top of the spinal cord: the connection or bridge between

the cerebrum and the cerebellum.
- Pituitary gland, situated under the brain: regulating the secretion of hormones.
- Limbic system, in the center of the brain: regulating emotions, such as anger, fear, elation, happiness, and sadness; also connected to the sex drive.
- Thalamus, part of the limbic system: the relay station between sensory input from the body and the frontal lobe.
- Hypothalamus, situated under the thalamus: regulating balance in temperature and fluid levels in the body; regulates endocrine hormones.
- Hippocampus, part of the limbic system: the short-term memory of the brain.
- Amygdala, part of the limbic system and situated next to the hippocampus: the alarm system of the brain, involved with aggression and fear.

Antidepressants, Stimulants and Medication for the Brain

The pharmacological industry has succeeded in developing many types of medication for use in conditions and disorders connected to brain dysfunction and the imbalance of neurotransmitters.

For instance, serotonin, noradrenalin, and dopamine are directly involved in the control of human emotions and moods. Usually, one or more of them cause a certain emotion or mood. A deficit of these substances can cause conditions such as depression, aggression, eating disorders, obsessive-compulsive disorders or other conditions.

A wide variety of antidepressants is available and they work on the principle that they –

- Stimulate the production of serotonin, dopamine, or noradrenalin; or

- Increase the sensitivity of the receptors on the receiving neuron's dendrites for these neurotransmitters; or
- Inhibit the neutralization of these neurotransmitters by certain enzymes in the brain fluid in order to increase the availability of the neurotransmitters artificially after they have delivered their message to the next neuron's dendrite.

Antidepressants, unfortunately, often have unpleasant side-effects by influencing other neurotransmitters, such as acetylcholine, negatively or by influencing the action of other hormones and enzymes in the body. Side-effects, such as nausea, head-aches, dizziness, high blood pressure, a decrease in the libido, digestive problems, weight gain, or sleeping disturbances, often occur. There are even known cases where antide-pressants have had the opposite effect and have driven people to suicide. Psychiatrists who prescribe antidepressants must often experiment with patients to find a type of antidepressant with the least side-effects for that particular patient.

Antidepressants work in only about 50% of the cases where they are administered. It has also been found that the use of antidepressants affects the cognitive abilities of even healthy people negatively.

The biggest problem with antidepressants is that they do not deal with the cause of the depression – they merely mask the symptoms and deaden the emotions – the negative emotions, but also the positive emotions.

A condition such as attention-deficit/hyperactivity disorder (ADHD) is sometimes kept under control by the use of stimulants such as Ritalin, Concerta, and Stratera. These medicines increase dopamine levels in the brain with the result that the patient can concentrate better, although they are also often accompanied by unpleasant side-effects.

Since certain types of schizophrenia are attributable to an excess of dopamine in the brain, these patients are treated with medication that blocks the production of dopamine. Patients with Parkinson's disease with a deficit of dopamine are often treated successfully with amino acids, including L-Dopa, from which the body can produce dopamine.

Patients with a GABA deficit may suffer from epilepsy or anxiety disorders. A drug such as Valium helps to increase the effects of GABA in the brain. GABA can also be administered in capsule form to decrease anxiety and panic attacks.

In many cases medical science is still in the dark about the reasons why certain medications help for certain conditions. Pharmaceutical companies – that make big profits from their patents – are engaged in continuous research to find new and more effective medications for various psychological disorders, to find out why these medications work and to avoid as many side-effects as possible.

Nutrition for the Brain
Because medication is often accompanied by unpleasant side-effects, and because it is unknown in certain cases why the medication does work, there has been a growing awareness of the fact that we can increase the availability of key neurotransmitters in the brain in other ways, namely by drastically increasing the patient's intake of certain nutrients. This approach is mainly due to the insights obtained by dieticians, although a number of medical practitioners and pharmacologists have also done pioneering work in this regard.

Pharmaceutical companies are not eager to support this approach because they cannot get patent rights on nutrients and there are, accordingly, no large profits to be made from the production and distribution of nutritional supplements. Large pharmacies, supermarket groups, and health stores have tapped into the growing market for these products, and one can find a variety of these preparations on their shelves.

The deficit or excess of certain neurotransmitters in people may sometimes be attributed to some or other genetic defect, with the result that they cannot metabolize the building blocks of these neurotransmitters from their daily diets.

Another factor that may also play a role is that the nutritional value of the food that we buy from supermarkets nowadays is less than in previous decades. Vegetables and fruit are cultivated on nutrient-depleted soil because crops are planted in the same fields year after year and their growth is artificially stimulated by chemical fertilizers. Many foods are sold in processed form and much of the nutritional value got lost during processing. The most well-known example is white bread, which consists mainly of empty carbohydrate calories.

It is recommended that every person take at least one multivitamin and mineral tablet every day to supplement or correct the deficiencies that occur in a typical diet.

Neurotransmitters are mostly manufactured in the body from certain amino acids (the building blocks of protein), while certain minerals and vitamins also play a role in the process. It helps to provide people with certain psychological disorders and addictions with ample quantities of nutrients in the form of supplements.

Serotonin, for instance, is manufactured in the body from the amino acid L-Tryptophane – or the variants 5-HTP/5-HT1. Because this amino acid occurs in many foodstuffs with protein it helps to drink a glass of warm milk at night to combat insomnia. The L-Tryptophane in the milk is converted into serotonin, and this has a calming effect. L-Tryptophane or 5-HTP/5-HT1, together with

Omega-3 fatty acids and sufficient minerals and vitamins, help in most cases of depression or other conditions that are connected to a serotonin deficiency.

GABA is an amino acid that doubles as an inhibitory neurotransmitter and it may be given directly to people with anxiety disorders, helping to alleviate the disorder in many cases.

It has been found that the supplementation of the necessary fatty acids, vitamins, and minerals can, to a significant extent, help to keep a condition such as ADHD in check. It has been found that regular doses of Omega-3 fatty acids, the building blocks of myelin – the stuff that forms the outer layer of neurons and which is involved in the firing of nerve impulses in the central nervous system – help patients with ADHD to concentrate better and pay better attention when spoken to.

A condition such as bipolar disorder is often treated with lithium, a chemical element, which may be regarded as a nutrient. Magnesium, another chemical element, has properties similar to lithium and may help with bipolar disorder, together with zinc, calcium, vitamin B-complex and vitamin C. The use of these substances will usually help the patient to need less medication.

Because addiction to drugs and alcohol lead to a decreased production of certain neurotransmitters, and because unpleasant withdrawal symptoms may result when the addictive substance is discontinued, it helps to provide the addicted person with mega doses of the necessary amino acids – together with the necessary quantities of fatty acids, minerals, and vitamins. These stimulate the production of the relevant neurotransmitters and help the patient to avoid many of the withdrawal symptoms.

Schizophrenia may also be kept under control by providing the necessary amino acids, minerals, and vitamins. There are different types of schizophrenia, and every type needs its own combination of nutritional supplements.

It is important that all patients refrain from ingesting diets with lots of sugar and carbohydrates. Several studies have shown that chronically elevated blood sugar levels due to a diet high in sugar and carbohydrates often leads to a worsening of the symptoms of ADHD, dyslexia, and dementia. High blood sugar levels are also often associated with aggression and criminal tendencies.

All the foregoing demonstrate that it is highly important for psychotherapists to monitor the diets of their patients. It is important to apply appropriate therapy in cases of emotional disorders, but the biological functioning of patients and their nutrition cannot be overlooked.

Implications for the Process of Communication
The architecture of the brain makes communication possible. The sender sends a message or information out – using speech, gestures, facial expressions, or by writing something. This message and its transmission take shape in various parts of the brain: the frontal lobes where rational thinking takes place, the temporal lobes where the long-term memory is stored, the speech areas of the brain where the thoughts or ideas are being transformed into words of some or other language, and the motor cortex where the muscles of the jaw and the mouth are activated to produce speech, where other muscles in the body are recruited for facial expressions or gestures or where the muscles in the arms and hands are used to write something.

The recipient of the message or information must use sense organs to receive the message or information – mainly the ears and eyes, although other sense organs may also be involved. The message must travel through various pathways through the auditory or visual cortexes, pass through the limbic system to pick up any emotional content and through the hippocampus – the short-term memory – to the frontal lobes to be decoded into understandable signals and eventually to the temporal lobes to be stored in the long-term memory.

A problem is often caused by the fact that the message traverses the limbic system before it reaches the frontal lobes and reaches full consciousness. That may result in almost instantaneous and instinctive reactions if it is perceived that the message contains an emotional flovor. The amygdala, the alarm system of the brain, may put in motion certain reactions, such as expressions of anger of fear – before the frontal lobes could have made a rational evaluation of the message. That often results in acts of aggression or the fight-or-flight reaction in order to ward off a perceived danger or threat.

It has been found that an over-active and enlarged amygdala may also interfere with communication. Children who have been exposed to traumatic experiences, such as cruelty, bullying, or prolonged sadness, may develop enlarged amygdalae. This gives them the tendency to avoid strange situations and new experiences due to a likelihood to react with fear or suspicion when confronted with such an experience or situation.

It may be difficult to communicate a message to people when it clashes with their previously-held convictions. They will, out of habit, reject any ideas that contradict their beliefs. They are usually not amenable to rational arguments to disprove their opinions.

People also have habitual ways of dealing with certain situations and they act in the same manner as in the past when confronted with certain events or messages – without thinking clearly about what the best reaction could or should have been.

This all means that a speaker or writer must formulate his message carefully to avoid misunderstandings or unwanted emotional reactions. He must deliver his message with enough conviction to make it credible and to help the recipient of the message to conclude that it will be safe and profitable to accept the content of the message.

When people experience strong emotions while receiving a message – joy, elation, relief, but also fear, sadness, or anger – that message is stored in more locations in the brain and is remembered better. That is why messages that are conveyed by means of beautiful and moving music may have a much greater impact than a simple spoken message.

Another aspect that plays a role in communication is empathy. Primates, including human beings and apes, have so-called mirror neurons in their brains. These neurons enable them to imitate the actions of others and to feel the same emotions displayed by others. This is the neurological basis for empathy – the ability to imagine and understand how another person might feel under certain circumstances. Empathy with its biological basis, therefore, makes virtues such as forgiveness/tolerance and compassion possible and helps the recipient of a message to understand the intentions of the sender so much better.

All the foregoing facts and arguments show that the brain is an extremely complex organ. Nevertheless, it works remarkably well, making daily life possible. It also enable gifted people to produce beautiful works of art, develop revolutionary scientific theories, or to perform super-human feats. Its compexity causes it also to be very vulnerable to a wide range of disorders and diseases.

At this stage, the following questions may be asked:

- Which neurological and psychological processes are involved in the experience of dying?
- What happens in the brain when somebody dies?
- Can the soul, the spirit, the ego, the self-consciousness, be located somewhere in the brain?

Answers to these questions will be provided in the pages that follow.

STAGES IN THE PROCESS OF DYING

It is generally accepted that cell death in the brain is a rapid and irreversible process when a person dies. Very soon after cutting off the supply of oxygen and blood to the brain, electrical activity and consciousness disappear, and after a few minutes the stored energy is used up and irreversible destruction occurs. Reasearches at the Yale School of Medicine in New Haven have succeeded, though, to keep certain parts of the brains of slaughtered pigs alive up to ten hours by providing these parts with the necessary nutrients and oxygen, with the object of studying these still-living parts in a laboratory. Although these parts stayed alive for some time, no sign of consciousness could be detected.[189]

Valuable psychological research has been done regarding the process of dying and the mourning process that follows after a loved one has passed on. Pioneering work was done by the late Elizabeth Kübler-Ross and her book On Death and Dying (1969) has been reprinted and translated many times. It will be instructive to give a summary of her model.

Kübler-Ross, a Swiss psychiatrist, studied many terminally-ill patients and found that there are the following stages in the processing of the news of impending death. These stages do not always follow in the same order and some stages may even be repeated:

Denial
The patient refuses to believe the verdict of death given by the medical practitioners. This news simply does not agree with his beliefs regarding himself.

Anger
After some time, the patient becomes angry – angry at the medical profession that hasn't found a cure for his condition, and anger directed towards God for allowing this tragedy to happen.

---

[189] Anon, "Researchers Restore Brain Functions after Death".

Depression
The patient becomes depressed, down-hearted, and mourns his approaching end. All emotional ties with others, all plans, and all expectations about the future must be abandoned and that causdes emotional pain.

Bargaining
The dying patient often makes wild promises towards God and other role players, including the medical personnel, in an effort to prolong life and ward off the inevitable end.

Acceptance
When all hope of recovery disappears, it becomes possible to accept that there is no hope and that death cannot be averted or avoided.

This model can also be applied to those left behind after the death of a loved one – or even during the process of accepting the news that no cure for the loved one's condition is available.[190]

NEUROPSYCHOLOGICAL VIEWS

The Soul, Mind, and Consciousness
The description of the human brain with its chemistry, electricity, functions, abilities, and architecture was necessary to demonstrate that neuroscientists haven't been able to find anything resembling an immortal soul within the brain – or anywhere else in the body, for that matter. Human actions and abilities, such as perfecption, thought, memory, movement, planning, innovation, and communication, can all be explained as functions or products of the all too material or physical brain – although the contents of perceptions, thoughts, memories, and communicated messages are, of course, invisible and not of a material nature. They form part of the realm

---

[190] Patrick Tyrrell *et al.*, "Kubler-Ross Stages of Dying".

of information, which is – by definition – immaterial.

Neuroscientists are unanimous in their conviction that the Platonic idea of a dualistic combination of a perishable and material human body and an indestructible and immortal soul or spirit lacks any scientific foundation. A few quotations to illustrate this:

- Carter: The idea that man is composed of a a body and a separate soul or mind "is now generally discounted."[191]
- Kolb and Wishaw: These authors reject the idea of a dualism between body and soul. "Thus, dualistrs who argue that mind and body interact causally cannot explain how." For contemporary neuroscientists, the human mind is not "a nonmaterial entity" but simply "a function of the brain."[192]
- Papineau and Selina: The theory of a dualistism where a soul or a mind inhabits a body has "the problem of explaining how two quite different substances can communicate causally. (…) This is the problem of seeing how a mind can affect matter without violating the principles of physics themselves."[193]
- Swaab: "All recent research shows that the combined activity of uncountable numbers of neurons in concert with a number of brain regions is the basis for consciousness."[194]
- Zilmer: "Researchers have found no single location for consciousness."[195]

All these quotations boil down to the following: All those who proclaim that functions such as (self-)consciousness, thought, memory, and perception belong to an immaterial spirit or soul and

---

[191] Carter *et al*, *The Brain Book*, 178.

[192] Kolb and Wishaw, *Fundamentals*, 7–8.

[193] Papineau and Selina, *Introducing Consciousness*, 64.

[194] Swaab, *Wij zijn ons Brein*, 209 (own translation from the Dutch).

[195] Zilmer *et al. Principles of Neurpsychoilogy*. 445.

that the brain inside the skull is only the conduit through which these thoughts, memories, consciousness, and perceptions flow, cannot explain how an immaterial spirit can connect with a material organ of the body, namely the brain. They cannot explain how an immaterial soul can store memories. All the available evidence demonstrates that memories are stored chemically in synapses in the brain.

All those who argue that consciousness is a function of the immaterial soul or spirit, cannot elucidate why and how consciousness disappears when people are sleeping, are drugged, slide into a coma, or suffer brain damage. Those who are convinced that a separate non-physical soul or spirit exists, apart from the physical body and brain, are unable to demonstrate how a person's mind, consciousness, emotions, intellectual functioning, or thoughts are affected by medication or nutrients, as has been explained above.

On the other hand, the phenomenon of a *conscious mind*, the ability or faculty of man of being aware of himself and of his environment, is a difficult subject for neuropsychologists. It is even difficult to provide an adequate definition for the concepts of *consciousness* or *mind*.

Young notes regarding the phenomenon of consciousness: "There are two major components, alertness and awareness, but they are strongly interconnected. Both alertness and awareness have multiple structural and functional components. Thus, the term consciousness, as it is commonly used clinically, is too broad and imprecise to be very useful."[196] This definition or description is, however, a tautology that doesn't say anything meaningful because it uses the words "alertness" and "awareness", which are merely synonyms for consciousness.

It is, however, more than abundantly clear that the mind or (self-)consciousness depends upon an intact and functioning brain.

---

[196] Young, "Consciousness".

Researchers have identified the brain structures mainly involved with the experience of (self-)consciousness – without being able to explain how these structures produce the mind or consciousness:

- The intact cortex (the outer layer of the cerebrum, containg the so-called grey matter) – especially those parts shown on the illustration below;
- An intact thalamus (the relay center of the brain between the cortex and other parts); and
- The intact connections between the cortex and the thalamus (the so-called white matter).

Young added:
> "Awareness requires the functional integrity of the ascending reticular activating system, thalamus, and cerebral cortex and is composed of a number of interconnected functions, including sensation, perception, attention, memory, self-awareness, motivation, executive frontal lobe functions, and associated cognitive operations. Awareness has multiple interdependent components and requires networking of numerous brain regions."[197]

It must be clear that consciousness or the mind depends on not one single brain structure, but on the interplay and coordination of several structures or subsystems.

It goes without saying that any damage to any of these parts due to a head injury, a stroke, toxic substances, epileptic seizures, cancerous tumors, or other lesions may impair consciousness in more than one way, even causing a long-lasting coma.[198]

---

[197] Young, "Awareness".
[198] Swaab, *Wij zijn ons Brein,* 187–89.

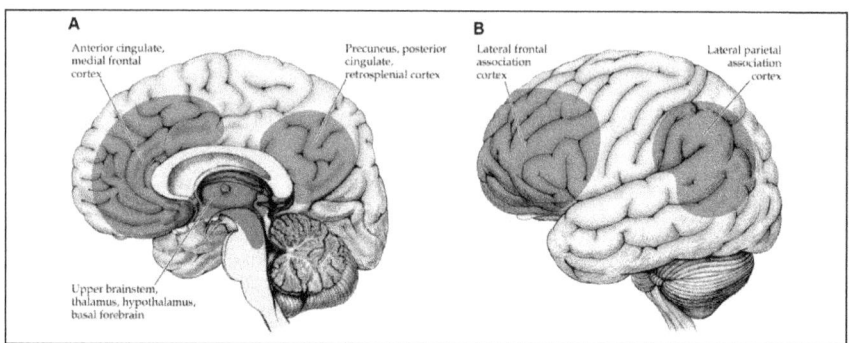

The Consciousness System: (A) Medial view and (B) lateral view of anatomical structures which regulate the level of consciousness.

The following neurotransmitters are also involved in alertness and awareness: choline, monoamines, and GABA.[199]

Mental Disorders

Neuroscience has established that mental disorders of all varieties – mood disorders, psychotic conditions, dementia, personality disorders, addictions, obsessions, compulsions, disorders of inattention, *etcetera*, are certainly not caused by devious demons or spiteful spirits, as described in the Bible. The Diagnostic and Statistical Manual of Mental Disorders, fifth edition (DSM-5), of the American Psychiatric Association (2013), as well as the International Classification of Diseases, tenth edition, of the World Health Organization (ICD-10), which are used world-wide, do not recognize spirit-infestation or demonic possession as a cause of any mental disorder. It must be stressed: according to the DSM-5, a neurological or neuropsychological basis for most or even all mental disorders have been discovered, although research is, of course, continuing.

The neurological mechanisms involved in mental disorders and diseases have been briefly touched upon in the part of this chapter dealing with the human brain.

---

[199] Goetz, "Alertness", 80.

NEAR-DEATH EXPERIENCES

Knowledge of the structure and functioning of the human brain enabled neuroscientists to explain phenomena such as a near-death experience (NDE) or a out-of-the-body experience (OBE).

People who have experienced an OBE or a NDE very often believe that they have had encounters with God, Jesus, deities, angels, deceased loved ones, and other supernatural entities. They often have the experience or impression of leaving their bodies behind, while their consciousness or soul travelled somewhere else. People who had these experiences usually regard them as spiritual experiences where they saw something of heaven or the afterlife briefly.[200]

The Apostle Paul reported that he was "caught up into the third heaven" during one of his visions. This third heaven must be explained as the dwelling of God, above the two lower strata of the heavens, filled with stars and clouds, according to the ancient cosmology (2 Cor 12: 2). It is likely that he experienced an OBE, perhaps the result of an epileptic fit.[201]

Neuroscientists are convinced that an OBE or NDE cannot be seen as proofs of an afterlife. There is absolutely no scientific evidence to support the idea that a person's mind or consciousness can get disengaged from the body and travel outside the body.

Experts explain these conditions as hallucinations, usually brought about by anoxia, the lack of oxygen to the brain for whatever reason, including cardiac arrest, serious injury, intense psychological trauma, drug overdoses, or epilepsy.[202]

---

[200] Cunningham, *Decoding the Language of God*, 210.
[201] Pretorius, *Jesus of Nazareth*, 127–37.
[202] Raypole, "What Really Happens Durig an Out-of-Body Experience?"; Sacks, *Hallucinations*, 260.

Although persons who have experienced an OBE or a NDE believe that they have reached heaven for a brief period, it must be concluded that such an experience is simply the resul of a (temporarily) malfunctioning brain.

REINCARNATION

Religions in Asia, as well as the ancient Greek philosophers Pythagoras and Plato, were or are supporters of the idea of reincarnation, the notion that a soul may survive death and be born into another body again.

There are reports of people who claim to remember such past lives, describing in detail what they purportedly experienced and did in their previous lives. Such anecdotes are seen as proof of the immortality of the soul and the transmigration of souls.[203]

There are psychologists who specialize in past life regression by means of hypnosis. According to them, some problems, such as anxiety, phobias, and trauma, may be the result of bad experiences in a previous life and that a process of hypnotherapy can rekindle those memories, enabling the patient to get a grip on his or her problems.[204]

Dr Ian Stevenson, a psychiatrist and founder of the Division of Perceptual Studies in the Faculty of Medicine at the University of Virginia, studied more or less 2 500 cases of suspected reincarnation, especially in children. According to him, he only tried to demonstrate the feasibility or possibility of reincarnation – not necessarily its reality. He encountered great skepticism and even opposition from the scientific community. He told his associates that he would place a locked combination lock in his locker and that he

---

[203] Division of Perceptual Studies, "Children who Report Memories".
[204] Healing Souls Hypnosis, "Past Life Regression".

would communicate the correct numbers to open the lock to them after his death, when he was possibly again reincarnated. Although he already died in 2007, the lock remained unopened in 2024.[205]

Hammond points out that careful research has demonstrated that past-life regression through hypnosis cannot be used as proof that people really had previous lives. So-called memories of past lives regularly prove to be forgotten memories of stories the persons heard or read somewhere and recalled during hypnosis, as if they experienced those events themselves.[206]

Roberta Temes quotes Dr Marvin Shabshin of the American Psychiatric Association (APA):

> "The APA believes that past-life regression is pure quakery. There is no accepted scientific evidence to support the existence of past lives, let alone the validity of past-life regression therapy."[207]

The APA Encyclopedia of Psychology states regarding past-life regression therapy:

> "Most hypnotherapists are skeptical of the practice and do not recognize it as a legitimate therapeutic tool."[208]

Nagaraj *et al.* concluded:

> "If reincarnation is to be examined from an unbiased scientific point of view, it is necessary first of all to find a way of bypassing such unscientific barriers as religious bias. Nei-

---

[205] Dowdey, "How Reincarnation Works".
[206] Hammond, *Handbook of Hypnotic Suggestions and Metaphors*, 512.
[207] Temes, *The Complete Idiot's Guide to Hypnosis*, 313.
[208] APA Encyclopedia of Psychology, "Past-life Regression".

ther there is strong objective evidence nor specific research methods that can discover the mystery of reincarnation."[209]

In other words: past-life regression therapy cannot be regarded as a valid therapeutic technique, which is not able to prove the reality of reincarnation. No other method has proved that souls can really be reincarnated, either.

All the available evidence demonstrates that memories are stored in the brain by meabs of chemical processes in the synapses. When the brain deteriorates due to dementia or when somebody suffers brain damage, memories – especially the short-term memory – disappear, never to be regained. There is just no possibility that an immaterial entity, such as a purportedly reincarnated soul, can retain and store memories of a past life.

THE MYSTERY OF CONSCIOUSNESS

Although neuroscientists have identified the structures in the human brain connected to consciousness, it is still a mystery how these structures can produce something like consciousness or the mind. A few quotations by neuroscientists may be necessary:

- Ratey informs us:

    "Despite the volumes that have been written on consciousness, we still don't know how to define it, or what brain activity gives rise to it."[210]

- Dr Michael Soso, a neurophysiologist of the University of Pitts-

---

[209] Nagaraj et al., *"The Mystery of Reincarnation"*.
[210] Ratey, *A User's Guide to the Brain*, 111.

burgh, writes about the mystery of consciousness:

> "Consciousness is a very hard problem. Not hard as in difficult, but hard as in impossible. No one really knows what it is, how it arises, or why it exists. (...) Consciousness is the mind's subjective experience of reality. It's what makes you feel pain when you stub your toe, joy when you see a rainbow, and boredom when you listen to me. It's also what makes you think, reflect, communicate, and create. Without consciousness, you would be a zombie, a robot, or a rock.
>
> "But how does the brain produce consciousness? How does a lump of flesh and blood generate something so immaterial and elusive? Well, that's the million-dollar question. Actually, scratch that. It's the billion-dollar question. Scientists and philosophers have been trying to answer it for centuries, and they still don't have a clue."[211]

- Kolb and Wishaw declare:

  > "Conscious experience is probably the most familiar mental process that we know, yet its workings remain mysterious. Everyone has a vague idea of what is meant by being conscious, but consciousness is easier to identify that to define." They, nevertheless, venture this definition: "[T]he level of responsiveness of the mind to impressions made by the senses ..."[212]

(This definition tells us nothing – it uses the concept "mind", which is simply a synonym for *consciousness*.)
- Russel reminds us:

---

[211] Soso, "Which parts of the brain are most responsible for consciousness?"
[212] Kolb and Wishaw, *Fundamentals,* 645.

"This is the paradox of consciousness. Its existence is undeniable, yet it remains totally inexplicable." The only definition he can provide is to call it "inner experience"[213] – which isn't very illuminating.

- Koch and Marcus note: "The final challenge, indubitably, will be how *subjective* feelings, how consciousness itself, emerges from the physical brain."[214]
- Horgan finds: "A theory of consciousness would represent the apogee – the culmination – of neuroscience."[215]

An effort will be made in the next chapter to offer an explanation of why consciousness, the mind, the ego, the "I" that is conscious of itself and of the world, will remain a mystery that cannot ever be solved.

---

[213] Russel, *From Science to God*, 27, 32.
[214] Koch and Marcus, "Neuroscience in 2054", 269.
[215] Horgan, *The End of Science*, 161.

Chapter 14
PHILOSOPHICAL PERSPECTIVES

SUMMARY OF VIEWS REGARDING THE AFTERLIFE

The previous chapters of this book provided some information about how ideas and views regarding the soul and the afterlife have been developing through the ages. Special attention was given to the Sacred Scriptures of Judaism, Christianity, and Islam, as well as the science of neuropsychology. At this point, it is necessary to provide a summary of all these points of view and to come to some conclusions regarding the current state of our knowledge about these matters.

Anumism

Animism is a primitive form of religion in which all aspects of reality are seen as animated by spirits – not only man, but also animals and inanimate objects. Contact with the spirits of ancestors are usually thought to be possible.

Mesopotamia

The souls of those who had passed on went to a netherworld where they could regain their old social status if their funerals were appropriate and those left behind mourned them long enough.

Egypt

The souls of important people, whose remains were mummified, were subjected to a test, the weighing of the heart. If it was found that they didn't have any serious criminal records, they were allowed to join the gods and their ancestors between the stars. If they failed the test or if their bodies were not mummified, their souls simply vanished into nothingness.

Persia
The soul had a pre-existence before birth. After death, this soul was examined by God and sent either to the House of Song, or the House of Lies. The enemy of God, Ahriman, will be destroyed at the end of time and the souls in the House of Lies will be saved or pardoned.

Greece
Initially, it was thought that the soul or spirit was merely the breath of a dead person. His ghost would descend to the netherworld. Later, the Greeks expected the souls of viruous and pious people to be rowed over the river Styx to the fields of Elysium, while evil and wicked people descended to Hades, the Abyss, where they were locked up.
    During the Hellenistic period, people could choose between various religions from the ancient world.

India
The religions of Hinduism and Buddhism believed in reincarnation, the rebirth of the soul of a dead person into another body. The cycle could be broken to reach nirvana, total rest and extinction.

Pre-Exilic Israel
The dead Israelites went to "Sheol", the abode of the dead, which may even be regarded as a general description of all graveyards or tombs where the dead were silent and unconscious, sleeping with their ancestors, and unable to have any relationships with God or the

living. They only lived on in the memories of their loved ones – not as individuals, each one with an identity and memories of life on earth. They were simply lifeless and liquidated.

Post-Exilic Israel

The post-exilic Judeans generally did not expect an afterlife – except for a veery few exceptions, which implied a survival after death as the Persians believed. The dead would simply turn to dust and ceased to exist when they died. The spirit or soul of man was seen as merely his breath, blood, or life force, which perished at death. God's heaven was thought to be above the stars, while the stars were regarded as angels. The netherworld, Sheol, contained the silent shadows or comatose and catatonic ghosts of the dead.

Apocryphal Literature

The books investigated in this category contain widely diverging ideas:

- Jesus Ben Sira thought that man just returned to dust after death.
- The Scond Book of Maccabees expected a resurrection with restored bodies.
- According to the Wisdom of Solomon, man is composed of an immortal soul and a mortal body. The soul is tested and tried by God after death and may be assigned either to heaven, or to hell (Hades).
- Enoch taught the dualism of body and soul as Plato did. The souls of the upright would be taken to heaven after death and Judgment Day, while the godless would be punished in hell, together with the fallen angels or demons who have been evicted from heaven.
- The Book of Jubilees did not foresee an afterlife where the faithful would be rewarded and the wicked be punished. This

reward or punishment would happen on a renewed earth. Satan and his demons are being kept in the Abyss in anticipation of Judgment Day.

Pythagoras
The school of Pythagoras believed in reincarnation or the transmigration of the souls of the dead. The world is ruled by numbers.

Plato
Plato subscribed to the popular idea that man is composed of two elements or substances – a mortal body and an immortal soul. The soul was thought to belong to the realm of eternal Ideas and that it would return thither after being liberated from the body at death. Reincarnation was a possibility.

Aristotle
The Greek philospher Aristotle rejected the dualism of body and soul. For him, the soul was merely the form of the body and both disintegrated at death, although the rational part of the human form or soul returned to the Realm of Reason, outside time and space, which realm may be seen as an impersonal God.

Stoics
The Stoic school consisted of deterministic materialists who didn't believe in an afterlife or an immortal soul.

Neo-Platonists
Philosophers and theologians who wrote in the Platonic tradition, retained Plato's dualism of body and soul. The body, part of the evil material world, was regarded as a prison from which the immortal soul had to be rescued at death. The soul returned to the realm of

spirits or to be united with an all-powerful deity.

Jesus of Nazareth
Jesus was convinced of the reality of heaven and hell as the destinations of saints and sinners after a future Judgment Day, although he also taught that man would reach his eternal destination directly after the moment of death. He was, however, not very clear about the state of the soul in the afterlife. At times he declared that one would arrive in heaven or hell with an intact body, but sometimes also with a crippled body. On other occasions he thought that only the immaterial soul would leave the body to enter the afterlife. On one occasion, he taught that the souls of the wicked would be destroyed after Judgment Day.

Paul of Tarsus
The self-appointed apsotle, Paul of Tarsus, accepted the Neo-Platonic dualism of a spirit or soul that is caught in a mortal body, the flesh with all its lusts and weaknesses. When Christ returns on Judgment Day, all the dead will be resurrected and the living will be transformed. Those who believed in Christ will be resurrected with spiritual or heavenly bodies, which are nothing but their spirits that were liberated from their bodies and made from stuff that differs fram ordinary matter, like the stars and planets, so that they will be able to enter heaven where they will be absorbed into God. The spirits of the godless will be sent to perdition and destruction, while Satan and all his followers will be eradicated or eliminated. Christ will abdicate his position and God will be all in all.

Later Gospels
The stories in the Synoptic Gospels regarding Jesus' resurrection after his crucifixion, are at odds with Paul's idea that he rose from

the grave with a transformed spiritual body – which is nothing bu an immaterial spirit. These gospels are adamant that he appeared with his ordinary earthly body made of matter.

Luke's two somewhat incompatible stories of Jesus' ascension into heaven may be regarded as pious fiction.

The later parts of the Gospel of John clearly taught the dualism of body and spirit in a Neo-Platonic tradition. The body, called (rotting) flesh and the seat of detestable desires, is the prison of the soul or spirit. Only the spirit will reach heaven after death if that person had believed in the Son of God.

John of Patmos

The prophet John of Patrmos accepted the dualism of body and soul of the Neo-Platonists. According to him, the soul is taken up to heaven directly after death where the martyrs and the faithful are in the presence of God. Satan and the spirits of evil people are stored in Hades, awaiting Judgment Day, after which Hades and hell will be abolished or cancelled to leave only a perfectly restored creation of God in the form of the New Jerusalem.

The Qur'an

Heaven, pictured as a beautiful garden or a city with gates, is the eternal destination of Muslim believers. Infidels and wicked people are destined to reach eternal punishment in hell after Judgment Day.

Some Conclusions

The ideas of animism and ancient religions can be discarded as mere irrational superstitions, without any scientific or rational backing. The Greek philosophers disagreed amongst themselves and it is impossible to choose between them, although the rationalism of Aristotle does seem to make some sense. The Platonic dualism of body and soul was accepted by Enoch, Jesus, and other early Christians, but this position is untennable because no possible or probable mechanism or method has ever been proposed, enabling a non-material entitiy, the soul or spirit, to interact with the material body and brain that operate with chemical processes and electricity.

It must also be concluded that there is no consistent view presented in the Hebrew and Christian scriptures. They provide widely different ideas and even flatly contradict each another. That leaves no other conclusion as that at least some of them must have had it wrong.

According to almost all of the Old Testament, man will simply turn to dirt after death, although his silent spirit, shadowy ghost, or ghastly shadow would descend to the netherworld, irrespective of his previous lifestyle. There are no immortal souls or spirits that experience a conscious afterlife.

In contrast, the New Testament portrays man as a combination of a perishable material body and an immaterial and immortal soul or spirit. At Judgment Day, the souls of the believers would be sent to heaven and sinners would be consigned to hell – although Paul thought that the souls of the believers would be amalgamated with God and that hell would eventually prove to be empty or obliterated. John of Patmos also thought that hell or Hades would be abolished or destroyed by becoming burnt-out in its own flames.

The Qur'an contains a very diluted and concrete version of some biblical ideas and can be dismissed as a document without much credibility.

Neurology and Neuropsychology
The practitioners of the scientific disciplines of neurology and neuropsychology are convinced that there is absolute no evidence of an immortal soul in man that survives death. They point out that those

who claim that the brain is only the channel or receiver of thoughts, perceptions, ideas, emotions, and (self-) consciousness coming from an immaterial soul or spirit, are not able to explain or demonstrate how an immaterial entity, such as the soul, is able to connect or communicate with the all-too material brain with its chemical and electrical processes and procedures. All the evidence demonstrate that the ego, the psyche, the mind, the self-consciousness, and the memories constituting the identity of a person are all somehow functions or products of the central nervous system.

Although a large body of insights and knowledge about the functioning of the brain has been collected, it proved to be impossible as yet to explain how the brain produces the mind, consciousness, the ego as the identity of a person with his memories, although research is ongoing.

In the following pages, an explanation will be given why the himan mind, ego, or consciousness continues to be such a mystery.

THE MYSTERIOUS MIND OR CONSCIOUSNESS

Dimensional Ontology

The Austrian psychiatrist and philosopher, Viktor Frankl (1905–1997), proposed a very interesting solution for the mind-body problem. He called it his "dimensional ontology".[216]

It cannot be denied that a human being has tangible and intangible aspects to his being. His body, including his brain, is tangible, physical, made of matter. But there are also intangible aspects, which may be called the psyche, such as thoughts, emotions, personality traits, mental abilities, and the conscious mind. The question is: how do we explain these intangible aspects?

---

[216] Frankl, *Das Menschenbild der Seelenheilkunde;* Frankl, "Grundriß der Existenzanalyse und Logoterapie".

The Paradox

We have a paradox: man is a unity, but also a multiplicity, consisting of a material body and an intangible psyche. This is, though, not an insoluble paradox. It may be worthwhile to look at the two figures pictured below:

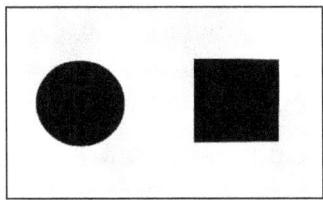

The illustration shows two two-dimensional geometrical figures: a square and a circle. Nobody of sound mind will confuse them with each other. One just cannot think that they represent the same thing.

If one leaves the two-dimensional level of the paper on which these figures are depicted and move to a three-dimensional level, one can immedietely see the unity and identity of the two figures without any problem.

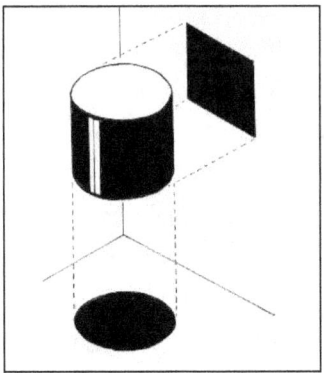

The second drawing shows a cylindrical object, such as a tin of canned fruit or marmelade, of which two shadows or projections are thrown onto the wall and onto the floor. One shadow is square and the other is circular. The cylinder is, however, one single object.

In the same way, one may illuminate the unity and the multiplicity of man. The cylinder may be regarded as a representation of the spirit of man – his hidden mind, consciousness, or ego. The psychiological aspects of man and the body can, in a certain sense, be regarded as projections of the spirit on a lower level. The spirit of man is not observable with our sense organs since it is hidden in an inaccessible dimension. On the other hand, the physical and psychological functions of man are observable. This duality is the reason why so many religions and philosophies taught an untenable dualism of soul and body.

The Ego and Time
The German theologian and philosopher, Karl Heim (1874–1958), convincingly maintained that all the efforts to fathom the mystery of the mind, consciousness, or the ego, fail to take the impoerance of the phenomenon of *time* into consideration.[217]

Nobody can deny that every normal human being possesses an identity, a personality, a self-consciousness, an ego. His identity is tied to his personal history and the recollections of his past. His past has molded him into the person he is at present.

We also experience other people as persons, beings with an ego, self-consiousness, or a mind – which is not one's self or own ego. One can only know one's own ego or the "I" that is conscious, but we accept that another person also has an ego or a consciousness. We even accept that some animals may have self-consciousness, memories, or an own identity. We may even communicate with animals, almost as if they are also human persons. The reason is that

---

[217] Heim, *Christian Faith and Natural Science;* Heim, *Glaube und Denken.*

animals also have brains.[218]

The reason why the spirit of man, his ego or "I", his consciousness, or mind, is not observable or cannot be investigated objectively is connected to the fact that the ego is in the present, while his body and psyche are already fixated in the past.

This must be explained as follows: Our sense organs can only observe objects that are in the past. The light that strikes somebody's eye so that he can see the thing from which the light travelled, needs time to advance from the observed object to the eye at a speed of $\pm 300\,000$ kilometers per second. In the case of stars in space, the light from them takes years to reach us. Astronomers can see galaxies with their telescopes of which the light waves needed millions or even billions of years to arrive on earth. This means that they do not observe those parts of the universe as they are at present, but as they were a very long time ago. They are literally looking back into the past.

The light from the sun needs seven minutes to strike the earth. The light from an object a meter away from somebody's eye, such as the computer screen in front of me while I am writing this, needs a tiny fraction of a second to travel that distance, but that is still a certain length of time.

In the same way, sound needs time to reach somebody's ear, just as I am listenening to Mozart's 40th symphony over the radio at

---

[218] Experiments have shown that animals with enough brain power, such as primates, are able to recognize themselves in mirrors and have self-awatreness. That is due to the fact that they have so-called mirror neurons in their brains, enabling them to have empathy and understand how others feel and think (Kolb and Wishaw, *Fundamentals,* 584–85).
A group of neuroscientists recently published the so-called *New York Declaration on Animal Consciousness* in which they stated that "there is strong scientific support for attributions of conscious experience to other mammals and to birds."

this moment.

Inside the brain, more time is needed for the nerve impulses to travel from the sense organs to certain centers before the observer can become conscious of what he sees or hears. Therefore, we can only observe the world as it was in the past, not as it is in the present, the moment of exactly "now".

The ego of man cannot, though, be observed since it is the ego itself that experiences and observes the objects in the past, while it is constantly gliding or sliding along in the present, the moment of "now". The ego can, therefore, never be in the past, only in the present and is never observable as if it were an object in the world.

The ego cannot experience itself, although every sane human being is aware of the fact that he is conscious of himself, as well as of the world. However, the ego can only experience the contents of consciousness, such as sensations, memories, thoughts, or even imaginary scenes – but not the consciousness as such. In the same way, no eye can see itself and no hand can grasp itself.

The physical and psychological aspects of man can be observed since they are already in the past at the moment of observation. Therefore, I can see my hands as they strike the keys of the computer in front of me as I write these words and I can feel my heart throbbing inside my chest. I can feel my reading glasses as they are resting upon my nose. These aspects are projections of the ego that were already fixated in the past and are, therefore, observable. The ego, the conscious "I", though, is always in the moment of "now".

Psychologists and neuroscientists have endeavored for decades to locate consciousness in the brain or to define consciousness in terms of brain activities – without success, as has been demonstrated in the previous chapter. Human consciousness, the ego, the "I" that observes, thinks, remembers, feels, imagines, plans, and experiences, simply cannot be observed and captured since it is not fixed in the past as all other objects are. It is, in other words, subjective and cannot be objectivized as objects in the world.

In the same way, we experience other persons as beings who also have an ego or self-awareness when we encounter them in the world. It has been explained in the second chapter that the so-called mirror neurons in our brains enable us to have empathy with others and to understand how they feel and think.

For these reasons, it is not possible to explain how the brain produces the mind, the ego, or (self-)consciousness.

In the same way, it will always remain a mystery how something like love is possible or how people can be moved by something beautiful. We know that love, romantic attraction between people, or the bond between a parent and a child, is somehow connected to the neurotransmitter and hormone oxytocin. This chemical substance, though, is not an adequate explanation for the mystery of love, a subjective experience. Likewse, the production of neurotransmitters such as dopamine and serotoning when somebody is moved by a beautiful piece of music, a beautiful natural scene, or a beautifyl human being or animal, is not enough to explain the exhiliration and excitement during such a subjective experience.

Human Knowledge

When all the preceding arguments and explanations are being kept in mind, it also sheds some light on the phenomenon of knowledge. Neuroscientists are convinced that memories are stored in the synapses, the connections between brain cells. The precise mechaniism has, though, eluded them so far, although there is evidence that it entails chemical processes.

Human knowledge does not consist of accurate mental images or copies of objects in the world outside man's consciousness. How will we ever know whether the *mental images* in our consciousness correspond with the objects in the *world*, the world outside our mind, which they are supposed to represent? We can only know that which is in our minds, in our own consciousness and memory. Our mental images are not like photos that we can take out and compare with the scene or object that was photographed. We can't compare our mental images with something "outside" the mind, since we only have access to our own mntal images inside our minds or consciousness.

Man, on the other hand, also does not have knowledge of a world he constructs or creates himself in his mind – otherwise he would only have known illusions and hallucinations.

Man knows the real world – but then as the world appears to him, as the world presents itself to the observer. He never gets a complete picture or representation since he only has a limited perspective on the world. His sense organs are not only receptors but also filters that do not register certain signals. Those aspects of the world that appears to him are also being interpreted and evaluated against the background of his memories, emotions, expectations, goals, interests, preferences, and dislikes.

It is, therefore, clear: the world does not appear in the same way to any two people. Since it is always the same world that appears to both of them, communication between them is possible.

Human knowledge consists of the contents of consciousness and stored memories that may be brought back into consciousness. To be truthful and accurate, this knowledge must correspond with the information that may be gathered about the world. This informatio is buried or embedded in all aspects of reality, namely that which can be said or described about a certain aspect of reality.

Truth or accurate facts are thus not, as is often being said, the correspondence between knowledge and being or reality; it is rather the correspondence on the one hand between the contents of a (human) consciousness or information that has been fixated or recorded by means of a code (for instance, letters on paper or in a computer's memory) and, on the other hand, the information that can be extracted from the world and can be expressed by means of visual images, spoken or written words, or other symbols.

Because it is always the *ego* that observes, interprets, and knows, we will never understand the nature of knowledge and memories fully. This *ego* is never available for observation or analysis, because it is the agent that does the observing and the analyzing.

In a same manner, human freedom will always stay a riddle since the *ego*, which is free and makes certain decisions and choices, stays hidden in the moment of "now", where it cannot be observed.

Surviving Death?

The question now arises: is this *ego*, the self-consciousness, spirit, or mind of a human being, something that can survive death? The answer of neuroscience is an emphatic and definite "no!", as has been demonstrated in the prevoious chapter. There are, though other reasons why it can be argued that nothing of man's mind or ego can survive death and enter an afterlife, either in heaven or in hell.

ETERNAL LIFE?

The Concept of Eternity

The notion of an everlasting existence in heaven or in hell, as found in certain parts of the Christian Bible and the Islamic Qur'an, must be classified as absurd, misguided, and impossible when these scriptures are scrutinized carefully and with an open mind.

According to the Bible, only God is eternal (Ps 90: 2; Heb 9: 14; 2 Pet 3: 8). We read in 1 Timn 1: 17 – "Now to the King eternal, immortal, invisible, to God who alone is wise, be honor and glory forever and ever." Rev 4: 8 mentions a heavenly song: "Holy, holy,

holy is the Lord God, the Almighty, who was and who is and who is to come."

God is, therefore, supposed to exists outside of time and space and is thought to be without beginning and end. Creation, on the other hand, had a beginning when God created it out of nothing, "in the beginning" (Gen 1: 1; John 1: 1–3), and it must, therefore, also come to an end somewhere in the future (Matt 24: 29–30; 2 Pet 3: 7). Time was created together with the universe "in the beginning" and time will again disappear when the universe dies.

This is also the view of contemporary cosmologists, who have demonstrated that our universe came into being between thirteen and fourteen billion years ago, by means of the "Big Bang". That was also when time was switched on and started moving forward, always in one direction, towards the future.[219]

Should it happen that humans, who are part of creation, enter an eternal mode of existence after death, then it must, of necessity, mean that they are dissolved or absorbed into the eternity of God, otherwise they cannot exist into all eternity, outside or without time. It is unthinkable that any entity that exists in time, be it a soul or a spirit, can leave the dimension of time without being annihilated. It just does not seem possible to "jump" from a temporal mode into an eternal or timeless mode.

Should that be the case, then it won't be possible to have an individual existence beyond death as the Bible sometimes promises. Paul must have realized this difficulty and, therefore, wrote that God will be "all in all" at the end. He, as well as John of Patmos, thought that hell would be abolished or wiped out, making the eternal punishment for sinners impossible. According to them, there can be no place for a hell filled with an evil devil and slimy sinful spirits in the restored creation after Judgment Day (1 Cor 15; Rev 20 and 22).

---

[219] Clark, *The Universe*, 27–35; Hawking, *The Grand Design*, 158–59, 196.

On the other hand, if souls do exist individually after death into an endless eternity, then it implies that they cannot have had a beginning either. Eternity is, per definition, timeless and without a beginning and an end – not a very, very, extremely long stretch of time.[220] That means that it is a puzzle how these souls could have escaped out of eternity and entered time at some point when being born as humans since eternity has no beginning and no end.

It is a mathematical impossibility that there can be any connection between anything finite and infinity or eternity. The mathematical concept of infinity (∞) cannot be used in any computation in which finite numbers appear. One may divide infinity any number of times, subtract from it, add to it, or multiply it, but it always stays infinity – except when infinity is divided by infinity, which produces a zero as the result.

Metaphysical infinity or eternity, likewise, cannot contain anything finite, such as the finite life of a human being. If people, who exist in time, leave this life through death, then it is just not possible that they can be converted into eternal or infinite beings, existing in an infinite mode, without beginning and end.

One must also ask: when does this promised eternal life start? Does it start directly after man has breathed his last breath and all brain activity has stopped? Or does it only start at Judgment Day with the resurrection? How is the transition from an existence in time to an existence outside time in eternity accomplished? Something of this sort simply does not seem to be possible since such a transition implies that that such an eternal existence must have had a beginning, which is not possible because eternity cannot contain a starting point somewhere, otherwise it would not be eternity.

Koetz summarized the position of the well-respected theolo-

---

[220] International Standard Bible Encyclopedia, "Eternity".

gian Karl Barth in this regard as follows:

> "There was a first moment of Creation in history, for which there was no previous moment, and likewise there will be a final moment, in a *twinkling of an eye*, for which there will be no subsequent moment. (...) There are no more happenings or occurrences in time once the final trump sounds, such that there will be no future consciousness or continuation of life beyond the last day. Eternal life means the 'eternalizing' of our past life, because there will be no continuation of time in any way."[221]

In other words: time will end at Judgment Day and all parts of creation, including man, will cease to exist.

It will be wrong to assume that this concept of eternity means that eternity must be totally empty. The following aspects of reality may be regarded as eternal or timeless: the axioms of mathematics, the axioms or rules of logics, the rules of natural justice, and the laws of nature as expressed by means of mathematical formulas. Nobody thought them out and it is inconceivable that there will ever be a condition where they do not apply. They may, therefore, be regarded as eternally valid, outside of time and immutable, even if no universe existed. They are, however, parts of the realm of meta-information, which is fundamentally different from the purported realm filled with the immortal and eternal souls of dead people.

It has already been noted that the world is composed of only four elements: matter or energy, time, space, and information. Meta-information is simply information about the phenomenon of information – the story behind the story, as it were.

---

[221] Koetz, "Karl Barth's Argument against Afterlife".

Pre-existence of the Soul?

Plato taught that the human soul had a pre-existence in the realm of Ideas before being born into a human body. The Persian religion had a similar idea. The scriptures are unclear on this point. It must be sipposed, though, that the soul that is thought to enter eternity after death, must be without a beginning and an end to be immortal and eternal.

One must, therefore, ask: Where did this eternal, indestructable, and immortal soul come from? Is it perhaps a spark from the fire that is God? How did this eternal, timeless, and immortal soul manage to get united with a mortal body that exists in time? Or was this soul only created at the moment of conception inside the mother's womb? If that is the case, then it is a time-bound entity, which cannot exist into all eternity after death. Both these possible origins for an immortal human soul create insoluble difficulties.

Some parts of the New Testament promise everlasting serenity for the souls of saints and endless suffering for the souls of sinners after death. This implies that the immortal souls of these saints and sinners must have existed from eternity to eternity – just as God. That means that they must be, somehow, part or aspects of the eternal God. But how a part of God, consisting of the immortal souls of unbelievers, atheists, cheaters, liars, and pagans, can undergo eternal punishment in hell does not seem to be compatible with the idea of a totally good, just, and loving God who supposedly cannot do any wrong and who doesn't deserve any punishment.

On the other hand, 1 Tim 6: 16 states that Jesus Christ "alone has immortality" (Greek: ὁ μόνος ἔχων ἀθανασίαν – *ho monon echon athanasian*). If that is the case, then nobody else can hope to gain everlasting or eternal ecstacy in heaven.

Likewise, according to Rev 20: 14, "death and Hades were thrown into the lake of fire." This amounts to an inner contradiction since the word *Hades* is often used in the New Testament for *hell* – here called rhe "lake of fire" (Matt 16: 18; Luke 10: 15; Luke 16: 23; Acts 2: 31; Rev 1: 18). This begs the question: how the hell can hell be thrown into hell? Does it mean that hell with its bonfires will burn out completely, or be eliminated, extinguished, and erased on Judgment Day? That seems to be the position of Paul of Tarsus and John of Patmos.

Hymns in Heaven?
The depiction of an existence in heaven by the departed saints in the book of Revelation seems to amount to an absurdity in another sense. One often reads in this book of the hymns being sung by the heavenly beings. Music can only be music if it has a beat – and that presupposes that it needs time to be performed. How can there be music in heaven if there is no time in heaven with its eternity?

These heavenly beings, who sing God's praise and enjoy unending joy, supposedly are conscious of their surroundings and of themselves, otherwise they would have forgotten the words of their hymns – in spite of having no brains.[222] Consciousness is always consciousness of something. The conscious mind cannot ever be empty – it is always filled with a mixture of sensations, memories, and thoughts, otherwise it would amount to unconsciousness. Sensations, memories, and thoughts can only exist in time – not in the timelessness of eternity. Therefore, it is just not possible that any Gospel songs are being sung in God's heaven.

The late neurologist Oliver Sacks wrote a book with the title, The River of Consciousness, in which he argued that consciousness is not an attribute of the brain but a process in which billions of

---

[222] According to John of Patmos, who wrote his book in Greek, the hymns that are being sung in heaven had Greek lyrics. One may ask: will the cheerful choir members also sing Chinese, Danish, Egyptian, or Zulu Gospel songs?

neurons play a role. Sensations and thoughts are mental processes that presuppose time where one moment is followed by another. Memories are always recollections of past events and that also presupposes the passage of time. Sacks added: "Our movements, our actions, are extended in time, as are our perceptions, our thoughts, the contents of consciousness."[223]

Therefore, a conscious existence after physical death, either in heaven, or in hell, in eternity, in a state of timelessness, just does not make sense and just cannot be possible. The notion of an eternal conscious existence of the individual in an afterlife simply cannot be accepted by any sensible and rational person.

Paganism?

Karl Barth, who rejected the idea of a never-ending state of and euphoria after Judgment Day, came to the following conclusion:

> "If we wish the New Testament had more to say about this [the afterlife] than the Old, it may well be that we are pursuing pagan dreams of a good time after death, and not letting the New Testament say the radically good thing which it has to say with the realism which it has in common with the Old Testament."[224]

This means that Barth thought that the idea of a happy existence in the afterlife is simply nothing but "pagan dreams".

The Bottom Line

We must conclude on account of all the foregoing facts and arguments as follows: heaven and hell, seen as the eternal destinations of the souls of dead people, do not exist and cannot exist and never

---

[223] Sacks, *The River of Consciousness*, 161.
[224] Barth, Karl. *Church Dogmatics III.2*, 625.

existed. Neither do humans have immortal souls. The reasons for these radical statements may be summurized as follows:

- The idea found in many religions, as well as in certain ancient philosophcal systems, that human beings possess immortal souls, united with mortal bodies, cannot be accepted because nobody can explain how these two fundamentally different enetities or elements could ever get connected and combined;
- The Sacred Scriptures contain so many conflicting, confusing, and contradictory thoughts about the human soul and the afterlife that they cannot be regarded as reliable sources of knowledge or insights in this regard;
- There are valid and solid scientific reasons for rejecting the idea that a human beings consists of a combination of a material body and an immaterial soul; all the evidence shows that consciousness, memory, the soul, the mind, the ego, is somehow produced by and dependent upon the physical brain;
- The concept of a continued, never-ending, and eternal existence for the human soul after death leads to various logical absurdities and untenable consequences; and
- It is understandable that people have the impression that their minds, egos, psyches, memories, and self-consciousness are somehow different from their physical bodies, since this inner core, the "I" or the "me" inside them, cannot be discovered or located anywhere, or observed and analyzed as if it were a material object, since it always exists in the moment of "now" – not in the past as all observable objects in the world. There is just no indication that this subjective and ungraspable "I" or the "me" can survive consciously without a brain after death.

Thus: there are no immortal souls that join the never-ending heavcenly choirs or the teams of stokers who shovel coals to keep the fires in hell's furnaces burning forever after they have been sent off with a beautiful and sad funeral. When man dies, he just turns to dust and dirt. His brain disintegrates and his mind, personality, and recollections vanish finally and forever.

* * * * *

> "For this we tell you by the word of the Lord, that we who are alive, who are left to the coming of the Lord, will in no way precede those who have fallen asleep. For the Lord himself will descend from heaven with a shout, with the voice of the archangel, and with God's trumpet. The dead in Christ will rise first, then we who are alive, who are left, will be caught up together with them in the clouds, to meet the Lord in the air. So we will be with the Lord forever " (1 Thess 4: 15–17).
>
> "But as it is written, 'Things which eye didn't see, and ear didn't hear, which didn't enter into the heart of man, whatever things God prepared for those who love him'" (1 Cor 2: 9).
>
> "When he opened the fifth seal, I saw underneath the altar the souls of those who had been killed for the word of God, and for the testimony which they held" (Rev 6: 9).
>
> "YHWH God formed man from the dust of the ground, and breathed into his nostrils the breath of life; and man became a living soul" (Gen 2: 7).
>
> "By the sweat of your face will you eat bread until you return to the ground, for out of it you were taken. For you are dust, and to dust you shall return" (Gen 3: 19).

"See now, I have taken it on myself to speak to the Lord, I who am but dust and ashes" (Gen 18: 27).

"But man dies, and is laid low. Yes, man gives up the spirit [breath], and where is he? As the waters fail from the sea, and the river wastes and dries up, so man lies down and doesn't rise; until the heavens are no more, they shall not awake, nor be roused out of their sleep (Job 14: 10–12).

"But man, despite his riches, doesn't endure. He is like the animals that perish" (Ps 49: 12).

"For all our days have passed away in your wrath. We bring our years to an end as a sigh. The days of our years are seventy, or even by reason of strength eighty years; yet their pride is but labor and sorrow, for it passes quickly, and we fly away (Ps 90: 9–10).

"Though the wicked spring up as the grass, and all the evil-doers flourish, they will be destroyed forever" (Ps 92: 7).

"You take away their breath: they die, and return to the dust" (Ps 104: 29).

"For that which happens to the sons of men happens to animals. Even one thing happens to them. As the one dies, so the other dies. Yes, they have all one breath; and man has no advantage over the animals: for all is vanity. All go to one place. All are from the dust, and all turn to dust again" (Eccl 3: 19–20).

"For the living know that they will die, but the dead don't know anything, neither do they have any more a reward; for the memory of them is forgotten. Also their love, their hatred, and their envy has perished long ago; neither have they any more a portion forever in anything that is done under the sun" (Eccl 9: 5–6).

> "The Lord created human beings from the earth, and makes them return to earth again" (Sir 17: 1).
>
> "... [A]ll mortals are dust and ashes" (Sir 17: 32).

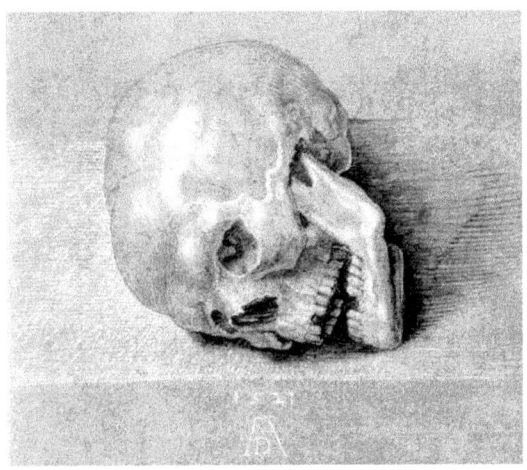

Albrecht Dürer: Study of a Skull (1521)

BIBLIOGRAPHY

EDITIONS AND TRANSLATIONS OF THE SCRIPTURES

The Bible

Passages from the Bible are quoted from the *World English Bible* as found on a CD with the title *The Bible Collection, Deluxe Edition*, and published by ValuSoft, a division of THQ Inc, Waconia MN, 2002.

    The above-mentioned CD also contains the Hebrew text of the Old Testament and the Greek text of the New Testament, as well as *Strong's Complete Greek & Hebrew Lexicon*. Other lexica utilized are mentioned under the heading of Other Publications.

    In addition, the following editions of the biblical text in the original languages were consulted:

Elliger, K. and W. Rudolph, eds. *Biblia Hebraica Stuttgartensia*. Stuttgart: Deutsche Bibelgesellschaft, 1997.

Nestle, E. and E. Nestle, eds. *Novum Testamentum Graece*. Stuttgart: Deutsche Bibelstiftung, 1981.

Apocrypha and Pseudepigrapha

Book of Enoch. From: The Apocrypha and Pseudepigrapha of the Old Testament. Tr. R.H. Charles Oxford: The Clarendon Press Section I. Chapters I-XXXVI.
    https://www.ccel.org/c/charles/otpseudepig/enoch/ENOCH_1.HTM

Book of Jubilees – Catholic Encyclopedia
    https://www.newadvent.org/cathen/08535a.htm

2 Maccabees, Bible, Revised Standard Version
    https://quod.lib.umich.edu/cgi/r/rsv/rsv-idx?type=DIV1&byte=4353562#:~:text=May%20God%20do%20good%20to,and%20may%20he%20bring%20peace.

Wisdom of Solomon, Kata Biblon, Greek Septuagint and Wiki English Translation.

https://en.katabiblon.com/us/index.php?text=LXX&book=Wsd&ch=1

The Qur'an
Quotations from the Qur'an were taken from the translation by MaulawI Sher 'Ali: The Holy Qur'an, Arabic Text and English Translation. Tilford, Surry: Islam International Publications Limited, 2021.
https://www.alislam.org/quran/Holy-Quran-English.pdf
Another translation that was consulted:
Rodwell,, J.M. and Alan Jones. *The Koran.* London: Phoenix, 1994.

OTHER LITERATURE:

Ahlström, G.W. "Prophecy". Chicago: Encyclopædia Britannica, 2010.
Anon. "Religion and Beliefs of the San".
https://southafrica.co.za/religion-and-beliefs-of-the-san.html
Anon, "Researchers Restore Brain Functions after Death".
https://www.msn.com/en-za/news/other/eesearchers restore brain functions after death (msn.com).
APA Encyclopedia of Psychology, "Past-life Regression".
https://dictionary.apa.org/past-life-regression.
Ardrey, Robert. *The Territorial Imperative: A Personal Inquiry into the Animal Origins of Property and Nations.* London: Collins, 1970.
Armstrong, Karen. *The Bible: The Biography.* London: Atlantic, 2007.
Barnes, Jonatha. "Plato". Chicago: Encyclopedia Brittanica, 2010.
Barth, Karl. *Church Dogmatics III.2 : The Doctrine of Creation.* Trans. G. W. Bromiley *et al.* London: T & T Clark, 2009.
Benedict, G. *The God Debate: A New Look at History's Oldest Argument.* London: Watkins, 2013.
Boshoff, Willem *et al. Geskiedenis en Geskrifte: die Literatuur van ou Israel.* Pretria: Protea, 2008.

Boudry, Martin. "The Sin of Scientism: Response to Clark". *Reports of The National Center for Science Education.* Sept–Oct 2015.

Bowman, Alan K. "Egypt, Ancient". Encyclopaedia Brittanica, Chicago: Encyclopaedia Brittanica, 2010.

Brunner, Helmut, & Peter F. Dorman. "Hieroglyphic Writing". Encyclopaedia Brittanica, Chicago: Encyclopaedia Brittanica, 2010.

Carbonaro, T.M. et al. "Magic Mushrooms Lift Depression in Cancer Patients". *Medical Brief,* 7 December 2016.
http://www.medicalbrief.co.za/archives/magic-mushrooms-lift-depression-cancer-patients/

Carter, Rita, *et al. The Braiun Book.* London: Penguin Random House, 2019.

Choksi, M. "Ancient Mesopotamian Beliefs in the Afterlife". World History Encyclopedia, 20 June 2014.

https://www.Ancient Mesopotamian Beliefs in the Afterlife

Clark, P. *et al. Lippincott's Illustrated Reviews: Pharmacology.* Baltimore: Wolters Kluwer Health, 2012.

Clark, Stuart. *The Universe,* London: Quercus, 2010.,

Cooke, Emily. "The Brain Can Store Nearly 10 Times More Data Than Previously Thought, Study Confirms". Live Science, 05.06.2024.
https://www.livescience.com/health/neuroscience/the-brain-can-store-nearly-10-times-more-data-than-previously-thought-study-confirms?utm_term=1EF9AB5E-4DB1-47F0-AABD-0CC5FBCC0EB9&lrh=a67410bc0161181ec536fc3d3b53cc33a0af584bec061fd0a23cd6b695d6aecf&utm_campaign=368B3745-DDE0-4A69-A2E8-62503D85375D&utm_medium=email&utm_content=A8ECDB03-3C5C-43F9-BB54-8955D8CF2C31&utm_source=SmartBrief

Craighead, W.E. and Nemeroff, C.B. *The Corsini Encyclopedia of Psychology and Behavioral Science, Volume 4.* New York: John Wiley and Sons, 2002.

Cunningham, G.C. *Decoding the Language of God.* New York: Prometheus, 2010.

Dawkins, Richard. "Good and Bad Reasons for Believing". In *How Things are: A Science Tool-Kit for the Mind*, edited by J. Brockman and K. Matson, K. London: Phoenix, 2001.

Department of Philosophy, Florida State University. "What is Philosophy?" https://philosophy.fsu.edu/undergraduate-study/why-philosophy/What-is-Philosophy

Department of Religion and Theology, Bristol Buddhist Studies, "Death and Dying in Buddhism". https://www.bristol.ac.uk/religion/buddhist-centre/projects/bdr/chaplains/online-guide.html#:~:text=Buddhists%20recognise%20that%20there%20is,to%20become%20free%20from%20samsara.

Division of Perceptual Studies, "Children who Report Memories of Pasrt Lives." https://med.virginia.edu/perceptual-studies/our-research/children-who-report-memories-of-previous-lives/

Doniger, Wendy, and Brian K. Smith, "Hinduism". Encyclopaedia Brittanica, Chicago: Encyclopaedia Brittanica, 2010.

Dowdey, Sarah. "How Reincarnation Works". https://people.howstuffworks.com/reincarnation.htm How Stuff Works.

Duchesne-Guillemin, Jacques. "Zoroastrianism". Encyclopaedia Britannica, Chicago: Encyclopaedia Britannica, 2010.

Encyclopaedia Brittanica. "Animism". Chicago: Encyclopedia Brittanica, 2010.

―――. "Astrology". Chicago: Encyclopædia Britannica, 2010.

―――. "Buddhism". Chicago: Encyclopædia Britannica, 2010.

―――. "Charon". Chicago: Encyclopædia Britannica, 2010.

―――. "Dehydration". Chicago: Encyclopædia Britannica, 2010.

―――. "Ecstacy". Chicago: Encyclopædia Britannica, 2010.

―――. "Gnosticism". Chicago: Encyclopædia Britannica, 2010.

―――. "Prophet". Chicago: Encyclopædia Britannica, 2010.

―――. "Mesopotamia". Chicago: Encyclopædia Britannica, 2010.

―――. "Mesopotamian Religion". Chicago: Encyclopædia Britannica, 2010.
―――. "Philo Judaeus". Chicago: Encyclopædia Britannica, 2010.
―――. "Philosophy". Chicago: Encyclopædia Britannica, 2010.
―――. "Platonism". Chicago: Encyclopædia Britannica, 2010.
―――. "Pythagoras". Chicago: Encyclopædia Britannica, 2010.
―――. "Styx". Chicago: Encyclopædia Britannica, 2010.
―――. "Sumer". Chicago: Encyclopædia Britannica, 2010.
Finkelstein, Israel, andNeil Asher Silberman. *The Bible Unearthed: Archeology's new Vision of Ancient Israel and the Orifin of its Sacred Texts.* New York: Touchstone, 2002.
Frankl, Viktor Emil. *Das Menschenbild der Seelenheilkunde: Kritik des Dynaminschen Psychologismus.* Stuttgart: Hippocrates, 1959.
―――. 1959b. "Grundriβ der Existenzanalyse und Logoterapie". In *Handbuch der Neurosenlehre und Psychotherapie*, edited by V.E. Frankl, V.E. Von Gebsattel and J.H. Schultz. München: Urban & Schwarzenberg, 1959.
Frazer, J.G. *The Golden Bough: A Study in Magic and Religion.* London: Macmillan, 1971.
Gauquelin, Michel. *Astrology and Science.* London: P. Davies, 1972.
Goetz, C.G. "Hallucinogens". In *Encyclopedia of the Neurological Sciences*, edited by M.J. Aminoff. Elsevier Science, 2003, 503–04.
Gottheil, Richard, and Enno Litmann. "Enoch, Books of (Ethiopic and Slavonic). *Jewish Encyclopedia..* https://www.jewishencyclopedia.com/articles/5773-enoch-books-of-ethiopic-and-slavonic
Grayling, A.C. *The God Argument: The Case Against Religion and for Humanism.* London: Bloomsbury, 2014.
Goetz, Chrisopher.G. "Alertness". In *Encyclopedia of the Neurological Sciences*, edited by M.J. Aminoff. Elsevier Science, 2003, 80–81.
Goetz, Chrisopher.G. "Hallucinogens". In *Encyclopedia of the Neurological Sciences*, edited by M.J. Aminoff. Elsevier Science, 2003, 503–04.

Goetz, Chrisopher.G. "Hallucinogens". In *Encyclopedia of the Neurological Sciences*, edited by M.J. Aminoff. Elsevier Science, 2003, 503–04.

Gottheil, R. and M. Kayserling. "Inquisition (Called also Sanctum Officium or Holy Office)". In *Jewish Encyclopedia*, 1906. http://www.jewishencyclopedia.com/articles/8122-inquisition

Graffin, Greg. and S. Olson. *Anarchy Evolution: Faith, Science and Bad Religion*. New York: Harper Collins, 2010.

Grayling, A.C. *The God Argument: The Case Against Religion and for Humanism*. London: Bloomsbury, 2014.

Greenwood, S. and R. Airey. *The Complete Illustrated Encyclopaedia of Witchcraft & Magic*. London: Hermes House, 2007.

Hallowell, B. *Shocking Porn 'Epidemic' Stats Reveal Details about Christian Consumption: 'A Very Real Addiction' that can 'Spiral Out Of Control'*. http://www.theblaze.com/stories/2014/08/28/shocking-statistics-about-porn-epidemic-and-christian-consumption-a-very-real-addiction-that-can-spiral-out-of-control/

Hammond, D. Croydon, *Handbook of Hypnotic Suggestions and Metaphors*. New York: Norton, 1990.

Hancock, Graham. *Supernatural: Meetings with the Ancient Teachers of Mankind*. London: Century, 2005.

Hawking, Stephen. *The Grand Design, New Answers to the Ultimate Questions of Life.* London: Transworld, 2011.

Healing Souls Hypnosis. "Past Life Regression". https://healingsoulhypnosis.com/12-things-you-should-know-about-a-past-life-regression/

Heim, Karl. *Christian faith and natural science* (tr N.H. Smith). New York : Harper & Row 1957.

Heim, Karl. *Glaube und Denken : Philosophische Grundlegung einer christlichen Lebensanschauung*. Wuppertal : Aussaat Verlag, 1975.

Hoffman, R.E. et al. "Transcranial Magnetic Stimulation of Left Temporal Cortex and Medication-Resistant Auditory Hallucinations. *Arch Gen Psychiatry,* Vol 60, January 2003: 49–56.
   http://www.neuro.hk/img/tmshallucinationsschizophrenia.pdf
Hengel, M. *Judentum und Hellenismus, Studien zu Ihrer Begegnung unter Besonderer Berücksichtigung Palästinas Bis zur Mitte des 2. Jh.s v. Chr.* Tübingen: Mohr Siebeck, 1973.
Heyns, Johan Adam, and Willie D. Jonker. *Op Weg met die Teologie.* Pretoria: N.G. Kerkboekhandel, 1974.
Humphrys, J. *In God we Doubt: Confessions of a Failed Atheist.* London: Hodder and Stoughton, 2007.
International Standard Bible Encyclopedia. "Eternity".
   https://www.biblestudytools.com/dictionary/eternity/
Jackson, "Man, God and Civilization." Benschville, IL: Lushena, 2001.
Jewish Virtual Library. "Death & Bereavement in Judaism: Ancient Burial Practices.
   https://www.jewishvirtuallibrary.org/ancient-burial-practices
Jenks, Gregory C. "Jesus and the Afterlife: Glimpses of Jewish Traditions in the Teachings of Jesus."
   https://www.academia.edu/5548747/Jesus_and_the_afterlife?email_work_card=title
Jones, A.R. "Ptolemy". Encyclopaedia Brittanice, Chicago: Encyclopædia Britannica, 2010.
Karoglou, Kiki. "Mystery Cults in the Greek and Roman World."
   In: *Heilbrunn Timeline of Art History.* New York: The Metropolitan Museum of Art, 2000–.
   http://www.metmuseum.org/toah/hd/myst/hd_myst.htm (October 2013)
Kennedy, Lesley. 6 Early Human Civilizations: Architecture, Agriculture, Art and More First Blossomed in These Cultures. History.com, February 6, 2024.

https://www.History.Com/News/First-Earliest-Human-Civilizations

Kenny, Sir Anthony, J.P. "Aristotle". Encyclopedia Brittanica, Chicago: Encyclopaedia Brittanica, 2010.

Koch, Christof, and Gary Marcus. "Neuroscience in 2064: A Look at the Last Century". In *The Future of the Brain: Essays by the World's Leading Neuroscientists.* Edited by Gary Marcus and and Jeremy Freeman, 255–70. Princeton: Princeton University Press, 2015.

Koetz, Wyatt. "Karl Barth's Argument Against Afterlife". https://postbarthian.com/2015/10/08/karl-barths-argument-against-afterlife/

Kohler, Kaufmann. "Immortality of the Soul". *Jewish Encyclopedia.* https://www.jewishencyclopedia.com/articles/8092-immortality-of-the-soul

Kolb, B., and I.Q. Whishaw. *Fundamentals of Human Neuro-psychology.* New York: Worth, 2009.

Louw, D.J. *Pastoraal en Ontmoeting: Ontwerp vir 'n Basisteorie, Antropologie, Metode en Terapie.* Pretoria: RGN, 1993.

Mackay, Danielle. "Ancient Greek Theories Of The Human Soul". The Collector, Mar 13, 2021 • https://www.thecollector.com/ancient-greek-theories-of-the-human-soul/

Makin, Simon. "Brain Scientists Finally Discover the Glue that Makes Memories Stick for a Lifetime". Scientific American, 28 August 2024. https://www.scientificamerican.com/article/brain-scientists-finally-discover-the-glue-that-makes-memories-stick-for-a/

Malina, Bruce J. *On the Genre and Message of Revelation: Star Visions and Sky Journeys*, Peabody, Ms, 1995.

Mallam, Sally. "Hinduism". *The Human Journey.* https://humanjourney.us/ideas/axial-age-thought/axial-age-religions-hinduism/?gad_source=1

Mark, Joshua. "Ancient Persian Religion." World History Encyclopedia https://www.worldhistory.org/Ancient_Persian_Religion/

Mark, Joshua. "Death and Afterlife in Ancient Persia". World History Encyclopedia. https://www.worldhistory.org/article/1485/death-and-the-afterlife-in-ancient-persia/

Martin, P. *Counting Sheep: The Science and Pleasures of Sleep and Dreams*. London: Flamingo, 2002.

McGregor, G.H.C. and A.C. Purdy. *Jew and Greek: Tutors unto Christ, the Jewish and Hellenistic Background of the New Testament*. London: Saint Andrew, 1959.

Mark, Joshua. "The After-Life In Ancient Greece". World History Encyclopedia. https://www.worldhistory.org/article/29/the-after-life-in-ancient-greece/

Meadow, M.J. and R.D. Kahoe. *Psychology of Religion*. New York: Harper & Row, 1984.

Mithen, S. *The Prehistory of the Mind: A Search for the Origins of Art, Religion and Science*. London: Thames and Hudsons, 1998.

Nagaraj, Anil Kumar Mysore, *et al.* "The Mystery of Reincarnation". Indian J Psychiatry. 2013 Jan; 55 (Suppl 2): S171–S176. doi: 10.4103/0019-5545.105519. https://www.ncbi.nlm.nih.gov/pmc/articles/PMC3705678/#:~:text=Reincarnation%20is%20the%20religious%20or,of%20the%20previous%20life's%20actions.

New World Encyclopedia. "Animism". https://www.newworldencyclopedia.org/entry/Animism

Oakes, Lorina and Lucia Gahlin. *Ancient Egypt*. Hermes, 2004.

Paine, Thomas. *The Age of Reason*. Reprint, London: Freethought, 1880. http://www.gutenberg.org/files/3743/3743-h/3743-h.htm

Peters, F.E. *The Harvest of Hellenism, a History of the Near East from Alexander the Great to the Triumph of Christianity*. London: Barnes and Noble, 1972.

Phillips, G. *The Moses Legacy: The Evidence of History*. London: Sidgwick & Jackson, 2002.

Pitts, M. *Hengeworld*. London: Arrow, 2000.

Rossouw, H.W. *Die Sin van die Lewe*. Cape Town: Tafelberg, 1981.

Rylaarsdam, J. C. et al. "Biblical Literature". Encyclopedia Brittanica, Chicago: Encyclopaedia Brittanica, 2010.

Papineau, David, and Howard Selina. *Introducing Consciousness.* Cambridge: Icon, 2005.

Peters, F.E.: *The Harvest of Hellenism, a History of the Near East from Alexander the Great to the Triumph of Christianity.* London, 1972.

Pollard, John R.T. "Greek Mythology". Encyclopaedia Brittanica. Chicago: Encyclopaedia Brittanica, 2010.

Pretorius, Albertus. *Jesus of Nazareth: A Deluded Messiah.* Eugene OR: Wipf & Stock, 2022.

––––. *The End of Christianity.* Eugene OR: Wipf & Stock, 2022.

––––. *The Gospels Explained: A Novel and Rational Guide to the Gospel Narratives.* Eugene, OR: Wipf & Stock, 2024.

––––. *To Hell with the Devil: An Analysis of the Scriptures' Teachings about Satan.* Eugene, OR: Resource, 2024.

––––. *Who, Where and What is God?* Eugene, OR: Wipf & Stock, 2022.

Raypole, Crystal. "What Really Happens During an Out-of-Body Experience?" *Healthline, 22 July 2022.* https://www.healthline.com/health/out-of-body-experience.

Reese, William L. *Pantheism.* Encyclopedia Brittanica, Chicago: Encyclopaedia Brittanica, 2010.

Sacks, Oliver. *Hallucinations.* London: Picador, 2013.

––––.*The River of Consciousness.* London: Picador, 2017.

Saunders, Jason Lewis. "Stoicism". Encyclopedia Brittanica, Chicago: Encyclopaedia Brittanica, 2010.

Schipper, Bernd. "Egyptian Influences on the Biblical Text". Bible Odyssey. https://www.bibleodyssey.org/articles/egyptian-influences-on-the-biblical-text/#:~:text=Psalm%20104%2C%20a%20creation%20psalm,(the%20Instruction%20of%20Amenemope).

Scholtz, Adelbert. *The Prophecies of Revelation : a Reconstruction of the Visions of John of Patmos.* Beau Basin, Mauritius: Lambert Academic, 2017

Seebauer, U. *Datura Stramonium.*

http://www.arscurandi.ca/stram.html

Segal, Alan F. *Life After Death: A History of the Afterlife in Western Religions*, Doubleday, 2004.

Shermer, Martin. *The Believing Brain: From Ghosts and Gods and Conspiracies – How we Construct Beliefs and Reinforce Them as Truths*. New York: St Martin's, 2011.

Smith, Jonathan. "Hellenistic Religion." Encyclopaedia Brittanica, Chicago: Encyclopaedia Brittanica, 2010.

Soso, Michael. "Which parts of the brain are most responsible for consciousness?" Quora, https://www.quora.com/Which-parts-of-the-brain-are-most-responsible-for-consciousness.

Spronk, Klaas. "Good Death and Bad Death in Ancient Israel According to Biblical Lore". Social Science & Medicine Volume 58, Issue 5, March 2004, 987–95. https://www.sciencedirect.com/science/article/abs/pii/S0277953603005744

Stace, W.T. *A Critical History of Greek Philosophy*. London: Macmillan, 1960.

Stenger, V.J. *The New Atheism: Taking a Stand for Science and Reason*. New York: Prometheus, 2009.

Stoker, H.G. *Beginsels en Metodes in die Wetenskap*. Johannesburg: Boekhandel De Jong, 1969.

Strauss, D.F.M. *Inleiding tot die Kosmologie*. Bloemfontein: Sacum, 1978.

Swaab, D. *Wij zijn ons Brein: van Baarmoeder tot Alzheimer*. Amsterdam: Uitgeverij Contact, 2010.

Swancutt, Katherine. "Animism". The Open Encyclopedia of Anthropology.
https://www.anthroencyclopedia.com/entry/animism.

Taylor, J.E. and D. Hay. "Astrology in Philo of Alexandria's De Vita Contemplativa: Paper Read at Aram Society for Syro-Mesopotamian Studies 29th International Conference on the Theme of Astrology in the Ancient Near East, Held at The University of Oxford, 08–10 July 2010".

file:///c:/users/user/downloads/astrology_in_philo_of_alexandrias_de_vit.pdf

Temes, R. *The Complete Idiot's Guide to Hypnosis*. Indianapolis: Alpha, 2000.

Albrecht Dürer: Harrowing of Hell or Christ in Limbo (1512)

Temple, R. *Netherworld*. London: Arrow, 2003.

Thesleff, Holger. "Pythagoreanism". Encyclopaedia Brittanica, Chicago: Encyclopaedia Brittanica, 2010.

Thiel, R. *And then There was Light*. New York: Knopf, 1958.

Tyrrell, Patrick, *et al.*, "Kübler-Ross Stages of Dying and Subsequent Models of Grief".

https://www.ncbi.nlm.nih.gov/books/NBK507885/
Von Ehrenkrook, Jason. "The Afterlife in Philo and Josephus".
https://www.academia.edu/4254181/The_Afterlife_in_Philo_and
_Josephus_Proofs_
Young, G. Bryan. "Awareness". In *Encyclopedia of the Neurological Sciences*, edited by M.J. Aminoff. Elsevier Science, 2003.
Young, G. Bryan. "Consciousness". In *Encyclopedia of the Neurological Sciences*, edited by M.J. Aminoff. Elsevier Science, 2003.
Zillmer, Eric A. *et al. Principles of Neuropsychoilogy.* Belmont CA: Wadsworth, 2008.

LIST OF ILLUSTRATIONS

Frontispiece
Albrecht Dürer: The Angels receiving a Soul into Heaven
  https://commons.wikimedia.org/wiki/File:Albrecht-Durer-7-Angels-with-Cross-6-Keys-Receive-A-Soul-Into-Heaven.jpg

Page viii
"Hell at last, yawning, received them whole" (drawing by Gustave Dore)
  https://www.wikiart.org/en/gustave-dore/hell-at-last-yawning-received-them-whole

Chapter 1
"Death" by Hendrick Andriessen – Museum of Fine Arts, Ghent
  https://en.wikipedia.org/wiki/Death

Chapter 2
Venus of Willendorf
  http://donsmaps.com/willendorf.html
Rock Art of the San
  https://africanrockart.org/south-africa/
Healing dance by a San tribe, Southern Afric
  https://medium.com/@abebaebrima/healing-dance-of-the-san-tribe-bda2fb9186af

Chapter 3
King Hammurabi receiving his royal insignia and laws from a god
  https://en.wikipedia.org/wiki/Hammurabi
Anubis weighing the soul
  Encyclopaedia Brittanica
The Fravahar (Farohar or Fravashi)
  https://delhiparsis.com/about-zoroastrianism/

LIST OF ILLUSTRATIONS

Bust of Zeus
    https://www.britannica.com/topic/Zeus

Chapter 4
Ancient family tombs in the country of Israel
    https://www.britannica.com/topic/Zeus

Chapter 5
The Beit Alpha Mosaic
    https://1.bp.blogspot.com/-0okrhto5gd0/t94a4giichi/aaaaaaaaaxs/z7wkosqedao/s1600/zodiac+2.jpg.
The Hebrew conception of the cosmos.
    http://patrickschreiner.com/?cat=18

Chapter 6
Gustave Doré: Satan thrown into the abyss by Michael
    https://www.thesmartset.com/my-hero-satan/

Chapter 7
Plato
    Encyclopaedia Brittanica
Aristotle
    Encyclopaefdia Brittanica
The reconstructed Stoa of Attalos
    https://athens-tourist-information.com/things-to-do/roman-agora/stoa-of-attalos

Chapter 8
The 17th-cent painting *Christ Crucified* by Diego Velázquez
    https://www.pxfuel.com/en/search?q=inri

Chapter 9
The apostle Paul

https://www.biblegateway.com/blog/2016/05/our-letters-to-the-church-series-is-complete-whats-next/paul-mosaic-ravenna-275x272x72/

Karl Barth. Encyclopedia Brittanica, 2010.

Chapter 11
An aerial photo of the Greek island of Nisyros
https://commons.wikimedia.org/wiki/File:Byzantinischer_Mosaizist_des_9._Jahrhunderts_001.jpg

Part of a mosaic depicting a procession of 26 saints or martyrs
https://hughellwood.files.wordpress.com/2011/09/47-ravenna-s-apollinare-nuovo1.jpg

An ancient winepress
http://www.ancient-origins.net/news-history-archaeology/innocent-boys-meticulously-excavated-1400-year-old-winepress-israel-003089

Mosaic of Christ in his glory
http://www.approachguides.com/blog/hidden-gem-in-istanbul-the-deesis-in-hagia-sophia/

Chapter 13
The human brain fits snugly within the skull and is protected by the skull
https://biox.stanford.edu/research/seed-grants/exploring-evolution-human-brain-development-cerebral-cortical-spheroids

A neuron, supported by glial cells
http://www.massageincolumbusohio.com/wp-content/uploads/2017/03/Glial-Cells.gif

A synapse
https://sites.google.com/site/boyswithoutfathers/home/synapse

Two hemispheres of the brain
https://steemit.com/brain/@halodad22/our-extraordinary-daughter

The different lobes of the cerebrum

https://humananatomyly.com/human-brain-parts-and-functions-diagram/human-brain-parts-and-functions-diagram-human-brain-parts-and-their-functions-human-anatomy-chart/

Structures and areas of the human brain, seen from the inside
http://madeinkibera.com/diagram-of-brain-parts-and-functions

The Consciousness System
https://www.researchgate.net/figure/The-consciousness-system-A-Medial-view-and-B-lateral-view-of-anatomical_fig1_259161336

Chapter 14

Drawings of geometric figures
Drawings done by the author

Albrecht Dürer: Study of a Skull
https://www.wikiart.org/en/albrecht-durer/skull

Bibliography

Albrecht Dürer: Harrowing of Hell
https://www.printed-editions.com/artist/albrecht-durer/harrowing-of-hell-christ-in-limbo-christopher-clark-fine-art/

The pilot of a small aircraft experienced engine trouble while in the air and had to bail out. Unfortunately, his parachute didn't open and he fell rapidly towards Mother Earth and that caused him to get blacked out. Fortunately, his fall was broken by some old-time telephone cables. When he regained consciousness, he was too afraid to open his eyes, uncertain of his fate. He groped and fumbled around him, felt the cables and exclaimed: "Thank heaven! It's not a shovel, but a harp!"

www.ingramcontent.com/pod-product-compliance
Lightning Source LLC
Chambersburg PA
CBHW050839230426
43667CB00012B/2068